Primary Source Reader
for World History

Volume I: To 1500

ELSA A. NYSTROM
Kennesaw State University

THOMSON
™
WADSWORTH

Australia • Canada • Mexico • Brazil • Singapore
Spain • United Kingdom • United States

THOMSON
WADSWORTH

Primary Source Reader for World History
Volume I: To 1500

Elsa A. Nystrom

Publisher: *Clark Baxter*
Assistant Editor: *Paul Massicotte*
Editorial Assistant: *Lucinda Bingham*
Technology Project Manager: *David Lionetti*
Marketing Manager: *Lori Grebe Cook*
Marketing Assistant: *Teresa Jessen*
Project Manager, Editorial Production: *Katy German*
Art Director: *Maria Epes*

Print Buyer: *Lisa Claudeanos*
Permissions Editor: *Sarah Harkrader*
Production Service: *Cadmus*
Copy Editor: *Megan A. Costello*
Cover Designer: *Laurie Anderson*
Cover Image: *Nimatallah/Art Resource, NY*
Cover Printer: *Transcontinental Printing/Interglobe*
Printer: *Transcontinental Printing/Louiseville*

Printed in Canada
1 2 3 4 5 6 7 09 08 07 06 05

For more information about our products, contact us at:
Thomson Learning Academic Resource Center
1-800-423-0563

For permission to use material from this text or product, submit a request online at
http://www.thomsonrights.com.

Any additional questions about permissions can be submitted by email to
thomsonrights@thomson.com.

Library of Congress Control Number: 2005926369

ISBN 0-495-00609-2

Thomson Higher Education
10 Davis Drive
Belmont, CA 94002-3098
USA

Asia (including India)
Thomson Learning
5 Shenton Way
#01-01 UIC Building
Singapore 068808

Australia/New Zealand
Thomson Learning Australia
102 Dodds Street
Southbank, Victoria 3006
Australia

Canada
Thomson Nelson
1120 Birchmount Road
Toronto, Ontario M1K 5G4
Canada

UK/Europe/Middle East/Africa
Thomson Learning
High Holborn House
50–51 Bedford Row
London WC1R 4LR
United Kingdom

Latin America
Thomson Learning
Seneca, 53
Colonia Polanco
11560 Mexico
D.F. Mexico

Spain (including Portugal)
Thomson Paraninfo
Calle Magallanes, 25
28015 Madrid, Spain

Contents

CHAPTER 2   THE GREAT RELIGIONS DEVELOP   19

CHAPTER 3   LAW, GOVERNMENT, AND WAR— 2000 BCE–500 CE   63

CHAPTER 4 SCIENCE, MEDICINE, AND TECHNOLOGY—2000 BCE–500 CE 89

CHAPTER 5 DAILY LIFE IN THE ANCIENT WORLD 109

CHAPTER 9 SCIENCE, MEDICINE AND TECHNOLOGY—500–1500 CE 193

CHAPTER 10 DAILY LIFE IN THE MEDIEVAL WORLD—500–1500 CE 207

CHAPTER 11   ARTS AND CULTURE— 500–1500 CE   237

Introduction

Primary source documents enhance the study of history. A primary source can be as simple as graffiti on a wall in Pompeii or as complex as the discourse of ancient philosophers. What primary sources are not is the synthesis of the past that is found in all history survey texts. Reading the actual words written or passed down orally through generations lets you into the mind of the writer so that you can make your own decision about the meaning of his or her words.

Many primary source documents are interesting and entertaining in their own right. However, in order to gain the most benefit from primary sources, you should learn as much about the origin and purpose of each document as possible.

This book contains a selection of documents that should enhance the study of world civilization It is intended to be used as a companion to a comprehensive world civilization text.

Most of the documents are brief, and they are arranged both topically and chronologically to allow you to more easily determine the similarities and differences that have existed between societies over time. The documents are also divided into two time periods—prehistory to 500 CE and 500 to 1500 CE.

Within each time period, primary sources are grouped under the following five headings: (1) Religion and Philosophy, (2) Law, Government, and War, (3) Science, Medicine, and Technology, (4) Daily Life, and (5) Arts and Culture. Under each heading, the documents are arranged from earliest to latest written. Within each section, there are documents that show both the commonalities and the differences between peoples over time. In the Daily Life section, the primary sources help to illuminate the role of women in various cultures and the interaction between male and female over time. Also included throughout the sections whenever possible are traveler's accounts of other cultures. In the Science, Medicine, and Technology section, in addition to more traditional documents, there is a series of writings that shows the development of medical theory and practice and how it has varied from East to West.

HOW TO READ PRIMARY DOCUMENTS

One of the common failings of historians and students alike is their willingness to believe that people who lived in the past were just like us. When reading these documents, you may well find that in some cases those who exist today only in the pages of history texts appear to have had concerns similar to our own.

Other documents, however, will give you exactly the opposite feeling. Then you will understand that you have to know more in order to make a valid judgment. What circumstances in that individual's life and society shaped his or her thoughts and values and made the creation of that document possible?

Perhaps the first question to ask when reading a primary source is where did the author get his or her information? It is also important to know who the author was and what position in society he or she occupied. Is it likely that the author had a bias that influenced his or her particular point of view? Why do you think the author wrote the document?

Other questions to ask are the following: What is the main argument being made? Does the document agree with your text or with other knowledge you may have of the subject?

For further information on how to read primary and secondary sources, see "The Historian's Toolbox" at *http://guides.library.fullerton.edu/historians_toolbox/index.html.*

Another Web site that contains links to a variety of peer-reviewed reference and world civilization sites is *http://www.merlot.org/Home.po.*

CHAPTER 1

Religion and Philosophy— 2000 BCE–500CE

All peoples since the beginning of time have sought to explain their existence and that of their world. Origin stories or sacred scripture have been treasured by every ethnic group since the first humans walked on Earth; these creation stories provide a much-desired rationale for living. The examples included in this section come from societies with vastly different cultures, climate, and terrain. Some of them are from societies with an oral rather than written tradition. These origin stories were an important part of their cultures and were passed orally through countless centuries; yet most were first recorded within the last few centuries. Although they are impossible to date accurately, an early version of each myth probably existed thousands of years ago. Creation stories also exist as some of the oldest examples of human writing, yet they too were likely first passed down orally for hundreds of years before they were transcribed.

As you read these accounts, look for commonalities between them. Some, especially the Book of Genesis, may be very familiar, whereas others will seem strange at first. Yet careful reading will reveal much about the concerns of the societies from which they came.

What elements, if any, do the creation stories share? Were any of the myths shaped by the geographic features of the area where they evolved? Does the relationship between people and their gods vary between myths? If so, why? Which of the myths seems to provide the most satisfactory solution to the problem of human existence? Why?

1

The Beginning of Life
(Aborigine)—ND

For perhaps 60,000 years, the Aborigines have lived in Australia. As hunter-gatherers, they have roamed the often barren land in tribal groups living in harmony with nature. Religion and spirituality are an important factor in their culture and myths. Rituals are passed orally from generation to generation. In Aboriginal belief, no one dies but rather becomes one with the present-day natural world. This mystical relationship between the present and the past is called "the Dreaming" or "Dreamtime." This myth, from Stadbroke Island near Queensland, features the Rainbow Serpent, an important fertility figure in Aboriginal culture. What role does the Rainbow Serpent take in this myth?

In the Dreamtime all the Earth lay sleeping. Nothing moved. Everything was quiet and still. The animals, birds and reptiles lay sleeping under the earth's crust.

Then one day the Rainbow Serpent awoke from her slumber and pushed her way through the earth's crust, moving the stones that lay in her way. When she emerged, she looked about her and then travelled over the land, going in all directions. She travelled far and wide, and when she grew tired she curled herself into a heap and slept. Upon the earth she left her winding tracks and the imprint of her sleeping body. When she had travelled all the earth, she returned to the place where she had first appeared and called to the frogs, "Come out!"

The frogs were very slow to come from below the earth's crust, for their bellies were heavy with water which they had stored in their sleep. The Rainbow Serpent tickled their stomachs, and when the frogs laughed, the water ran all over the earth to fill the tracks of the Rainbow Serpent's wanderings—and that is how the lakes and rivers were formed. Then the grass began to grow, and trees sprang up, and so life began on earth.

All the animals, birds, and reptiles awoke and followed the Rainbow Serpent, the Mother of Life, across the land. They were happy on earth, and each lived and hunted for food with his own tribe. The kangaroo, wallaby and emu tribes lived on the plains. The reptile tribes lived among the rocks and stones, and the bird tribes flew through the air and lived in the trees.

From Oodgeroo Nunukul, *Stadbroke Dreamtime*. Pymblie, Australia: Angus & Robertson, 1992, p. 59-61.

The Rainbow Serpent made laws that all were asked to obey, but son grew quarrelsome and were troublemakers. The Rainbow Serpent scolded them, saying, "Those who keep my laws I shall reward well. I shall give to them a human form. They and their children and their children's children shall roam this earth for ever. This shall be their land. Those who break my laws I shall punish. They shall be turned to stone, never to walk the earth again."

So the law-breakers were turned to stone, and became mountains and hills, to stand for ever and watch over the tribes hunting for food at their feet.

But those who kept her laws she turned into human form, and gave each of them his own totem of the animal, bird or reptile whence they came. So the tribes knew themselves by their own totems: the kangaroo, the emu, the carpet snake, and many, many more. And in order that none should starve, she ruled that no man should eat of his own totem, but only of other totems. In this way there was food for all.

So the tribes lived together in the land given to them by the Mother of Life, the Rainbow Serpent; and they knew that the land would always be theirs, and that no one should ever take it from them.

2

A View of Creation From the Boshongo (Bantu)—ND

The Bantu peoples began a migration from western Africa around 1000 BCE, with some reaching southern Africa by 400 CE. The Boshongo are a member of the Bantu language family. Bantu languages are spoken by many tribes in sub-Saharan Africa; the most common is Swahili. The Boshongo were both farmers and hunter-gatherers who had a strong oral tradition. Their creation story is one of many to come from the Bantu peoples. What values seem to be most important to the Boshongo in this story?

In the beginning, in the dark, there was nothing but water. And Bumba was alone. One day Bumba was in terrible pain. He retched and strained and vomited up the sun. After that light spread over everything. The heat of the

From Maria Leach, *The Beginning: Creation Myths Around the World.* New York: Funk & Wagnalls, 1956, p. 145–146.

sun dried up the water until the black edges of the world began to show. Black sandbanks and reefs could be seen. But there were no living things.

Bumba vomited up the moon and then the stars, and after that the night had its light also.

Still Bumba was in pain. He strained again and nine living creatures came forth; the leopard named Koy Bumba, and Pongo Bumba the crested eagle, the crocodile, Ganda Bumba, and one little fish named Yo; next, old Kono Bumba, the tortoise, and Tsetse, the lightning, swift, deadly, beautiful like the leopard, then the white heron, Nyanyi Bumba, also one beetle, and the goat named Budi.

Last of all came forth men. There were many men, but only one was white like Bumba. His name was Loko Yima.

The creatures themselves then created all the creatures. The heron created all the birds of the air except the kite. He did not make the kite. The crocodile made serpents and the iguana. The goat produced every beast with horns. Yo, the small fish, brought forth all the fish of all the seas and waters. The beetle created insects.

Then the serpents in their turn made grasshoppers, and the iguana made the creatures without horns.

Then the three sons of Bumba said they would finish the world. The first, Nyonye Ngana, made the white ants; but he was not equal to the task, and died of it. The ants, however, thankful for life and being, went searching for black earth in the depths of the world and covered the barren sands to bury and honour their creator.

Chonganda, the second son, brought forth a marvelous living plant from which all the trees and grasses and flowers and plants in the world have sprung. The third son, Chedi Bumba, wanted something different, but for all his trying made only the bird called the kite.

Of all the creatures, Tsetse, lightning, was the only trouble-maker. She stirred up so much trouble that Bumba chased her into the sky. Then mankind was without fire until Bumba showed the people how to draw fire out of trees. 'There is fire in every tree,' he told them, and showed them how to make the firedrill and liberate it. Sometimes today Tsetse still leaps down and strikes the earth and causes damage.

When at last the work of creation was finished, Bumba walked through the peaceful villages and said to the people, 'Behold these wonders. They belong to you.' Thus from Bumba, the Creator, the First Ancestor, came forth all the wonders that we see and hold and use, and all the brotherhood of beasts and man.

3

The Woman Who Fell From the Sky (Huron)—ND

The Huron, or Wyandot, originally lived in central Ontario. Mortal enemies of the Iroquois, they were eventually driven from their land in 1650 CE. Some went to Quebec and others fled to the Ohio Valley and later to Kansas. In pre-Columbian days, the Huron numbered perhaps 40,000 and lived in fortified villages of about 1,000 people. The spiritual world was very important to the Huron way of life. Why might a female be an important figure in the Huron story of creation?

In the beginning there was nothing but the water, a wide sea, which was peopled by various animals of the kind that live in and upon the water. It happened then that a woman fell down from the upper world. Two loons, which were flying over the water, happened to look up and see her falling. To save her from drowning they hastened to place themselves beneath her, joining their bodies together so as to form a cushion for her to rest on. In this way they held her up, while they cried with a loud voice to summon the other animals to their aid. The cry of the loon can be heard a great distance, and the other creatures of the sea heard it, and assembled to learn the cause of the summons. Then came the tortoise . . . , a mighty animal, which consented to relieve the loons of their burden. They placed the woman on the back of the tortoise, charging him to take care of her. The tortoise then called the other animals to a grand council, to determine what should be done to preserve the life of the woman. They decided that she must have earth to live on. The tortoise directed them all to dive to the bottom of the sea and endeavor to bring up some earth. Many attempted it—the beaver, the muskrat . . ., and others—but without success. Some remained so long below that when they rose they were dead. The tortoise searched their mouths, but could find no trace of earth. At last the toad went down, and after remaining a long time rose, exhausted and nearly dead. On searching his mouth the tortoise found in it some earth, which he gave to the woman. She took it and placed it carefully around the edge of the tortoise's shell. When thus placed, it became the beginning of dry land. The land grew and extended on every side, forming at last a great country, fit for vegetation. All was sustained by the tortoise, which still supports the earth.

From Horatio Hale, "Huron Folklore," *The Journal of American Folklore*, Vol. 1, No. 3, October–December 1888, p. 180–182.

When the woman fell she was pregnant with twins. When these came forth they evinced opposite dispositions, the one good, the other evil. Even before they were born the same characters were manifested. They struggled together, and their mother heard them disputing. The one declared his willingness to be born in the usual manner, while the other malignantly refused, and, breaking through his mother's side, killed her. She was buried, and from her body sprang the various vegetable productions which the new earth required to fit it for the habitation of man. From her head grew the pumpkin-vine; from her breasts the maize; from her limbs the bean. Meanwhile the twins grew up, showing in all they did their opposing inclinations. The name of the good one was Tijuskeha, which means . . . something like . . . good man. The evil brother was Tawiskarong, meaning flinty, an allusion probably to his hard and cruel nature. They were not men, but supernatural beings, who were to prepare the world to be the abode of men. Finding that they could not live together, they separated, each taking his own portion of the earth. Their first act was to create animals of various kinds. The bad brother made fierce and monstrous creatures, proper to terrify and destroy mankind—serpents, panthers, wolves, bears, all of enormous size, and huge mosquitoes, "as large as turkeys." Among other things he made an immense toad, which drank up all the fresh water that was on the earth. In the meantime the good brother, in his province, was creating the innocent and useful animals. Among the rest he made the partridge. To his surprise, the bird rose in the air and flew toward the territory of Tawiskarong. Tijuskeha asked him were he was going. The bird replied that he was going to look for water, as there was none left in that land, and he heard there was some in the dominion of Tawiskarong. Tijuskeha then began to suspect mischief. He followed the course which the partridge had taken and presently reached the land of his evil brother. Here he encountered the snakes, ferocious brutes, and enormous insects which his brother had made, and overcame them. Finally he came to the monstrous toad, which he cut open, letting the water flow forth. He did not destroy the evil animals—perhaps had not the power to do so—but he reduced them in size, so that men would be able to master them.

The spirit of his mother warned him in a dream to beware of his evil brother, who would endeavor to destroy him by treachery. Finally they encountered [one another], and as it was evident that they could not live together on the earth, they determined to decide by a formal combat . . . which of them should remain master of the world. It was further agreed that each should make known to the other the only weapon by which he could be overcome. This extraordinary article of their agreement was probably made necessary by the fact that without such a disclosure the contest would have lasted forever. The good brother declared that he could be destroyed only by being beaten to death with a bag full of corn, beans, or some other product of the bread kind; the evil brother rejoined that he could be killed only by the horn of a deer or of some other wild animal. . . . Tawiskarong [. . .] set upon his brother with a bag of corn [and] chased him about the ground, and pounded him until he was nearly lifeless and lay as if dead. He revived, however, and recovering his strength, pursued in turn his evil brother, beating him with a deer's horn until he killed him. But the slain combatant was not utterly destroyed. He reappeared after death to his brother, and told him that he had gone to the far west, and that thenceforth all the races of men after death would go to the west, like him.

4

The Book of Genesis— ca. 1000 BCE

In the West, the Book of Genesis is the certainly the best-known creation story. Both historic and religious in intent, Genesis is the first book of the Judeo-Christian Old Testament and the first book of the Hebrew Torah. The oldest books of the Old Testament were probably passed down orally by the Jews living in (Palestine) the Middle East until they were transcribed somewhere between 1000 and 600 BCE. In Genesis, unlike in other creation stories, the origin myths, a single God created the world and its inhabitants. How does the concept of monotheism impact the relationship between God and man?

CHAPTER 1

In the beginning God created the heaven and the earth.

And the earth was without form, and void; and darkness *was* upon the face of the deep. And the Spirit of God moved upon the face of the waters.

And God said, Let there be light: and there was light.

And God saw the light, that it *was* good: and God divided the light from the darkness.

And God called the light Day, and the darkness he called Night.

And the evening and the morning were the first day.

And God said, Let there be a firmament in the midst of the waters, and let it divide the waters from the waters.

And God made the firmament, and divided the waters which *were* under the firmament from the waters which *were* above the firmament: and it was so.

King James Version of the Holy Bible, Book of Genesis.

And God called the firmament Heaven. And the evening and the morning were the second day.

And God said, Let the waters under the heaven be gathered together unto one place, and let the dry *land* appear: and it was so.

And God called the dry *land* Earth; and the gathering together of the waters called he Seas: and God saw that *it was* good.

And God said, Let the earth bring forth grass, the herb yielding seed, *and* the fruit tree yielding fruit after his kind, whose seed *is* in itself, upon the earth: and it was so.

And the earth brought forth grass, and herb yielding seed after his kind, and the tree yielding fruit, whose seed *was* in itself, after his kind: and God saw that *it was* good.

And the evening and the morning were the third day.

And God said, Let there be lights in the firmament of the heaven to divide the day from the night; and let them be for signs, and for seasons, and for days, and years:

And let them be for lights in the firmament of the heaven to give light upon the earth: and it was so.

And God made two great lights; the greater light to rule the day, and the lesser light to rule the night: *he made* the stars also.

And God set them in the firmament of the heaven to give light upon the earth,

And to rule over the day and over the night, and to divide the light from the darkness: and God saw that *it was* good.

And the evening and the morning were the fourth day.

And God said, Let the waters bring forth abundantly the moving creature that hath life, and fowl *that* may fly above the earth in the open firmament of heaven.

And God created great whales, and every living creature that moveth, which the waters brought forth abundantly, after their kind, and every winged fowl after his kind: and God saw that *it was* good.

And God blessed them, saying, Be fruitful, and multiply, and fill the waters in the seas, and let fowl multiply in the earth.

And the evening and the morning were the fifth day.

And God said, Let the earth bring forth the living creature after his kind, cattle, and creeping thing, and beast of the earth after his kind: and it was so.

And God made the beast of the earth after his kind, and cattle after their kind, and every thing that creepeth upon the earth, after his kind: and God saw that *it was* good.

And God said, Let us make man in our image, after our likeness: and let them have dominion over the fish of the sea, and over the fowl of the air, and over the cattle, and over all the earth, and over every creeping thing that creepeth upon the earth.

So God created man in his *own* image, in the image of God created he him; male and female created he them.

And God blessed them, and God said unto them, Be fruitful, and multiply, and replenish the earth, and subdue it: and have dominion over the fish of the sea, and over the fowl of the air, and over every living thing that moveth upon the earth.

And God said, Behold, I have given you every herb bearing seed, which *is* upon the face of all the earth, and every tree, in the which *is* the fruit of a tree yielding seed; to you it shall be for meat.

And to every beast of the earth, and to every fowl of the air, and to every thing that creepeth upon the earth, wherein *there* is life, *I have given* every green herb for meat: and it was so.

And God saw every thing that he had made, and, behold, *it was* very good. And the evening and the morning were the sixth day.

CHAPTER 2

Thus the heavens and the earth were finished, and all the host of them.

And on the seventh day God ended his work which he had made; and he rested on the seventh day from all his work which he had made.

And God blessed the seventh day, and sanctified it: because that in it he had rested from all his work which God created and made.

These *are* the generations of the heavens and of the earth when they were created, in the day that the LORD God made the earth and the heavens,

And every plant of the field before it was in the earth, and every herb of the field before it grew: for the LORD God had not caused it to rain upon the earth, and *there was* not a man to till the ground.

But there went up a mist from the earth, and watered the whole face of the ground.

And the LORD God formed man *of* the dust of the ground, and breathed into his nostrils the breath of life; and man became a living soul.

And the LORD God planted a garden eastward in Eden; and there he put the man whom he had formed.

And out of the ground made the LORD God to grow every tree that is pleasant to the sight, and good for food; the tree of life also in the midst of the garden, and the tree of knowledge of good and evil.

And a river went out of Eden to water the garden; and from thence it was parted, and became into four heads.

The name of the first *is* Pi'son: that *is* it which compasseth the whole land of Hav'i-lah, where *there is* gold;

And the gold of that land *is* good: there is bdellium and the onyx stone.

And the name of the second river *is* Gi'hon: the same *is* it that compasseth the whole land of E-thi-o'pi-a.

And the name of the third river *is* Hid'dekel: that *is* it which goeth toward the east of Ass-yr'i-a. And the fourth river *is* Euphra'tes.

And the LORD God took the man, and put him into the garden of Eden to dress it and to keep it.

And the LORD God commanded the man, saying, Of every tree of the garden thou mayest freely eat:

But of the tree of the knowledge of good and evil, thou shalt not eat of it: for in the day that thou eatest thereof thou shalt surely die.

And the LORD God said, It is not good that the man should be alone; I will make him an help meet for him.

And out of the ground the LORD God formed every beast of the field, and every fowl of the air; would call them unto Adam to see what he would call them; and whatsoever Adam called every living creature, that was the name thereof. And Adam gave names to all cattle, and to the fowl of the air, and to every beast of the field; but for Adam there was not found an help meet for him.

And the LORD God caused a deep sleep to fall upon Adam, and he slept: and he took one of his ribs, and closed up the flesh instead thereof;

And the rib, which the LORD God had taken from man, made he a woman, and brought her unto the man.

And Adam said, This is now bone of my bones, and flesh of my flesh: she shall be called Woman, because she was taken out of Man.

Therefore shall a man leave his father and his mother, and shall cleave unto his wife: and they shall be one flesh.

And they were both naked, the man and his wife, and were not ashamed.

5

The Story of Pan Gu (Chinese)—ND

A complex civilization has existed in China for perhaps 10,000 years. For most of that time, the elites have had some form of pictographic writing not dependent on an alphabet, which later evolved into Chinese characters. Although handed down orally for centuries, the story of Pan Gu was likely transcribed by a Daoist writer, Ho Kung, in the fourth century CE. Some scholars feel this story is not native to China but instead came from the Miao or another ethnic minority living in Chinese territory. Do you see any similarities between Pan Gu and the Miao creation myth?

From Fotopoulou Sophia, NewsFinder.org, Feb. 9, 2003.

Pan Gu and Nu Wa

Long, long ago, when heaven and earth were still one, the entire universe was contained in an egg-shaped cloud. All the matter of the universe swirled chaotically in that egg. Deep within the swirling matter was Pan Gu, a huge giant who grew in the chaos. For 18,000 years he developed and slept in the egg. Finally one day he awoke and stretched, and the egg broke to release the matter of the universe. The lighter purer elements drifted upwards to make the sky and heavens, and the heavier impure elements settled downwards to make the earth.

In the midst of this new world, Pan Gu worried that heaven and earth might mix again; so he resolved to hold them apart, with the heavens on his head and the earth under his feet. As the two continued to separate, Pan Gu grew to hold them apart. For 18,000 years he continued to grow, until the heavens were 30,000 miles above the earth. For much longer he continued to hold the two apart, fearing the return of the chaos of his youth. Finally he realized they were stable, and soon after that he died.

With the immense giant's death, the earth took on new character. His arms and legs became the four directions and the mountains. His blood became the rivers, and his sweat became the rain and dew. His voice became the thunder, and his breath became the winds. His hair became the grass, and his veins became the roads and paths. His teeth and bones became the minerals and rocks, and his flesh became the soil of the fields. Up above, his left eye became the sun, and his right eye became the moon. Thus in death, as in life, Pan Gu made the world as it is today.

Many centuries later, there was a goddess named Nu Wa who roamed this wild world that Pan Gu had left behind, and she became lonely in her solitude. Stopping by a pond to rest, she saw her reflection and realized that there was nothing like herself in the world. She resolved to make something like herself for company.

From the edge of the pond she took some mud and shaped it in the form of a human being. At first her creation was lifeless, and she set it down. It took life as soon as it touched the soil, however, and soon the human was dancing and celebrating its new life. Pleased with her creation, Nu wa made more of them, and soon her loneliness disappeared in the crowd of little humans around her. For two days she made them, and still she wanted to make more. Finally she pulled down a long vine and dragged it through the mud, and then she swung the vine through the air. Droplets of mud flew everywhere and, when they fell, they became more humans that were nearly as perfect as the ones she had made by hand. Soon she had spread humans over the whole world. The ones she made by hand became the aristocrats, and the ones she made with the vine became the poor common people.

Even then, Nu Wa realized that her work was incomplete, because as her creations died she would have to make more. She solved this problem by dividing the humans into male and female so they could reproduce and save her from having to make new humans to break her solitude.

Many years later, Pan Gu's greatest fear came true. The heavens collapsed so that there were holes in the sky, and the earth cracked, letting water rush from below to flood the earth. At other places fire sprang forth from the earth, and everywhere wild beasts emerged from the forests to prey on the people. Nu Wa drove the beasts back and healed the earth. To fix the sky, she took stones of many colors from the river and built a fire in which she melted them. She used the molten rock to patch the holes in the sky, and she used the four legs of a giant turtle to support the sky again. Exhausted by her labors, she soon lay down to die and, like Pan Gu, from her body came many more features to adorn the world that she had restored.

6

Creation Story (Miao)—ND

The Miao, a minority group living in southwest China, migrated there about 4,500 years ago, perhaps from Mongolia or Tibet. A friendly hospitable people, they have many unique celebrations involving music and dance. With no written language, they have preserved their legends in verses, which are often sung at festivals. The following creation story comes from the Black Miao; they received this name because of the dark-colored clothes they wore. Why might a society with an oral tradition relate their sacred legends in verse and song?

Miao Creation Story

> Who made heaven and earth?
> Who made insects?
> Who made men?
> Made male and made female?
> I who speak don't know.

> Heavenly King made heaven and earth,
> Ziene made insects,
> Ziene made men and demons,
> Made male and made female.
> How is it you don't know?

Adapted by D.L. Ashliman from E.T.C. Werner, *Myths and Legends of China* (London: George G. Harrap and Company, 1922), p. 406-408.

How made heaven and earth?
How made insects?
How made men and demons?
Made male and made female?
I who speak don't know.

Heavenly King was intelligent,
Spat a lot of spittle into his hand,
Clapped his hands with a noise,
Produced heaven and earth,
Tall grass made insects,
Stories made men and demons,
Made men and demons,
Made male and made female.

7

Creation Hymn From the Rig Veda (Indo-European)—1500 BCE

An early agricultural society existed in the fertile Indus valley thousands of years before the arrival of the Indo-European Aryans around 2000 BCE. The Aryans were fierce warriors who conquered the local inhabitants and eventually created the Vedic civilization. The creation hymn from the Rig Veda contains the foundation of what would eventually become the Hindu religion.

At first was neither Being nor Nonbeing.
There was not air nor yet sky beyond.
What was wrapping? Where? In whose protection?
Was Water there, unfathomable deep?

There was no death then, nor yet deathlessness;
of night or day there was not any sign.
The One breathed without breath by its own impulse.
Other than that was nothing at all.

From Raimundo Panikkar, "The Vedic Experience: Mantramanjari," Motilal Banarsidas Publishers. Reprinted by permission of the publisher.

Darkness was there, all wrapped around by darkness,
and all was Water indiscriminate, Then
that which was hidden by Void, that One, emerging,
stirring, through power of Ardor, came to be.

In the beginning Love arose,
which was primal germ cell of mind.
The Seers, searching in their hearts with wisdom,
discovered the connection of Being in Nonbeing.

A crosswise line cut Being from Nonbeing.
What was described above it, what below?
Bearers of seed there were and mighty forces,
thrust from below and forward move above.

Who really knows? Who can presume to tell it?
Whence was it born? Whence issued this creation?
Even the Gods came after its emergence.
Then who can tell from whence it came to be?

That out of which creation has arisen,
whether it held it firm or it did not,
He who surveys it in the highest heaven,
He surely knows – or maybe He does not!

8

The Creation of the World (India)—7th century BCE

The Upanishads ("those who sit near") are written in a format that implies discourse between teacher and student. They come out of the Vedic scripture, but they show a more sophisticated approach to creation as well as an increased awareness of the soul, life and death, and reincarnation, which is similar to that found in the Hindu religion. The earliest were written (in Sanskrit) in the seventh century BCE and the latest around the

From *The Principal Upanishads*, ed. and trans. by S. Radhakrishnan (New York: Harper & Row, 1953).

time of Buddha (fifth century BCE). How do these creation stories differ from some of the others you have read? What differences do you find between these two documents, which came from the same society but perhaps a thousand years apart?

ACCORDING TO THE UPANISHADS

1. There was nothing whatsoever here in the beginning. By death indeed was this covered, or by hunger, for hunger is death. He created the mind, thinking 'let me have a self' (mind). Then he moved about, worshiping. From him, thus worshiping, water was produced. . . .

2. . . . That which was the froth of the water became solidified; that became the earth. On it he [i.e., death] rested. From him thus rested and heated (from the practice of austerity) his essence of brightness came forth (as) fire.

3. He divided himself threefold (fire is one-third), the sun one-third and the air one-third. He also is life [lit., breath] divided threefold, . . . (*Brihad-aranyaka Upanishad,* 1, 2, 1-3.)

1. The Sun is Brahman-this is the teaching. An explanation thereof (is this). In the beginning this (world) was non-existent. It became existent. It grew. It turned into an egg. It lay for the period of a year. It burst open. Then came out of the eggshell, two parts, one of silver, the other of gold. That which was of silver is this earth; that which was of gold is the sky. What was the outer membrane is the mountains; that which was the inner membrane is the mist with the clouds. What were the veins were the rivers. What was the fluid within is the ocean. (*Chandogya Upanishad,* III, 19, 1-2.)

1. In the beginning, my dear, this was Being alone' one only without a second. Some people say 'in the beginning this Was non-being alone, one only; without a second. From that non-being, being was produced.'

2. But how, indeed, my dear, could it be thus? said he [i.e., the sage Uddalaka], how could being be produced from non-being? On the contrary, my dear, in the beginning this was being alone, one only, without a second.

3. It thought, May I be many, may I grow forth. It sent forth fire. That fire thought, May I be many, may I grow forth. It sent forth water. . . .

4. That water thought, May I be many, may I grow forth. It sent forth food. . . .

(*Chandogya Upanishad,* VI, 2, 1-4.)

9

Hesiod's Theogony (Greek)— 1st century BCE

The difficult mountainous terrain of Greece produced a series of heroes, poets, and philosophers from the eighth century BCE to the Roman conquest, in the first century BCE. Hesiod was a poet who lived during the mythic "dark ages" of Greece ca. 700 BCE. Scholars do not agree that Hesiod was a real person or that all the poems attributed to him were actually his work. Little is known about his life except through his surviving work. Although there is no absolute proof that Hesiod wrote "Theogony," it is very similar in style to another poem, "Works and Days," which is considered authentic. The gods Hesiod wrote about were anthropomorphic and willful. From what you have learned about ancient Greek culture, do you think Hesiod's version of creation was shaped by the struggle for existence on the Greek peninsula?

First of all, the Void (Chaos) came into being, next broad-bosomed Earth, the solid and eternal home of all, and Eros [Desire], the most beautiful of the immortal gods, who in every man and every god softens the sinews and overpowers the prudent purpose of the mind. Out of Void came Darkness and black Night, and out of Night came Light and Day, her children conceived after union in love with Darkness. Earth first produced starry Sky, equal in size with herself, to cover her on all sides. Next she produced the tall mountains, the pleasant haunts of the gods, and also gave birth to the barren waters, sea with its raging surges–all this without the passion of love. Thereafter she lay with Sky and gave birth to Ocean with its deep current. Coeus and Crius and Hyperion and Iapetus; Thea and Rhea and Themia [Law] and Mnemosyne [Memory]; also golden-crowned Phoebe and lovely Tethys. After these came cunning Cronus, the youngest and boldest of her children; and he grew to hate the father who had begotten him. Earth also gave birth to the violent Cyclopes-Thunderer, Lightner, and bold Flash-who made and gave to Zeus the thunder and the lightning bolt. They were like the gods in all respects except that a single eye stood in the middle of their foreheads, and their strength and power and skill were in their hands. There were also born to Earth and Sky three more children, big, strong, and horrible, Cottus and Briareus and Gyes. This unruly brood had a hundred monstrous hands sprouting from their shoulders, and fifty heads on top of their shoulders growing from their sturdy bodies. They had monstrous strength to match their huge size.

From *Hesiod's Theogony*, trans. by Norman O. Brown (New York: Liberal Arts Press, 1953).

Of all the children born of Earth and Sky these were the boldest, and their father hated them from the beginning. As each of them was about to be born, Sky would not let them reach the light of day; instead he hid them all away in the bowels of Mother Earth. Sky took pleasure in doing this evil thing. In spite of her enormous size, Earth felt the strain within her and groaned. Finally she thought of an evil and cunning stratagem. She instantly produced a new metal, grey steel, and made a huge sickle. Then she laid the matter before her children; the anguish in her heart made her speak boldly, 'My children, you have a savage father; if you will listen to me, we may be able to take vengeance for this evil outrage: he was the one who started using violence.'

This was what she said: but all the children were gripped by fear, and not one of them spoke a word. Then great Cronus, the cunning trickster, took courage and answered his good mother with these words: 'Mother, I am willing to undertake and carry through your plan. I have no respect for our infamous father, since he was the one who started using violence.'

This was what he said, and enormous Earth was very pleased. She hid him in ambush and put in his hands the sickle with jagged teeth, and 'instructed him fully in her plot. Huge Sky came drawing night behind him and desiring to make love; he lay on top of Earth stretched all over her. Then from his ambush his son reached out with his left hand and with his right took the huge sickle with its long jagged teeth and quickly sheared the organs from his own father and threw them away. The drops of blood that spurted from them were all taken in by Mother Earth, and in the course of the revolving years she gave birth to the powerful Erinyes [Spirits of Vengeance] and the huge Giants with shining armour and long spears. As for the organs themselves, for a long time they drifted round the sea just as they were when Cronus cut them off with the steel edge and threw them from the land into the waves of the ocean; then white foam issued from the divine flesh, and in the foam a girl began to grow. First she came near to holy Cythera, then reached Cyprus, the land surrounded by sea. There she stepped out, a goddess, tender and beautiful, and round her slender feet the green grass shot up. She is called Aphrodite by gods and men because she grew in the froth, and also Cytherea, because she came near to Cythera, and the Cyprian, because she was born in watery Cyprus. Eros [Desire] and beautiful Passion were her attendants both at her birth and at her first going to join the family of the gods. The rights and privileges assigned to her from the beginning and recognized by men and gods are these; to preside over the whispers and smiles and tricks which girls employ, and the sweet delight and tenderness of love. Great Father Sky called his children the Titans, because of his feud with them: he said that they blindly had tightened the noose and had done a savage thing for which they would have to pay in time to come.

The Great Religions Develop

Although many religions invoke the story of a great flood, the development of religion in the ancient world varied greatly from continent to continent. Isolated tribal groups retained their animist beliefs. In India, however, Hinduism and later Buddhism advocated a more otherworldly view. Except during a brief period of monotheism, Egypt clung to the old gods. The Judeo-Christian religion, on the other hand, kept its Mosaic foundation in monotheism while trying to spread a doctrine of peace and love throughout a warring Roman empire. In some religions, a concern for what happened to the physical body after death also emerged at this time.

Does the Hymn to the Sun share any commonalities with the Hindu, Buddhist, and Christian documents?

Is the philosophy of Confucius, Dao, and Mencius concerned with religion as we know it? Why or why not?

Why was the Edict of Milan so important to the spread of Christianity?

What might Saint Jerome have in common with Buddha?

How does the Egyptian *Book of the Dead* compare with that of Tibet?

10

The Flood, From the *Epic of Gilgamesh*—ca. 2000 BCE

The Epic of Gilgamesh *contains one of several accounts of a universal flood from various parts of the ancient world that parallels the more familiar account in Genesis. Gilgamesh was likely a real person (that is, the King of Uruk in Babylon), and this story of his life was written on clay tablets in Sumerian cuneiform. This flood story, written several thousand years before Genesis, is believed by some scholars to have influenced the Hebrew version. If this is the case, then there are some striking differences, as well as many similarities, between the two accounts. What are the main differences between the two versions?*

"'Tear down thy house, build a ship!
Let riches go, seek Life,
Despise possessions, save thy life!
Bring living things of all kinds into the ship!
The ship that thou art to build,
Be its measurements strictly laid out,
For its length and its breadth to match—
On the holy lake set it at anchor!'

"When a shimmer of morning shone,
I began to do what Ea had ordered.
On the fifth day
I planned the form of the ship:
Its walls measured one hundred and twenty ells.
And one hundred and twenty ells
Measured the rim of its roof.
I planned the bows and made a drawing,
I gave it six stories,
Divided it sevenfold on the outside,
Divided it ninefold on the inside,
And hammered calk-plugs amidships.
I chose me out a pole,
And laid ready what I needed. . . .
Before sunset the ship was finished.
All that I had I laded upon it,

From *Gilgamesh, Epic of Old Babylonia*, trans. by William Ellery Leonard (New York: Viking Press, 1934).

All that I had of silver I laded upon it,
I laded upon it all that I had of gold,
I laded upon it all that I had
Of living things of all kinds.
I made my whole family and kin
To go aboard the ship;
Cattle of the field, animals of the field,
All handworkers I made go aboard.
Shamash had given me the appointed time:
'Of an evening will the Sender of darkness
Let a cloudburst stream from on high.
Then enter the ship and close thy door.'
This appointed time came on.
The Sender of darkness
Of an evening let a cloudburst come down.
I observed the look of the tempest,
I was afraid to gaze on the tempest,
I went within the ship and shut my gate.
To the pilot of the ship,
The shipman Pusur-Amurri,
I gave over the giant ship with all it held. . . .
All one day raged the southstorm,
Roared hastening along,
And made the waters reach the hills.
The waters fell upon men like a battle,
No one seeth the other;
From above in heaven
One could no more make out man and man.
The gods were afraid before the stormflood,
Fled, and mounted up to the heaven of Anu.
The gods cringe down like dogs,
Cowering on the ground.
Ishtar shrieks like a woman in birth-pangs,
The lovely-voiced lady of the gods yells aloud:
'The times before are indeed turned to earth,
Because I myself in the gods' assembly
Gave the ill counsel!
How could I in the gods' assembly
Give such ill counsel,
To decree the fight
For the destruction of my mankind?
I alone give birth to my mankind.
Now they fill, like the spawn of the fish, the sea!'
The gods of the Anunnaki weep with her,
The gods are bowed down, sit weeping there.
Their lips are shut.

"Six days and six nights swirls the stormflood,
And the southstorm is a weight on the land.
As the seventh day came on,
The southstorm gave up the fight,
Which it had fought like an army.
The sea grew quiet, and gathered up its waters.
The stormflood ceased.
I looked for the tempest, all had become still.
The whole race of man was turned to earth.
Like a flat roof were the plains.
Then I opened a hatch,
And light streamed into my face.
I sat me down weeping,
And my tears ran over my face.
I gazed about for solid earth
In the dominions of the sea.
After twelve hours an island emerged.
The ship drove for Mount Nissir.
Mount Nissir holds the ship fast
And keeps it from rocking.
One day, a second day, Mount Nissir
Holds the ship fast and keeps it from rocking.
A third and fourth day Mount Nissir
Holds the ship fast and keeps it from rocking.
A fifth, a sixth day Mount Nissir
Holds the ship fast and keeps it from rocking.

"As the seventh day came on,
I held a dove outside and set it free;
The dove flew forth and came back.
She found no resting-place, so she turned home.
I held a swallow outside and set it free;
The swallow flew forth and came back.
She found no resting-place, so she turned home.
I held a raven outside and set it free;
The raven flew forth, saw the water run dry,
He feeds, scrapes, croaks, and turns not home.

"Then I let all out unto the four winds,
And offered a sacrifice,
Set up a burnt-offering
On the top of the mountain. . . .
The gods savoured the smell,
The gods savoured the sweet smell;
The gods foregathered, like flies,
Above the maker of the offering. . . .

"As Ellil came nigh, he saw the ship.
Then Ellil grew wroth and was angry at the gods:

'Someone hath escaped, a living soul!
No man was to have remained alive in this ruin.'
Ninurta opens his mouth and speaks,
He says to the hero Ellil:
'Can anyone devise plans except Ea?
Why, Ea understands every matter!'
Ea opens his mouth and speaks,
Says to the hero Ellil:
'Thou hero and wise one among the gods,
How couldst thou without heed
Rouse up a stormflood?
He who doeth sin let him bear his sin,
He who doeth sacrilege let him bear his sacrilege;
Yet see to it that he be not destroyed,
Be long-suffering that he be not rooted out. . . .
I myself have not betrayed
The secret of the great gods.
I let Utnapishtim, the Very-Wise, see dream-pictures,
And so the secret of the great gods he learned.
Ye now, devise counsel for him.'
"Then Ea went aboard the ship,
Took me by the hands, led me onto the land,
And had my wife kneel down at my side.
He stepped into our midst,
Touched our foreheads and blessed us." . . .

11

The Flood, From Genesis— 1st century BCE

The hero of the Genesis flood story, Noah, was both the head of an important Semitic family and the first cultivator of vineyards. He was chosen by God to continue the human race after all evildoers had perished in the great flood. Jesus would later reference the flood as a symbol of baptism. Only in the Genesis flood story is the action of God related to sinfulness. How does this make the flood narrative in Genesis stand out from other flood stories?

King James Version of the Holy Bible, Book of Genesis.

CHAPTER 6

1 When men began to multiply on the face of the ground, and daughters were born to them, 2 the sons of God saw that the daughters of men were fair; and they took to wife such of them as they chose. 3 Then the LORD said, "My spirit shall not abide in man for ever, for he is flesh, but his days shall be a hundred and twenty years." 4 The Nephilim were on the earth in those days, and also afterward, when the sons of God came in to the daughters of men, and they bore children to them. These were the mighty men that were of old, the men of renown.

5 The LORD saw that the wickedness of man was great in the earth, and that every imagination of the thoughts of his heart was only evil continually. 6 And the LORD was sorry that he had made man on the earth, and it grieved him to his heart. 7 So the LORD said, "I will blot out man whom I have created from the face of the ground, man and beast and creeping things and birds of the air, for I am sorry that I have made them." 8 But Noah found favor in the eyes of the LORD.

9 These are the generations of Noah. Noah was a righteous man, blameless in his generation; Noah walked with God. 10 And Noah had three sons, Shem, Ham, and Japheth.

11 Now the earth was corrupt in God's sight, and the earth was filled with violence. 12 And God saw the earth, and behold, it was corrupt; for all flesh had corrupted their way upon the earth. 13 And God said to Noah, "I have determined to make an end of all flesh; for the earth is filled with violence through them; behold, I will destroy them with the earth. 14 Make yourself an ark of gopher wood; make rooms in the ark, and cover it inside and out with pitch. 15 This is how you are to make it: the length of the ark three hundred cubits, its breadth fifty cubits, and its height thirty cubits. 16 Make a roof for the ark, and finish it to a cubit above; and set the door of the ark in its side; make it with lower, second, and third decks. 17 For behold, I will bring a flood of waters upon the earth, to destroy all flesh in which is the breath of life from under heaven; everything that is on the earth shall die. 18 But I will establish my covenant with you; and you shall come into the ark, you, your sons, your wife, and your sons' wives with you. 19 And of every living thing of all flesh, you shall bring two of every sort into the ark, to keep them alive with you; they shall be male and female. 20 Of the birds according to their kinds, and of the animals according to their kinds, of every creeping thing of the ground according to its kind, two of every sort shall come in to you, to keep them alive. 21 Also take with you every sort of food that is eaten, and store it up; and it shall serve as food for you and for them." 22 Noah did this; he did all that God commanded him.

CHAPTER 7

1 Then the LORD said to Noah, "Go into the ark, you and all your household, for I have seen that you are righteous before me in this generation. 2 Take with you seven pairs of all clean animals, the male and his mate; and a pair of

the animals that are not clean, the male and his mate; 3 and seven pairs of the birds of the air also, male and female, to keep their kind alive upon the face of all the earth. 4 For in seven days I will send rain upon the earth forty days and forty nights; and every living thing that I have made I will blot out from the face of the ground." 5 And Noah did all that the LORD had commanded him.

6 Noah was six hundred years old when the flood of waters came upon the earth. 7 And Noah and his sons and his wife and his sons' wives with him went into the ark, to escape the waters of the flood. 8 Of clean animals, and of animals that are not clean, and of birds, and of everything that creeps on the ground, 9 two and two, male and female, went into the ark with Noah, as God had commanded Noah. 10 And after seven days the waters of the flood came upon the earth.

11 In the six hundredth year of Noah's life, in the second month, on the seventeenth day of the month, on that day all the fountains of the great deep burst forth, and the windows of the heavens were opened. 12 And rain fell upon the earth forty days and forty nights. 13 On the very same day Noah and his sons, Shem and Ham and Japheth, and Noah's wife and the three wives of his sons with them entered the ark, 14 they and every beast according to its kind, and all the cattle according to their kinds, and every creeping thing that creeps on the earth according to its kind, and every bird according to its kind, every bird of every sort. 15 They went into the ark with Noah, two and two of all flesh in which there was the breath of life. 16 And they that entered, male and female of all flesh, went in as God had commanded him; and the LORD shut him in.

17 The flood continued forty days upon the earth; and the waters increased, and bore up the ark, and it rose high above the earth. 18 The waters prevailed and increased greatly upon the earth; and the ark floated on the face of the waters. 19 And the waters prevailed so mightily upon the earth that all the high mountains under the whole heaven were covered; 20 the waters prevailed above the mountains, covering them fifteen cubits deep. 21 And all flesh died that moved upon the earth, birds, cattle, beasts, all swarming creatures that swarm upon the earth, and every man; 22 everything on the dry land in whose nostrils was the breath of life died. 23 He blotted out every living thing that was upon the face of the ground, man and animals and creeping things and birds of the air; they were blotted out from the earth. Only Noah was left, and those that were with him in the ark. 24 And the waters prevailed upon the earth a hundred and fifty days.

CHAPTER 8

1 But God remembered Noah and all the beasts and all the cattle that were with him in the ark. And God made a wind blow over the earth, and the waters subsided; 2 the fountains of the deep and the windows of the heavens were closed, the rain from the heavens was restrained, 3 and the waters receded from the earth continually. At the end of a hundred and fifty days the waters had

abated; 4 and in the seventh month, on the seventeenth day of the month, the ark came to rest upon the mountains of Ar'arat. 5 And the waters continued to abate until the tenth month; in the tenth month, on the first day of the month, the tops of the mountains were seen.

6 At the end of forty days Noah opened the window of the ark which he had made, 7 and sent forth a raven; and it went to and fro until the waters were dried up from the earth. 8 Then he sent forth a dove from him, to see if the waters had subsided from the face of the ground; 9 but the dove found no place to set her foot, and she returned to him to the ark, for the waters were still on the face of the whole earth. So he put forth his hand and took her and brought her into the ark with him. 10 He waited another seven days, and again he sent forth the dove out of the ark; 11 and the dove came back to him in the evening, and lo, in her mouth a freshly plucked olive leaf; so Noah knew that the waters had subsided from the earth. 12 Then he waited another seven days, and sent forth the dove; and she did not return to him any more.

13 In the six hundred and first year, in the first month, the first day of the month, the waters were dried from off the earth; and Noah removed the covering of the ark, and looked, and behold, the face of the ground was dry. 14 In the second month, on the twenty-seventh day of the month, the earth was dry. 15 Then God said to Noah, 16 "Go forth from the ark, you and your wife, and your sons and your sons' wives with you. 17 Bring forth with you every living thing that is with you of all flesh—birds and animals and every creeping thing that creeps on the earth—that they may breed abundantly on the earth, and be fruitful and multiply upon the earth." 18 So Noah went forth, and his sons and his wife and his sons' wives with him. 19 And every beast, every creeping thing, and every bird, everything that moves upon the earth, went forth by families out of the ark.

20 Then Noah built an altar to the LORD, and took of every clean animal and of every clean bird, and offered burnt offerings on the altar. 21 And when the LORD smelled the pleasing odor, the LORD said in his heart, "I will never again curse the ground because of man, for the imagination of man's heart is evil from his youth; neither will I ever again destroy every living creature as I have done. 22 While the earth remains, seedtime and harvest, cold and heat, summer and winter, day and night, shall not cease."

CHAPTER 9

1 And God blessed Noah and his sons, and said to them, "Be fruitful and multiply, and fill the earth. 2 The fear of you and the dread of you shall be upon every beast of the earth, and upon every bird of the air, upon everything that creeps on the ground and all the fish of the sea; into your hand they are delivered. 3 Every moving thing that lives shall be food for you; and as I gave you the green plants, I give you everything. 4 Only you shall not eat flesh with its life, that is, its blood. 5 For your lifeblood I will surely require a reckoning;

of every beast I will require it and of man; of every man's brother I will require the life of man. 6 Whoever sheds the blood of man, by man shall his blood be shed; for God made man in his own image. 7 And you, be fruitful and multiply, bring forth abundantly on the earth and multiply in it."

8 Then God said to Noah and to his sons with him, 9 "Behold, I establish my covenant with you and your descendants after you, 10 and with every living creature that is with you, the birds, the cattle, and every beast of the earth with you, as many as came out of the ark. 11 I establish my covenant with you, that never again shall all flesh be cut off by the waters of a flood, and never again shall there be a flood to destroy the earth." 12 And God said, "This is the sign of the covenant which I make between me and you and every living creature that is with you, for all future generations: 13 I set my bow in the cloud, and it shall be a sign of the covenant between me and the earth. 14 When I bring clouds over the earth and the bow is seen in the clouds, 15 I will remember my covenant which is between me and you and every living creature of all flesh; and the waters shall never again become a flood to destroy all flesh. 16 When the bow is in the clouds, I will look upon it and remember the everlasting covenant between God and every living creature of all flesh that is upon the earth." 17 God said to Noah, "This is the sign of the covenant which I have established between me and all flesh that is upon the earth."

12

The Great Flood, From Ovid's *Metamorphosis*—1st century CE

Ovid (Publius Ovidius Naso) (43 BCE-17 CE) was a Roman of the equestrian class who served as an administrator in Rome for many years. He was a wealthy man and somewhat of a rake who enjoyed the social life of Rome. His main interest was writing poetry. Ars Amatoria *satirized Roman society, whereas the legends of Greek mythology were preserved in* Metamorphosis. *Unfortunately, at the age of 50, Ovid offended Emperor Augustus and was exiled to Tomi on the Black Sea (modern Romania), where he lived unhappily until his death in 17 CE. This account of a great flood comes from* Metamorphosis. *How does it compare with other examples of flood narrative? Do all the flood narratives share some elements in common?*

From *The Metamorphosis of Ovid*, trans. by Mary M. Innes, Penguin Books UK, 1995, book 1.

Looking down from his kingdom in the sky, Jove saw that mankind was now hopelessly violent and cruel. He called together his council, and they came to him forthwith, traveling that famous bright path across heaven's vault, the Milky Way. Jove angrily demanded that the utterly corrupt human race be destroyed, promising that afterward he himself would supervise the creation of a new stock of men. The gods sadly agreed that only this extreme act would solve the threat of mankind's wickedness.

Jove was about to strike the earth with a barrage of thunderbolts when he realized that the conflagration caused by such an attack might threaten heaven itself, so he resolved to destroy the earth's inhabitants by water instead of by fiery lightning. To this end he fettered the North Wind, then charged the South Wind to bring forth endless rains. Jove's brother Neptune, god of the seas, caused the tides and the waves to rise upon the land and the rivers to overflow their banks.

Man and beast alike fell prey to the ever-rising flood. Orchards and planted fields were washed away. Houses and other buildings were either demolished by the crashing waves or submerged beneath a sea that had no shores. Not even the temples and sacred images were spared. The birds themselves, their wings finally tiring from continuous flight, in the end were forced to surrender to watery graves.

In the end only one place on earth remained above water: the twin summits of Mount Parnassus. It was here that the small boat carrying Deucalion and his wife Pyrrha ran aground. They alone had survived the great deluge.

When Jove saw that only one man and one woman were still alive on earth, and that this husband and this wife were virtuous people, both true worshippers, he released the North Wind and caused it to dissipate the storms and clouds. Then Neptune called upon Triton to recall the tides and waves with a signal from his conch-shell trumpet.

The earth was now restored, but lifeless, desolate, and empty. Deucalion and Pyrrha, seeing that they were the only living beings left on earth, sought guidance by going together to the Waters of Cephissus, which were again flowing in their usual channel. They sprinkled themselves with this holy water, then entered the temple and asked for assistance. The answer came through an oracle that they should leave the temple and scatter behind them their mothers' bones.

Deucalion could not believe his ears, and Pyrrha stated aloud that she would never dishonor her mother's spirit by thus disturbing her bones. Deucalion, however, thought that the words of the oracle were not to be taken literally, that the mother mentioned was not a human mother, but rather mother earth, and that the bones to be scattered were stones from the earth's body. Deciding to put this interpretation to the test, Deucalion and Pyrrha scattered behind them stones from the earth.

No one would believe what happened afterward, if it were not for the testimony of ancient legends. The stones, once thrown to the ground, lost their hardness and assumed human forms. Those scattered by Deucalion became male, and those scattered by Pyrrha became female. And thus the earth was repopulated.

Then through the natural process of warmth and moisture and earth reacting with one another the lower animals were reborn as well. Yes, fire and water are opposites, but moist heat is the source of all living things. Creation comes about through the resolution of opposing forces.

13

Hymn to the Nile—ca. 2500 BCE

This hymn was composed near the end of the Old Kingdom. The Nile River brought life to Egypt in many ways. The first people in this area settled along its banks and learned to use its annual flood to irrigate and fertilize their crops. The fish and waterfowl the river harbored were a valuable source of protein. Despite the hordes of crocodiles that lived in its depths, the Nile was essential to the well-being of all Egyptians. The writer of this hymn refers to the Nile as a god. What god-like powers does he give the river?

Praise to thee, O Nile, that issueth from the earth, and cometh to nourish Egypt. Of hidden nature, a darkness in the daytime. . . .

That watereth the meadows, he that Rē[1] hath created to nourish all cattle. That giveth drink to the desert places, which are far from water; it is his dew that falleth from heaven.

Beloved of Kēb,[2] director of the corngod; that maketh to flourish every workshop of Ptah.[3]

Lord of fish, that maketh the waterfowl to go upstream. . . .

That maketh barley and createth wheat, so that he may cause the temples to keep festivals.

If he be sluggish,[4] the nostrils are stopped up,[5] and all men are improverished; the victuals of the gods are diminished, and millions of men perish.

"*Hymn to the Nile*," trans. by A. M. Blackman as printed in Sources of World Civilization, ed. by Oliver and Johnson, Prentice Hall, 1994.

1 The sun-god.

2 The earth-god.

3 Ptah, the craftsman, who fashions everything, could effect nothing without the Nile.

4 On the occasion of a deficient inundation.

5 Men no longer breathe and live.

If he be niggardly the whole land is in terror and great and small lament. . . . Khnum[6] hath fashioned him. When he riseth, the land is in exultation and every body is in joy. All jaws begin to laugh and every tooth is revealed.

He that bringeth victuals and is rich in food, that createth all that is good. The revered, sweet-smelling. . . . That createth herbage for the cattle, and giveth sacrifice to every god, be he in the underworld, in heaven, or upon earth. . . . That filleth the storehouses, and maketh wide the granaries, that giveth things to the poor.

He that maketh trees to grow according to every wish, and men have no lack thereof; the ship is built by his power, for there is no joinery with stones. . . .

. . . thy young folk and thy children shout for joy over thee, and men hail thee as king. Unchanging of laws, when he cometh forth in the presence of Upper and Lower Egypt. Men drink the water. . . .

He that was in sorrow is become glad, and every heart is joyful. Sobk,[7] the child of Neith, laugheth, and the divine Ennead, that is in thee, is glorious.

Thou that vomitest forth, giving the fields to drink and making strong the people. He that maketh the one rich and loveth the other. He maketh no distinctions, and boundaries are not made for him.

Thou light, that cometh from the darkness! Thou fat for his cattle. He is a strong one, that createth. . . .

. . . one beholdeth the wealthy as him that is full of care, one beholdeth each one with his implements. . . . None that (otherwise) goeth clad, is clad,[8] and the children of notables are unadorned. . . .

He that establisheth right, whom men love. . . . It would be but lies to compare thee with the sea, that bringeth no corn. . . . no bird descendeth in the desert. . . .

Men begin to play to thee on the harp, and men sing to thee with the hand.[9] Thy young folk and thy children shout for joy over thee, and deputations to thee are appointed.

He that cometh with splendid things and adorneth the earth! That causeth the ship to prosper before men; that quickeneth the hearts in them that are with child; that would fain have there be a multitude of all kinds of cattle.

When thou art risen in the city of the sovereign, then men are satisfied with a goodly list.[10] "I would like lotus flowers," saith the little one, "and all manner of things," saith the . . . commander, "and all manner of herbs," say the children. Eating bringeth forgetfulness of him.[11] Good things are scattered over the dwelling. . . .

When the Nile floodeth, offering is made to thee, cattle are slaughtered for thee, a great oblation is made for thee. Birds are fattened for thee, antelopes are hunted for thee in the desert. Good is recompensed unto thee.

---

6 The ram-headed god, who fashions all that is.

7 Sobk has the form of a crocodile and will originally have been a water-god, who rejoices in the inundation.

8 For hard work, clothes are taken off.

9 It is an old custom to beat time with the hand while singing.

10 *I.e.,* a multitude of good things.

11 The Nile.

Offering is also made to every other god, even as is done for the Nile, with incense, oxen, cattle, and birds (upon) the flame. The Nile hath made him his cave in Thebes, and his name shall be known no more in the underworld. . . .

All ye men, extol the Nine Gods, and stand in awe of the might which his son, the Lord of All, hath displayed, even he that maketh green the Two River-banks. Thou art verdant, O Nile, thou art verdant. He that maketh man to live on his cattle, and his cattle on the meadow! Thou art verdant, thou art verdant: O Nile, thou art verdant.

14

Hymn to the Sun—ca. 1340 BCE

Amenhotep IV (1350-1334 BCE) was perhaps the first monotheist. He attempted to introduce the worship of only one god, Aten (the Sun), who was creator of all and the source of all goodness. The Egyptian people did not willingly embrace this concept, nor did the priests who served the many anthropomorphic Egyptian deities. Aten-worship ended with the death of Amenhotep, who had changed his name to Akenaten in honor of his god. Some scholars believe that Hebrew Psalm 104, which gives the Lord some of the Sun's attributes, was influenced by this hymn.

Thy dawning is beautiful in the horizon of heaven,
O living Aton,[1] Beginning of life!
When thou risest in the eastern horizon of heaven,
Thou fillest every land with thy beauty;
For thou art beautiful, great, glittering, high over the earth;
Thy rays, they encompass the lands, even all thou hast made.
Thou are Rē, and thou has carried them all away captive;
Thou bindest them by thy love.
Though thou art afar, thy rays are on earth;
Though thou art on high, thy footprints are the day.

When thou settest in the western horizon of heaven,
The world is in darkness like the dead.

"*Hymn to the Sun*," trans. by James H. Breasted as printed in Sources of World Civilization, ed. by Oliver and Johnson, Prentice Hall, 1994.

1 [One of the names given to the sun god—*Ed.*]

They sleep in their chambers,
Their heads are wrapt up,
Their nostrils stopped, and none seeth the other.
Stolen are all their things, that are under their heads,
While they know it not.
Every lion cometh forth from his den,
All serpents, they sting.
Darkness reigns,
The world is in silence,
He that made them has gone to rest in his horizon.

Bright is the earth,
When thou risest in the horizon,
When thou shinest as Aton by day.
The darkness is banished,
When thou sendest forth thy rays,
The Two Lands[2] are in daily festivity,
Awake and standing upon their feet,
For thou hast raised them up.
Their limbs bathed, they take their clothing;
Their arms uplifted in adoration to thy dawning.
Then in all the world, they do their work.

All cattle rest upon their herbage,
All trees and plants flourish,
The birds flutter in their marshes.
Their wings uplifted in adoration to thee.
All the sheep dance upon their feet,
All winged things fly,
They live when thou has shone upon them.

The barques sail up-stream and down-stream alike.
Every highway is open because thou hast dawned.
The fish in the river leap up before thee,
And thy rays are in the midst of the great sea.

Thou art he who creates the man-child in woman,
Who makest seed in man,
Who giveth life to the son in the body of his mother,
Who soothest him that he may not weep,
A nurse even in the womb.
Who giveth breath to animate every one that he maketh.
When he cometh forth from the body . . . on the day of his birth,
Thou openest his mouth in speech.
Thou suppliest his necessities.

---

2 [Upper and Lower Egypt—*Ed.*]

When the chicklet crieth in the eggshell,
Thou givest him breath therein, to preserve him alive.
When thou has perfected him
That he may pierce the egg,
He cometh forth from the egg,
To chirp with all his might;
He runneth about upon his two feet,
When he hath come forth thereform.
How manifold are thy works!
They are hidden from before us,
O thou sole god, whose powers no other possesseth.
Thou didst create the earth according to thy desire.
While thou wast alone:
Men, all cattle large and small,
All that are upon the earth,
That go about upon their feet;
All that are on high,
That fly with their wings.
The countries of Syria and Nubia,
The land of Egypt;
Thou settest every man in his place,
Thou suppliest their necessities.
Every one has his possessions,
And his days are reckoned.
Their tongues are divers in speech,
Their forms likewise and their skins,
For thou divider, hast divided the peoples.

Thou makest the Nile in the Nether World,
Thou bringest it at thy desire, to preserve the people alive.
O lord of them all, when feebleness is in them,
O lord of every house, who risest for them,
O son of day, the fear of every distant land,
Thou makest also their life.
Thou has set a Nile in heaven,
That it may fall for them,
Making floods upon the mountains, like the great sea;
And watering their fields among their towns.
How excellent are thy designs, O lord of eternity!
The Nile in heaven is for the strangers,
And for the cattle of every land, that go upon their feet;
But the Nile, it cometh from the Nether World for Egypt.

Thus thy rays nourish every garden,
When thou risest they live, and grow by thee.
Thou makest the seasons, in order to create all thy works:
Winter bringing them coolness,

And the heat of summer likewise.
Thou has made the distant heaven to rise therein,
In order to behold all that thou didst make,
While thou wast alone,
Rising in thy form as living Aton,
Dawning, shining afar off and returning.
Thou makest the beauty of form, through thyself alone.
Cities, towns and settlements,
On highway or on river,
All eyes see thee before them.
For thou art Aton of the day over the earth.

Thou art in my heart,
There is no other that knoweth thee,
Save thy son Ikhnaton.
Thou hast made him wise in thy designs
And in thy might.
The world is in thy hand,
Even as thou hast made them.
When thou hast risen, they live:
When thou settest, they die.
For thou art duration, beyond thy mere limbs,
By thee man liveth,
And their eyes look upon thy beauty
Until thou settest.
All labour is laid aside,
When thou settest in the west;
When thou risest, they are made to grow . . . for the king.

Since thou didst establish the earth,
Thou hast raised them up for thy son,
Who came forth from thy limbs,
The king, living in truth,
The lord of the Two Lands Nefer-khepure-Rē, Wan-Rē,
The son of Rē, living in truth, lord of diadems,
Ikhnaton, whose life is long;
And for the great royal wife, his beloved,
Mistress of the Two Lands, Nefer nefru aton, Nofretete,
Living and flourishing for ever and ever.

15

The Book of the Dead
(Egypt)—ca. 1600 BCE

The Egyptian Book of the Dead *is actually a series of chapters that contain a collection of magic spells and formulas dedicated to aiding the dead in their journey to the underworld. They not only proclaim the virtues of the deceased, but they also provide the protection of the gods, as well as passwords and clues for a safe journey. The charms and formulas were sold on papyri that could be ordered before death and were usually later glued to the underside of the sarcophagus lid. Egyptians considered life to be good and wanted to continue it after death. Does* The Book of the Dead *provide proof that the Egyptian religion had an ethical component? How? How much do you think ancient Egyptians relied on magic to gain the favor of the gods?*

THE PROTESTATION OF GUILTLESSNESS

What is said on reaching the Broad-Hall of the Two Justices, absolving X of every sin which he has committed, and seeing the faces of the gods:

Hail to thee, O great god, lord of the Two Justices! I have come to thee, my lord, I have been brought that I might see thy beauty. I know thee; I know thy name and the names of the forty-two gods who are with thee in the Broad-Hall of the Two Justices, who live on them who preserve evil and who drink their blood on that day of reckoning up character in the presence of Wenofer. Behold, "Sati-mertifi, Lord of Justice," is thy name. I have come to thee; I have brought thee justice; I have expelled deceit for thee.

I have not committed evil against men.
I have not mistreated cattle.
I have not blasphemed a god.
I have not done violence to a poor man.
I have not done that which the gods abominate.
I have not defamed a slave to his superior.
I have not made (anyone) sick.
I have not made (anyone) weep.
I have not killed.
I have given no order to a killer.
I have not caused anyone suffering.

From *Ancient Near Eastern Texts Relating to the Old Testament* 2nd ed., ed. by James B. Pritchard (Princeton, NJ: Princeton University Press, 1955).

I have not cut down on the food-(income) in the temples.
I have not damaged the bread of the gods.
I have not taken the loaves of the blessed (dead).
I have not had sexual relations with a boy.
I have not defiled myself.
I have neither increased or diminished the grain-measure.
I have not taken milk from the mouths of children.
I have not driven cattle away from their pasturage.
I have not snared the birds of the gods.
I have not caught fish in their marshes.
I have not held up the water in its season.
I have not built a dam against running water.
I have not driven away the cattle of the god's property.
I have not stopped a god on his procession.

I am pure! My purity is the purity of the great benu-bird which is in Herakleopolis, because I am really that nose of the Lord of Breath, who makes all men to live, on that day of filling out the Eye (of Horus) in Heliopolis, in the second month of the second season, the last day, in the presence of the lord of this land. I am the one who has seen the filling out of the Eye in Heliopolis. Evil will never happen to me in this land or in this Broad-Hall of the Two justices, because I know the names of these gods who are in it, the followers of the great god. . . .

INSTRUCTIONS FOR THE
USE OF THE SPELL

To be done in conformance with what takes place in this Broad-Hall of the Two Justices. This spell is to be recited when one is clean and pure, clothed in (fresh) garments, shod with white sandals, painted with stibium, and anointed with myrrh, to whom cattle, fowl, incense, bread, beer, vegetables have been offered. Then make thou this text in writing on a clean pavement with ochre smeared with earth upon which pigs and (other) small cattle have not trodden. As for him on whose behalf this book is made, he shall be prosperous and his children shall be prosperous, without greed, because he shall be a trusted man of the king and his courtiers. Loaves, jars, bread, and joints of meat shall be given to him from the altar of the great god. He cannot be held back at any door of the west, (but) he shall be ushered in with the Kings of Upper and Lower Egypt, and he shall be in the retinue of Osiris.

Right and true a million times.

16

Chandogya Upanishad— 3rd century BCE

At the end of the Vedas, *the Chandogya Upanishad addresses the mysticism and specu-lations about reality and the individual soul that characterize the Upanishads in a didac-tic manner. In this story, a son returns from school after spending years studying the* Vedas *and feels himself superior in knowledge to his father. The father then shows the son that there is more to understanding than learning. What point is the father trying to make?*

NINTH KHANDA

The unitary World-Soul, the immanent reality of all things and of man

1. 'As the bees, my dear, prepare honey by collecting the essences of differ-ent trees and reducing the essence to a unity, [2]. as they are not able to dis-criminate "I am the essence of this tree," "I am the essence of that tree"—even so, indeed, my dear, all creatures here, though they reach Being, know not "We have reached Being."

3. Whatever they are in this world whether tiger, or lion, or wolf, or boar, or worm, or fly, or gnat, or mosquito, that they become.

4. That which is the finest essence—this whole world has that as its soul. That is Reality. That is Ātman (Soul). That art thou, Śvetaketu.'

'Do you, sir, cause me to understand even more.'

'So be it, my dear,' said he.

THIRTEENTH KHANDA

1. 'Place this salt in the water. In the morning come unto me.'

Then he did so.

Then he said to him: 'That salt you placed in the water last evening—please bring it hither.'

Then he grasped for it, but did not find it, as it was completely dissolved.

From The Chandogya Upanishad in R.E. Hume, ed., *The Thirteen Principal Upanishads,*
(Bombay: Oxford University Press).

2. 'Please take a sip if it from this end,' said he. 'How is it?'

'Salt.'

'Take a sip from the middle,' said he. 'How is it?'

'Salt.'

'Take a sip from that end,' said he. "How is it?'

'Salt.'

'Set it aside. Then come unto me.'

He did so, saying, 'It is always the same.'

Then he said to him: 'Verily, indeed, my dear, you do not perceive Being here. Verily, indeed, it is here.

3. That which is the finest essence—this whole world has that as its soul. That is Reality. That is Ātman (soul). That are thou, Śvetaketu.'

17

Benares Sermon of Buddha— 6th century BCE

The Benares Sermon of Buddha is similar to Jesus' Sermon on the Mount in that it contains the core of Buddhist teaching, just as the essence of Christianity is contained in the Sermon on the Mount. Buddha (Siddhartha Guatama) was born in Southern Nepal in 563 BCE. The son of a king, he renounced his family and inheritance and sought enlightenment as a monk. After a period of self-denial and asceticism, he realized that asceticism in itself had no meaning. Exhausted in body, he found enlightenment in the middle way while sitting under a Bodhi tree (or Tree of Life). Returning home, he became a teacher and gave his first sermon at Benares. He traveled northern India for 45 years teaching both rich and poor before dying peacefully at the age of 80. How does this sermon illustrate the otherworldly aspects of Buddhism as compared to Chinese philosophy?

There are two extremes, O brethren, which a holy man should avoid—the habitual practice of . . . self-indulgence, which is vulgar and profitless . . . and the habitual practice of self-mortification, which is painful and equally profitless.

From The Benares Sermon of Buddha in Lewis Browne, ed., *The World's Great Scriptures* (New York: Macmillan, 1946).

There is a middle path, O brethren, discovered by the Tathagata (Buddha)—a path which opens the eyes, and bestows understanding, which leads to peace of mind, to the higher wisdom, to full enlightenment, to Nirvana. Verily! it is this noble eightfold path; that is to say:

> Right views;
> Right aspirations;
> Right speech;
> Right conduct;
> Right livelihood;
> Right effort;
> Right mindfulness; and
> Right contemplation.

This, O brethren, is that middle path, avoiding these two extremes, discovered by the Tathagata—that path which opens the eyes, and bestows understanding, which leads to peace of mind, to the higher wisdom, to full enlightenment, to Nirvana!

Now this, O brethren, is the noble truth concerning suffering.

Birth is attended with pain, decay is painful, disease is painful, death is painful. Union with the unpleasant is painful, painful is separation from the pleasant; and any craving that is unsatisfied, that too is painful. In brief, the five aggregates that spring from attachment (the conditions of individuality and their cause) are painful

This, then, O brethren, is the noble truth concerning suffering.

Now this, O brethren, is the noble truth concerning the origin of suffering.

Verily, it is that thirst (or craving), causing the renewal of existence, accompanied by sensual delight, seeking satisfaction now here, now there—that is to say, the craving for the gratification of the passions, or the craving for a future life, or the craving for success in this present life.

This then, O brethren, is the noble truth concerning the origin of suffering.

Now this, O brethren, is the noble truth concerning the destruction of suffering. Verily, it is the destruction, in which no passion remains, of this very thirst; the laying aside of, the getting rid of, the being free from, the harboring no longer of this thirst. This then, O brethren, is the noble truth concerning the destruction of suffering.

Now this, O brethren, is the noble truth concerning the way which leads to the destruction of sorrow. Verily! it is this noble eightfold path . . .

. . . as soon, O brethren, as my knowledge and insight were quite clear regarding each of these four noble truths . . . then did I become certain that I had attained to the full insight of that wisdom which is unsurpassed in the heavens or on earth, among the whole race of Samanas and brahmins or of gods or men.

And now this knowledge and this insight has arisen within me. Immovable is the emancipation of my heart. This is my last existence. There will now be no rebirth for me!

18

The Tibetan Book of the Dead— 8th century CE

The Tibetan Book of the Dead is an ancient Tibetan Buddhist text that was finally transcribed in the eighth century CE. The book is a guide for those who are in the period between death and the next rebirth; it was read to the dying to help them achieve liberation. How does the Buddhist view of death differ from that of the Egyptians?

DEATH AND INTERMEDIATE STATES

Bardo Thodol, 'The Tibetan Book of the Dead,' is a guide for the dead and dying. The first part, called Chikhai Bardo, describes the moment of death. The second part, Chonyid Bardo, deals with the states which supervene immediately after death. The third part, Sidpa Bardo, concerns the onset of the birth instinct and of prenatal events.

When the expiration hath ceased, the vital-force will have sunk into the nerve-centre of Wisdom [1] and the Knower [2] will be experiencing the Clear Light of the natural condition [3]. Then the vital force, being thrown backwards and flying downwards through the right and left nerves [4] the Intermediate State (Bardo) momentarily dawns.

The above [directions] should be applied before [the vital force hath] rushed into the left nerve [after first having traversed the navel nerve-centre].

The time [ordinarily necessary for this motion of the vital-force] is as long as the inspiration is still present, or about the time required for eating a meal.

Then the manner of application [of the instructions] is:

When the breathing is about to cease, it is best if the Transference hath been applied efficiently; if [the application] hath been inefficient, then [address the deceased] thus:

O nobly-born [so and so by name], the time hath now come for thee to seek the Path [in reality]. Thy breathing is about to cease. Thy guru hath set

---

1 The 'nerve-centres' are the 'psychic centres' (*cakra*). The 'nerve-centre of wisdom' is located in the heart-centre (*anahata-cakra*).

2 'Knower,' i.e. the mind in its knowing functions.

3 The mind in its natural, or primal, state.

4 That is, the 'psychic nerves,' *pingala-nadi* and *ida-nadi*.

thee face to face before with the Clear Light; and now thou art about to experience in its Reality in the Bardo state, wherein all things are like the void and cloudless sky, and the naked, spotless intellect is like unto a transparent vacuum without circumference or centre. At this moment, know thou thyself-, and abide in that state. I, too, at this time, am setting thee face to face.

Having read this, repeat it many times in the ear of the person dying, even before the expiration hath ceased, so as to impress it on the mind [of the dying one].

If the expiration is about to cease, turn the dying one over on the right side, which posture is called the 'Lying Posture of a Lion.' The throbbing of the arteries [on the right and left side of the throat] is to be pressed.

If the person dying be disposed to sleep, or if the sleeping state advances, that should be arrested, and the arteries pressed gently but firmly. Thereby the vital-force will not be able to return from the median-nerve and will be sure to pass out through the Brahmanic aperture.[5] Now the real setting-face-to-face is to be applied.

At this moment, the first glimpsing of the Bardo of the Clear Light of Reality, which is the Infallible Mind of the Dharma-Kaya, is experienced by all sentient beings.

After the expiration hath completely ceased, press the nerves of sleep firmly; and, a lama, or a person higher or more learned than thyself, impress in these words, thus:

Reverend Sir, now that thou art experiencing the Fundamental Clear Light, try to abide in that state which now thou art experiencing.

And also in the case of any other person the reader shall set him face-to-face thus:

O nobly-born [so-and-so], listen. Now thou art experiencing the Radiance of the Clear Light of Pure Reality. Recognize it. O nobly-born, thy present intellect, in real nature void, not formed into anything as regards characteristics or colour, naturally void, is the very Reality, the All-Good.

Thine own intellect, which is now voidness, yet not to be regarded as of the voidness of nothingness, but as being the intellect itself, unobstructed, shining, thrilling, and blissful, is the very consciousness, the All-good Buddha.

Thine own consciousness, not formed into anything, in reality void, and the intellect, shining and blissful,-these two,-are inseparable. The union of them is the Dharma-Kaya state of Perfect Enlightenment.[6]

Thine own consciousness, shining, void, and inseparable from the Great Body of Radiance, hath no birth, nor death, and is the Immutable Light-Buddha Amitabha.

Knowing this is sufficient. Recognizing the voidness of thine own intellect to be Buddhahood, and looking upon it as being thine own consciousness, is to keep thyself in the [state of the] divine mind of the Buddha.

---

5 *Brahmarandhra, the fissure on the top of the cranium identified with sutura frontalis.*

6 *From the union of the two states of mind, or consciousness, is born the state of Perfect Enlighten-ment, Buddhahood. The Dharma-Kaya ('Body of Truth') symbolizes the purest and the highest state of being, a state of supramundane consciousness.*

Repeat this distinctly and dearly three or [even] seven times. That will recall to the mind [of the dying one] the former [i.e. when living] setting-face-to-face by the guru. Secondly, it will cause the naked consciousness to be recognized as the Clear Light; and, thirdly, recognizing one's own self [thus], one becometh permanently united with the Dharma-Kaya and liberation will be certain.

[if when dying, one is familiar with this state, the wheel of rebirth is stopped and liberation is instantaneously achieved. But such spiritual efficiency is so very rare that the normal mental condition of the dying person is unequal to the supreme feat of holding on to the state in which the Clear Light shines. There follows a progressive descent into lower and lower states of the Bardo existence, and finally rebirth. immediately after the first state of Chikhai Bardo comes the second stage, when the consciousness-principle leaves the body and says to itself. 'Am I dead, or am I not dead?' without being able to determine.]

But even though the Primary Clear Light be not recognized, the Clear Light of the second Bardo being recognized, Liberation will be attained. If not liberated even by that, then that called the third Bardo or the Chonyid Bardo dawneth.

In this third stage of the Bardo, the karmic illusions come to shine. It is very important that this Great setting-face-to-face of the Chonyid Bardo be read: it hath much power and can do much good.

About this time [the deceased] can see that the share of food is being set aside, that the body is being stripped of its garments, that the place of the sleeping-rug is being swept;[7] can hear all the weeping and wailing of his friends and relatives, and, although he can see them and can hear them calling upon him, they cannot hear him calling upon them, so he goeth away displeased.

At that time, sounds, lights, and rays–all three–are experienced. These awe, frighten, and terrify, and cause much fatigue. At this moment, this setting-face-to-face with the Bardo [during the experiencing] of Reality is to be applied. Call the deceased by name, and correctly and distinctly explain to him, as follows:

O nobly-born, listen with full attention, without being distracted: There are six states of Bardo, namely: the natural state of Bardo while in the womb; the Bardo of the dream-state; the Bardo of ecstatic equilibrium, while in deep meditation; the Bardo of the moment of death; the Bardo [during the experiencing] of Reality, the Bardo of the inverse process of samsaric existence. These are the six.

O nobly-born, thou wilt experience three Bardos, the Bardo of the moment of death, the Bardo [during the experiencing] of Reality, and the Bardo while seeking rebirth. Of these three, up to yesterday, thou hadst experienced the Bardo of the moment of death. Although the Clear Light of Reality dawned upon thee, thou wert unable to hold on, and so thou hast to wander here. Now henceforth thou art going to experience the [other] two, the Chonyid Bardo and the Sidpa Bardo.[8] Thou wilt pay undistracted attention to that with which I am about to set thee face to face, and hold on;

---

7 *The references are (1) to the share of food being set aside for the deceased during the funeral rites; (2) to his corpse being prepared for the shroud; (3) to his bed or sleeping-place.*

8 *The Chonyid Bardo is the intermediate state during the experiencing of Reality. The Sidpa Bardo represents the state wherein the deceased is seeking rebirth.*

O nobly-born, that which is called death hath now come. Thou art departing from this world, but thou art not the only one; [death] cometh to all. Do
not cling, in fondness and weakness, to this life. Even though thou clingest out
of weakness, thou hast not the power to remain here. Thou wilt gain nothing
more than wandering in this *Samsara*.[9] Be not attached [to this world]; be not
weak. Remember the Precious Trinity.[10]

O nobly-born, whatever fear and terror may come to thee in the Chonyid
Bardo, forget not these words; and, bearing their meaning at heart, go forwards:
in them lieth the vital secret of recognition:

Alas! when the Uncertain Experiencing of Reality is dawning upon me here,

With every thought of fear or terror or awe for all [apparitional appearances] set aside,

May I recognize whatever [visions] appear, as the reflections of mine own consciousness;

May I know them to be of the nature of apparitions in the Bardo: When at this all-
important moment [of opportunity] of achieving a great end.

May I not fear the bands of Peaceful and Wrathful [Deities], mine own thought-forms.

Repeat thou these [verses] dearly, and remembering their significance as
thou repeatest them, go forwards, [O nobly-born]. Thereby, whatever visions
of awe or terror appear, recognition is certain; and forget not this vital secret
art lying therein.

O nobly-born, when thy body and mind were separating, thou must have
experienced a glimpse Of the Pure Truth, subtle, sparkling, bright dazzling,
glorious, and radiantly awesome, in appearance like a mirage moving across a
landscape in spring-time in one continuous stream of vibrations. Be not
daunted thereby, nor terrified, nor awed. That is the radiance of thine own
true nature. Recognize it.

From the midst of that radiance, the natural sound of Reality, reverberating
like a thousand thunders simultaneously sounding, will come. That is the
natural sound of thine own real self. Be not daunted thereby, nor terrified,
nor awed.

The body, which thou hast now is called the thought-body of propensi-
ties.[11] Since thou hast not a material body of flesh and blood, whatever may
come,-sounds, lights, or rays,-are, all three, unable to harm thee: thou art incapable of dying. It is quite sufficient for thee to know that these apparitions are
thine own thought-forms. Recognize this to be the Bardo.

O nobly-born, if thou dost not now recognize thine own thoughtforms,
whatever of meditation or of devotion thou mayest have performed while in
the human world-if thou hast not met with this present teaching-the lights
will daunt thee, the sounds will awe thee, and the rays will terrify thee.
Shouldst thou not know this an important key to the teachings,-not being able
to recognize the sounds, lights, and rays,-thou wilt have to wander in the
Samsara.

---

9 *Samsara, the universal becoming.*

10 *That is, the Buddha, the Dharma (= the Law, the Doctrine), the Samgha (the entire community*
of monks and hermits).

11 *'Thought-body' or 'mind-body' born of the past worldly existence.*

19

Sayings From the *Book of Dao* by Lao Tsu—5th century BCE

Some believe that Lao Tsu was a mythical person, but others think he was a real official who held several important government positions, including curator of the royal library. "Dao" roughly translated means "the path." In his writings, Lao Tsu looked for a way to avoid the constant warfare that existed in China during his lifetime. In some ways, Daoism is a combination of philosophy and psychology; it advises living in harmony with nature instead of following the rigid rules of society. This was contrary to Confucian belief that people should acknowledge their civic duty and live as good citizens and neighbors. In 440 CE, Daoism was adopted as the state religion of China. Why do you think many Chinese at this time turned to a philosophy so contrary to the Confucian way of life?

KNOWING THE ETERNAL LAW

Attain the utmost in Humility;
Hold firm to the basis of Quietude.
The myriad things take shape and rise to activity,
　　But I watch them fall back to their repose.
Like vegetation that luxuriantly grows
　　But returns to the root (soil) from which it springs.

To return to the root is Repose;
　　It is called going back to one's Destiny.
Going back to one's Destiny is to find the Eternal Law.
　　To know the Eternal Law is Enlightenment.
And not to know the Eternal Law
　　Is to court disaster.

He who knows the Eternal Law is tolerant;
Being tolerant, he is impartial;
Being impartial, he is kingly;
Being kingly, he is in accord with Nature;
Being in accord with Nature, he is in accord with Dao;
Being in accord with Dao, he is eternal,
And his whole life is preserved from harm.

From The Book of Tao in *The Wisdom of China and India*, ed. by Lin Yutang (New York: Random House, 1942).

RULERS

Of the best rulers
    The people (only) know that they exist;
The next best they love and praise;
The next they fear;
And the next they revile.

    When they do not command the people's faith,
    Some will lose faith in them,
    And then they resort to oaths!
But (of the best) when their task is accomplished, their work done,
The people all remark, "We have done it ourselves."

RACING HORSES

When the world lives in accord with Dao,
Racing horses are turned back to haul refuse carts.
When the world lives not in accord with Tao,
Cavalry abounds in the countryside.

There is no greater curse than the lack of contentment.
No greater sin than the desire for possession.
Therefore he who is contented with contentment shall be always content.

HARD AND SOFT

When man is born, he is tender and weak;
    At death, he is hard and stiff.
When the things and plants are alive, they are soft and supple;
When they are dead, they are brittle and dry.
    Therefore hardness and stiffness are the companions of death,
    And softness and gentleness are the companions of life.

Therefore when an army is headstrong, it will lose in battle.
When a tree is hard, it will be cut down.
    The big and strong belong underneath.
    The gentle and weak belong at the top.

20

Sayings of Confucius—6th century BCE

Confucius was a contemporary of Buddha, slightly younger than Lao Tsu, whose writings became the foundation of Chinese civilization for 25 centuries. His philosophy was adopted by the Han dynasty as the official moral and political doctrine of the Chinese state. Other than showing concern for others and living as a good citizen, Confucius stressed the importance of correct conduct and the belief that profit is not a proper motive for action. Why might Confucian philosophy be suited as a governing policy for a populous state? How might Confucian beliefs have kept China from becoming a modern industrialized state until the twentieth century?

The Master said: "I will not be afflicted at men's not knowing me; I will be afflicted that I do not know men."

The Master said, "At fifteen I had my mind bent on learning.

At thirty, I stood firm.

At forty, I had no doubts.

At fifty, I knew the decrees of heaven.

At sixty, my ear was an obedient organ *for the reception* of truth.

At seventy, I could follow what my heart desired, without transgressing what was right."

The Master said, "It is virtuous manners which constitute the excellence of a neighborhood. If a man in selecting a residence do not fix on one where such prevail, how can he be wise?"

The Master said, "A scholar, whose mind is set on truth, and who is ashamed of bad clothes and bad food, is not fit to be discoursed with."

The Master said, "The superior man, in the world, does not set his mind for anything, or against anything: what is right he will follow."

The Master said, "The superior man thinks of virtue; the small man thinks of comfort. The superior man thinks of the sanctions of law; the small man thinks of favors *which he may receive.*"

The Master said, "*A man should say,* I am not concerned that I have no place,—I am concerned how I may fit myself for one. I am not concerned that I am not known,—I seek to be worthy to be known."

From Confucian Sayings in *The Ideas that Have Influenced Civilization*, Vol. 1, ed. by Oliver J. Thatcher (Milwaukee, WI: Roberts-Manchester, 1901).

The Master said, "The mind of the superior man is conversant with righteousness; the mind of the mean man is conversant with gain."

The Master said, "The cautious seldom err."

The Master said, "They who know *the truth* are not equal to those who love it, and they who love it are not equal to those who find delight in it."

The Master said, "I would not have him act with me, who will unarmed attack a tiger, or cross a river without a boat, dying without any regret. My associate must be the man who proceeds to action full of solicitude, who is fond of adjusting his plans, and then carries them into execution."

The things in reference to which the Master exercised the greatest caution were—fasting, war, and sickness.

The Master said, "When I walk along with two others, they may serve me as my teachers. I will select their good qualities and follow them, their bad qualities and avoid them."

There were four things which the Master taught,—letters, ethics, devotion of soul, and truthfulness.

The Master said, "A sage it is not mine to see; could I see a man of real talent and virtue, that would satisfy me."

Tsze-chang asked what constituted intelligence. The Master said, "He with whom neither slander that gradually soaks *into the mind*, nor statements that startle like a wound in the flesh, are successful, may be called intelligent indeed. Yea, he with whom neither soaking slander nor startling statements are successful, may be called far-seeing."

Tsze-loo asked how a sovereign should be served. The Master said, "Do not impose on him, and, moreover, withstand him to his face."

Some one said, "What do you say concerning the principle that injury should be recompensed with kindness?"

The Master said, "With what then will you recompense kindness?

Recompense injury with justice, and recompense kindness with kindness."

Tsze-kung asked, saying, "Is there one word which may serve as a rule of practice for all one's life?" The Master said, "Is not RECIPROCITY such a word? What you do not want done to yourself, do not do to others."

The Master said, "The superior man is correctly firm, and not firm merely."

Confucius said, "There are three things of which the superior man stands in awe. He stands in awe of the ordinances of Heaven. He stands in awe of great men. He stands in awe of the words of sages."

21

Mencius—4th century BCE

The Chinese call Mencius "the second sage." Like Confucius, he was unsuccessful in getting a ruler to follow his philosophies. During his lifetime, the Chinese government adopted Confucion philosophy but only after his death. Mencius believed that rulers were given the mandate of Heaven (the gods) to bring peace and order to the people. Unlike Confucius, he taught that the people could revolt against rulers who did not fulfill this promise. Why do you think such a "Western" idea might have originated in ancient China?

Mencius said to the king Hsüan of Ch'î, 'Suppose that one of your Majesty's ministers were to entrust his wife and children to the care of his friend, while he himself went into Ch'û to travel, and that, on his return, he should find that the friend had let his wife and children suffer from cold and hunger;—how ought he to deal with him?' The king said, 'He should cast him off.'

Mencius proceeded, 'Suppose that the chief criminal judge could not regulate the officers under him, how would you deal with him?' The king said, 'Dismiss him.'

Mencius again said, 'If within the four borders of your kingdom there is not good government, what is to be done?' The king looked to the right and left, and spoke of other matters.

THE GREAT MAN

To dwell in the wide house of the world, to stand in the correct seat of the world, and to walk in the great path of the world; when he obtains his desire for office, to practice his principles for the good of the people; and when that desire is disappointed, to practice them alone; to be above the power of riches and honours to make dissipated, of poverty and mean condition to make swerve from principle, and of power and force to make bend:—these characteristics constitute the great man.

From Mencius in *The Chinese Classics*, 2nd ed., Vol. II, edited by James Legge (Oxford: Clarendon Press, 1895).

SIMPLICITY

'Halls several times eight cubits high, with beams projecting several cubits;—these, if my wishes were to be realized, I would not have. Food spread before me over ten cubits square, and attendants and concubines to the amount of hundreds;—these, though my wishes were realized, I would not have. . . .'

Mencius said, 'To nourish the mind there is nothing better than to make the desires few.'

22

A Legalist View of Life—3rd century BCE

Legalism was the harshest of ancient China's major philosophies. It placed the rule of law over everyone, even the rulers. Legalist philosophy was founded by Han Feizu, who had been educated in the Confucian tradition. Although previous Chinese laws existed only in the minds of the rulers, under Legalism the law code was written and the code itself ran the state. The king and his ministers were merely administrators. Punishments were harsh because the Legalists had a pessimistic view of the world. They believed that people needed a strong ruler or would grow lazy and disrespectful. China was unified under the legalist Qin emperor, but his rule was unpopular. The succeeding Han dynasty turned back to Confucian philosophy. How does Legalism differ from Confucian and Daoist philosophy?

If orders are made trim, laws never deviate; if laws are equable, there will be no culprit among the officials. Once the law is fixed, nobody can damage it by means of virtuous words. If men of merit are appointed to office, the people will have little to say; if men of virtue are appointed to office the people will have much to talk about. The enforcement of laws depends upon the method of judicial administration. Who administers judicial affairs with ease . . . attains supremacy. . . . Whoever procrastinates in creating order, will see his state dismembered.

From Han Fei-Tzu, The Complete Works, 2 vols. trans. by W. K. Liao (London: Arthur Probsthain, 1959), Vol. II, p. 322–333.

Govern by penalties; wage war by rewards; and enlarge the bounties so as to put the principles of statecraft into practice. If so, there will be no wicked people in the state nor will there by any wicked trade at the market. If things are many and trifles are numerous, and if farming is relaxed and villainy prevails, the state will certainly be dismembered.

If the people have a surplus of food, make them receive rank by giving grain to the state. If only through their own effort they can receive rank, then farmers will not idle.

If a tube three inches long has no bottom, it can never be filled. Conferring office and rank or granting profit and bounty without reference to merit, is like a tube having no bottom.

If the state confers office and bestows rank, it can be said to devise plans with complete wisdom and wage war with complete courage. Such a state will find a rival. Again, if the state confers office and bestows rank according to merit, then rules will be simplified and opponents barred; this can be said to abolish government by means of government, abolish words by means of words, and bestow rank according to merit. Therefore the state will have much strength and none else in All-under-Heaven will dare to invade it. When its soldiers march out, they will take the objective and, having taken it, will certainly be able to hold it. When it keeps its soldiers in reserve and does not attack, it will certainly become rich.

The affairs of the government, however small, should never be abandoned. For instance, office and rank are always obtained according to the acquired merit; though there may be flattering words, it will be impossible thereby to make any interference in the state affairs. This is said to be "government by figures." For instance, in attacking with force, ten points are taken for every point given out; but in attacking with words, one hundred are lost for every one marched out. If a state is fond of force, it is called hard to attack; if a state is fond of words, it is called easy to attack.

If the ability of the official is equal to his post, if his duty is lightened and he never reserves any surplus energy in mind, and if he does not shift any responsibility of additional offices back to the ruler, then there will be no hidden grudge inside. If the intelligent ruler makes the state affairs never mutually interfere, there will be no dispute; if he allows no official to hold any kind of additional post, everybody will develop his talent or skill; and if he allows no two persons to share the same meritorious achievement, there will be no quarrel.

If penalties are heavy and rewards are few, it means that the superior loves the people, wherefore the people will die for rewards. If rewards are many and penalties are light, it means that the superior does not love the people, wherefore the people will never die for rewards.

If the profit issues from one outlet only, the state will have no rival; if it issues from two outlets, its soldiers will be half useful; and if the profit comes from ten outlets, the people will not observe the law. If heavy penalties are clear and if the people are always well disciplined and then if men are engaged in case of emergency, the superior will have all the advantage.

In inflicting penalties light offences should be punished severely; if light offences do not appear, heavy offences will not come. This is said to be to abolish penalties by means of penalties. And the state will certainly become strong. If crimes are serious but penalties are light, light penalties breed further troubles. This is said to create penalties through penalties, and such a state will infallibly be dismembered.

The sage in governing the people considers their springs of action, never tolerates their wicked desires, but seeks only for the people's benefit. Therefore, the penalty he inflicts is not due to any hatred for the people but to his motive of loving the people. If penalty triumphs, the people are quiet; if reward over-flows, culprits appear. Therefore the triumph of penalty is the beginning of order; the overflow of reward, the origin of chaos.

Indeed, it is the people's nature to delight in disorder and detach themselves from legal restraints. Therefore, when the intelligent sovereign governs the state, if he makes rewards clear, the people will be encouraged to render meritorious services; if he makes penalties severe, the people will attach themselves to the law. If they are encouraged to render meritorious services, public affairs will not be obstructed; if they attach themselves to the law, culprits will not appear. Therefore, he who governs the people should nip the evil in the bud; he who commands troops, should inculcate warfare in the people's mind. If prohibitions can uproot causes of villainy, there will always be order; if soldiers can imagine warfare in mind, there will always be victory. When the sage is governing the people, he attains order first, wherefore he is strong; he prepares for war first, wherefore he wins.

Indeed, the administration of the state affairs requires the attention to the causes of human action so as to unify the people's mental trends; the exclusive elevation of public welfare so as to stop self-seeking elements, the reward for denunciation of crime so as to suppress culprits; and finally the clarification of laws so as to facilitate governmental procedures. Whoever is able to apply these four measures, will become strong; whoever is unable to apply these four measures, will become weak. Indeed, the strength of the state is due to the administration of its political affairs; the honour of the sovereign is due to his supreme power. Now, the enlightened ruler possesses the supreme power and the administrative organs; the ignoble ruler possesses both the supreme power and the administrative organs, too. Yet the results are not the same, because their standpoints are different. Thus, as the enlightened ruler has the supreme power in his grip, the superior is held in high esteem; as he unifies the administrative organs, the state is in order. Hence law is the origin of supremacy and penalty is the beginning of love.

Indeed, it is the people's nature to abhor toil and enjoy ease. However, if they pursue ease, the land will waste; if the land wastes, the state will not be in order. If the state is not orderly, it will become chaotic. If reward and penalty take no effect among the inferiors, government will come to a deadlock. Therefore, he who wants to accomplish a great achievement but hesitates to apply his full strength, can not hope for the accomplishment of the achievement; he who wants to settle the people's disorder but hesitates to change their traditions, can not hope to banish the people's disorder. Hence there is no constant method for the government of men. The law alone leads to political order. If laws are adjusted to the time, there is good government. If government fits the age, there will be great accomplishment. Therefore, when the people are naive, if you regulate them with fame, there will be good government; when everybody in the world is intelligent, if you discipline them with penalties, they will obey. While time is moving on, if laws do not shift accordingly, there will be misrule; while abilities are diverse, if prohibitions are not changed, the state will be dismembered. Therefore, the sage in governing the people makes laws move with time and prohibitions change with abilities. Who can exert his forces to land-utilization, will become rich; who can rush his forces at enemies, will become strong. The strong man not obstructed in his way will attain supremacy.

Therefore, the way to supremacy lies in the way of shutting culprits off and the way of blocking up wicked men. Who is able to block up wicked men, will eventually attain supremacy. The policy of attaining supremacy relies not on foreign states' abstention from disturbing your state, but on their inability to disturb your state. Who has to rely on foreign powers' abstention from disturbing his state before he can maintain his own independence, will see his state dismembered; who relies on their inability to disturb his state and willingly enacts the law, will prosper.

Therefore, the worthy ruler in governing the state follows the statecraft of invulnerability. When rank is esteemed, the superior will increase his dignity. He will accordingly bestow rewards on men of merit, confer ranks upon holders of posts, and appoint wicked men to no office. Who devotes himself to practical forces, gets a high rank. If the rank is esteemed, the superior will be honoured. The superior, if honoured, will attain supremacy. On the contrary, if the state does not strive after practical forces but counts on private studies, its rank will be lowered. If the rank is lowered, the superior will be humbled. If the superior is humbled, the state will be dismembered. Therefore, if the way of founding the state and using the people can shut off foreign invaders and block up self-seeking subjects, and if the superior relies on himself, supremacy will be attained. . . .

In general, wherever the state is extensive and the ruler is honourable, there laws are so strict that whatever is ordered works and whatever is prohibited stops. Therefore, the ruler of men who distinguishes between ranks and regulates bounties, makes laws severe and thereby makes the distinction strict.

Indeed, if the state is orderly, the people are safe; if affairs are confused, the country falls into peril. Who makes laws strict, hits on the true nature of mankind; who makes prohibitions lenient, misses the apparent fact. Moreover, everybody is, indeed, gifted with desperate courage. To exert desperate courage to get what one wants, is human nature. Yet everybody's likes and dislikes should be regulated by the superior. Now the people like to have profit and bounty and hate to be punished; if the superior catches their likes and dislikes and thereby holds their desperate courage under control, he will not miss the realities of affairs.

However, if prohibitions are lenient and facts are missed, reward and penalty will be misused. Again, when governing the people, if you do not regard conformity to law as right, you will eventually observe no law. Therefore, the science and philosophy of politics should by all means emphasize the distinction between degrees of penalty and of reward.

Who governs the state, should always uphold the law. In life there are ups and downs. If any ruler goes down, it is because in regulating rewards and penalties he makes no distinction between different degrees. Who governs the state, always distinguishes between reward and punishment. Therefore, some people might regard the distinction between reward and punishment as distinction, which should not be called distinction in the strict sense.

As regards the distinction made by the clear-sighted ruler, it is the distinction between different grades of reward and of punishment. Therefore, his subjects respect laws and fear prohibitions. They try to avoid crime rather than dare to expect any reward. Hence the saying: "Without expecting penalty and reward the people attend to public affairs."

For this reason, the state at the height of order is able to take the suppression of villainy for its duty. Why? Because its law comprehends human nature and accords with the principles of government.

If so, how to get rid of delicate villainy? By making the people watch one another in their hidden affairs. Then how to make them watch one another? By implicating the people of the same hamlet in one another's crime. When everyone knows that the penalty or reward will directly affect him, if the people of the same hamlet fail to watch one another, they will fear they may not be able to escape the implication, and those who are evil-minded, will not be allowed to forget so many people watching them. Were such the law, everybody would mind his own doings, watch everybody else, and disclose the secrets of any culprit. For, whosoever denounces a criminal offence, is not held guilty but is given a reward; whosoever misses any culprit, is definitely censured and given the same penalty as the culprit. Were such the law, all types of culprits would be detected. If the minutest villainy is not tolerated, it is due to the system of personal denunciation and mutual implication.

Indeed, the most enlightened method of governing a state is to trust measures and not men. For this reason, the tactful state is never mistaken if it does not trust the empty fame of men. If the land within the boundary is always in order it is because measures are employed. If any falling state lets foreign soldiers walk all over its territory and can neither resist nor prevent them, it is because that state trusts men and uses no measures. Men may jeopardize their own country, but measures can invade others' countries. Therefore, the tactful state spurns words and trusts laws.

Broadly speaking, it is hard to uncover a crooked merit that appears to fulfil the promise; it is hard to disclose the feature of the fault that is ornamented with beautiful words. Therefore, penalty and reward are often misled by doubledealers. What is alleged to be fulfilling the promise but is hard to uncover, is a villainous merit. Any minister's fault is hard to disclose, because its motive is missed. However, if by following reason you can not disclose the false merit and by analyzing feelings you are still deceived by the villainous motive, then can both reward and punishment have no mistake respectively?

For such reasons, false scholars establish names inside, while itinerants devise plans outside, till the stupid and the coward mix themselves with the brave and the clever. Inasmuch as the false path is customary, they are tolerated by their age. Therefore, their law does not work and their penalty affects nobody. If so, both reward and penalty have to be double-dealings.

Therefore, concrete facts have their limits of extension, but abstract principles involve no accurate measures. The absence of such measures is due not to the law but to the abandonment of law and the dependence on cleverness. If the law is abandoned and cleverness is employed, how can the appointee to office perform his duty? If duty and office are not equivalent to each other, then how can the law evade mistakes and how can penalty evade troubles? For this reason reward and punishment will be thrown into confusion and disorder, and the state policy will deviate and err, because neither penalty nor reward has any clear distinction of degree as in the difference between black and white.

23

The Ten Commandments— ca. 1000 BCE

After fleeing enslavement in Egypt, the Israelites under the leadership of Moses wandered the desert for a long time. The Old Testament recounts how they were provided daily with food (manna) and water by their God. Moses eventually led the Israelites to the foot of Mount Sinai, where he received the Ten Commandments. They were written by the hand of God on two tablets of stone. These commandments became the foundation of Mosaic Law and the Judeo-Christian religion. Both a legal code and a statement of belief, the commandments form the keystone of Christianity and Judaism. Why do you think receiving the tablets from the hand of God was important to the followers of Moses? What similarities exist between the Ten Commandments and the Bernares Sermon of Buddha?

From the Revised Standard Version of the Bible, Exodus, Reading 19 and 20. Copyright 1946, 1952, 1971 by the Division of Christian Education of the National Council of the Churches of Christ of USA.

16 On the morning of the third day there were thunders and lightnings, and a thick cloud upon the mountain, and a very loud trumpet blast, so that all the people who were in the camp trembled. 17 Then Moses brought the people out of the camp to meet God; and they took their stand at the foot of the mountain. 18 And Mount Sinai was wrapped in smoke, because the LORD descended upon it in fire; and the smoke of it went up like the smoke of a kiln, and the whole mountain quaked greatly. 19 And as the sound of the trumpet grew louder and louder, Moses spoke, and God answered him in thunder. 20 And the LORD came down upon Mount Sinai, to the top of the mountain; and the LORD called Moses to the top of the mountain, and Moses went up. 21 And the LORD said to Moses, "Go down and warn the people, lest they break through to the LORD to gaze and many of them perish. 22 And also let the priests who come near to the LORD consecrate themselves, lest the LORD break out upon them." 23 And Moses said to the LORD, "The people cannot come up to Mount Sinai; for thou thyself didst charge us, saying, 'Set bounds about the mountain, and consecrate it.'" 24 And the LORD said to him, "Go down, and come up bringing Aaron with you; but do not let the priests and the people break through to come up to the LORD, lest he break out against them." 25 So Moses went down to the people and told them.

CHAPTER 20

1 And God spoke all these words, saying,

2 "I am the LORD your God, who brought you out of the land of Egypt, out of the house of bondage.

3 "You shall have no other gods before me.

4 "You shall not make for yourself a graven image, or any likeness of anything that is in heaven above, or that is in the earth beneath, or that is in the water under the earth; 5 you shall not bow down to them or serve them; for I the LORD your God am a jealous God, visiting the iniquity of the fathers upon the children to the third and the fourth generation of those who hate me, 6 but showing steadfast love to thousands of those who love me and keep my commandments.

7 "You shall not take the name of the LORD your God in vain; for the LORD will not hold him guiltless who takes his name in vain.

8 "Remember the sabbath day, to keep it holy. 9 Six days you shall labor, and do all your work; 10 but the seventh day is a sabbath to the LORD your God; in it you shall not do any work, you, or your son, or your daughter, your manservant, or your maidservant, or your cattle, or the sojourner who is within your gates; 11 for in six days the LORD made heaven and earth, the sea, and all that is in them, and rested the seventh day; therefore the LORD blessed the sabbath day and hallowed it.

12 "Honor your father and your mother, that your days may be long in the land which the LORD your God gives you.

13 "You shall not kill.

14 "You shall not commit adultery.

15 "You shall not steal.

16 "You shall not bear false witness against your neighbor.

17 "You shall not covet your neighbor's house; you shall not covet your neighbor's wife, or his manservant, or his maidservant, or his ox, or his ass, or anything that is your neighbor's."

18 Now when all the people perceived the thunderings and the lightnings and the sound of the trumpet and the mountain smoking, the people were afraid and trembled; and they stood afar off, 19 and said to Moses, "You speak to us, and we will hear; but let not God speak to us, lest we die." 20 And Moses said to the people, "Do not fear; for God has come to prove you, and that the fear of him may be before your eyes, that you may not sin."

21 And the people stood afar off, while Moses drew near to the thick darkness where God was. 22 And the LORD said to Moses, "Thus you shall say to the people of Israel: 'You have seen for yourselves that I have talked with you from heaven. 23 You shall not make gods of silver to be with me, nor shall you make for yourselves gods of gold. 24 An altar of earth you shall make for me and sacrifice on it your burnt offerings and your peace offerings, your sheep and your oxen; in every place where I cause my name to be remembered I will come to you and bless you. 25 And if you make me an altar of stone, you shall not build it of hewn stones; for if you wield your tool upon it you profane it. 26 And you shall not go up by steps to my altar, that your nakedness be not exposed on it.'

24

Sermon on the Mount— ca. 27 CE

Found in the gospel of Matthew in the New Testament of the Bible, this sermon was given by Jesus at the beginning of his ministry. In it he expands on Jewish teaching and the Ten Commandments. Jesus, unlike other teachers and prophets of the time, brought his message directly to the ordinary people in various locations throughout Jerusalem. The following document contains the core of Christian belief in a simple and easy to understand form. How does it compare with the Benares Sermon of Buddha? How does Jesus expand on the earlier Jewish moral standard, the Ten Commandments?

Then Jesus was led up by the Spirit into the wilderness to be tempted by the devil. And he fasted forty days and forty nights, and afterward he was hungry. And the tempter came and said to him, "If you are the Son of God, command these stones to become loaves of bread." But he answered, "It is written,

'Man shall not live by bread alone, but by every word that proceeds from the mouth of God.'"

Then the devil took him to the holy city, and set him on the pinnacle of the temple, and said to him. "If you are the Son of God, throw yourself down; for it is written,

'He will give his angels charge of you,'

and

'On their hands they will bear you up, lest you strike your foot against a stone.'"

Jesus said to him, "Again it is written, 'You shall not tempt the Lord your God.'" Again, the devil took him to a very high mountain, and showed him all the kingdoms of the world and the glory of them; and he said to him, "All these I will give you, if you will fall down and worship me." Then Jesus said to him, "Begone, Satan! for it is written,

'You shall worship the Lord your God and him only shall you serve.'"

Then the devil left him, and behold, angels came and ministered to him.

From that time Jesus began to preach, saying, "Repent, for the kingdom of heaven is at hand."

As he walked by the Sea of Galilee, he saw two brothers, Simon who is called Peter and Andrew his brother, casting a net into the sea; for they were fishermen. And he said to them, "Follow me, and I will make you fishers of men." Immediately they left their nets and followed him. And going on from there he saw two other brothers, James the son of Zebedee and John his brother, in the boat with Zebedee their father, mending their nets, and he called them. Immediately they left the boat and their father, and followed him.

And he went about all Galilee, teaching in their synagogues and preaching the gospel of the kingdom and healing every disease and every infirmity among the people. So his fame spread throughout all Syria, and they brought him all the sick, those afflicted with various diseases and pains, demoniacs, epileptics, and paralytics, and he healed them. And great crowds followed him from Galilee and the Decapolis and Jerusalem and Judea and from beyond the Jordan.

Seeing the crowds, he went up on the mountain, and when he sat down his disciples came to him. And he opened his mouth and taught them, saying:

"Blessed are the poor in spirit, for theirs is the kingdom of heaven.

"Blessed are those who mourn, for they shall be comforted.

"Blessed are the meek, for they shall inherit the earth.

"Blessed are those who hunger and thirst for righteousness, for they shall be satisfied.

"Blessed are the merciful, for they shall obtain mercy.

"Blessed are the pure in heart, for they shall see God.

"Blessed are the peacemakers, for they shall be called sons of God.

"Blessed are those who are persecuted for righteousness' sake, for theirs is the kingdom of heaven.

"Blessed are you when men revile you and persecute you and utter all kinds of evil against you falsely on my account. Rejoice and be glad, for your reward is great in heaven, for so men persecuted the prophets who were before you.

"You are the salt of the earth; but if salt has lost its taste, how shall its saltness be restored? It is no longer good for anything except to be thrown out and trodden under foot by men.

"You are the light of the world. A city set on a hill cannot be hid. Nor do men light a lamp and put it under a bushel, but on a stand, and it gives light to all in the house. Let your light so shine before men, that they may see your good works and give glory to your Father who is in heaven.

"Think not that I have come to abolish the law and the prophets; I have come not to abolish them but to fulfill them. For truly, I say to you, till heaven and earth pass away, not an iota, not a dot, will pass from the law until all is accomplished. Whoever then relaxes one of the least of these commandments and teaches men so, shall be called least in the kingdom of heaven; but he who does them and teaches them shall be called great in the kingdom of heaven. For I tell you, unless your righteousness exceeds that of the scribes and Pharisees, you will never enter the kingdom of heaven.

"You have heard that it was said to the men of old, 'You shall not kill; and whoever kills shall be liable to judgment.' But I say to you that every one who is angry with his brother shall be liable to judgment; whoever insults his brother shall be liable to the council, and whoever says, 'You fool!' shall be liable to the hell of fire. So if you are offering your gift at the altar, and there remember that your brother has something against you, leave your gift there before the altar and go; first be reconciled to your brother, and then come and offer your gift. Make friends quickly with your accuser, while you are going with him to court, lest your accuser hand you over to the judge, and the judge to the guard, and you be put in prison; truly, I say to you, you will never get out till you have paid the last penny.

"You have heard that it was said, 'You shall not commit adultery.' But I say to you that every one who looks at a woman lustfully has already committed adultery with her in his heart.

"If your right eye causes you to sin, pluck it out and throw it away; it is better that you lose one of your members than that your whole body be thrown into hell. And if your right hand causes you to sin, cut it off and throw it away; it is better that you lose one of your members than that your whole body go into hell.

"It was also said, 'Whoever divorces his wife, let him give her a certificate of divorce.' But I say to you that every one who divorces his wife, except on the ground of unchastity, makes her an adulteress; and whoever marries a divorced woman commits adultery.

"Again you have heard that it was said to the men of old, 'You shall not swear falsely, but shall perform to the Lord what you have sworn.' But I say to you, Do not swear at all, either by heaven, for it is the throne of God, or by the earth, for it is his footstool, or by Jerusalem, for it is the city of the great King. And do not swear by your head, for you cannot make one hair white or black. Let what you say be simply 'Yes' or 'No'; anything more than this comes from evil.

"You have heard that it was said, 'An eye for and eye and a tooth for a tooth.' But I say to you. Do not resist one who is evil. But if any one strikes you on the right cheek, turn to him the other also; and if any one would sue you and take your coat, let him have your cloak as well and if any one forces you to go one mile, go with him two miles. Give to him who begs from you, and do not refuse him who would borrow from you.

"You have heard that it was said, 'You shall love your neighbor and hate your enemy.' But I say to you, Love your enemies and pray for those who persecute you, so that you may be sons of your Father who is in heaven; for he makes his sun rise on the evil and on the good, and sends rain on the just and on the unjust. For if you love those who love you, what reward have you? Do not even the tax collectors do the same? And if you salute only your brethren, what more are you doing than others? Do not even the Gentiles do the same? You, therefore, must be perfect, as your heavenly Father is perfect.

25

Edict of Milan—313 CE

The Edict of Milan was a proclamation issued by the western Roman emperor Constantine and his fellow (eastern) Roman emperor Licinius at Milan in 313 CE. The Edict gave Christianity legal status equal to Paganism. In addition, Christians were no longer to be persecuted, tortured, or killed because of their faith. Why was this edict so important to the development of Christianity within the Roman Empire?

From The Edict of Milan, 313 A.D., in *The Ideas that Have Influenced Civilization*, Vol. IV, ed. by Oliver J. Thatcher (Milwaukee, WI: Roberts-Manchester, 1901).

Finally, under the co-emperors Constantine and Licinius, governmental toleration was granted.

When we, Constantine and Licinius, emperors had an interview at Milan, and conferred together with respect to the good and security of the commonweal, it seemed to us that, amongst those things that are profitable to mankind in general, the reverence paid to the Divinity merited out first and chief attention, and that it was proper that the Christians and all others should have liberty to follow that mode of religion which to each of them appeared best; so that that God, who is seated in heaven, might be benign and propitious to us, and to every one under our government. And therefore we judged it a salutary measure, and one highly consonant to right reason, that no man should be denied leave of attaching himself to the rites of the Christians, or to whatever other religion his mind directed him, that thus the supreme Divinity, to whose worship we freely devote ourselves, might continue to vouchsafe His favor and beneficence to us. And accordingly we give you to know that, without regard to any provisos in our former orders to you concerning the Christians, all who choose that religion are to be permitted, freely and absolutely, to remain in it, and not to be disturbed any ways, or molested. And we thought fit to be thus special in the things committed to your charge, that you might understand that the indulgence which we have granted in matters of religion to the Christians is ample and unconditional; and perceive at the same time that the open and free exercise of their respective religions is granted to all others, as well as to the Christians. For it befits the well-ordered state and the tranquility of our times that each individual be allowed, according to his own choice, to worship the Divinity; and we mean not to derogate aught from the honor due to any religion or its votaries. Moreover, with respect to the Christian we formerly gave certain orders concerning the places appropriated for their religious assemblies; but now we will that all persons who have purchased such places . . . do restore them to the Christians, without money demanded or price claimed . . .

26

The Joys of Asceticism by Saint Jerome—4th century CE

Born to a wealthy pagan family, Jerome (334–420 CE) studied in Rome, where he converted to Christianity. A scholarly monk, he spent most of his life in the desert as a solitary recluse. There, he undertook a revision of the Latin Bible and wrote many other works of Christian scholarship. Considered a Father of the Church, he is the patron saint of archivists and librarians. Why does Jerome recommend the life of an ascetic?

EXTENDING YOUR UNDERSTANDING
OF MEDIE

. . . O desert, bright with the flowers of Christ! O solitude, whence comes the stones of which, in the Apocalypse, the city of the great king is built! O wilderness, gladdened with God's especial presence! What keeps you in the world, my brother, you who are above the world? How long shall gloomy roofs oppress you? How long shall smoky cities immure you? Believe me, I have more light than you. Sweet it is to lay aside the weight of the body and to soar into the pure bright ether. Do you dread poverty? Christ calls the poor blessed. Does toil frighten you? No athlete is crowned but in the sweat of his brow. Are you anxious as regards food? Faith fears no famine. Do you dread the bare ground for limbs wasted with fasting? The Lord lies there beside you. Do you recoil from an unwashed head and uncombed hair? Christ is your true head. Does the boundless solitude of the desert terrify you? In the spirit you may walk always in Paradise. Do but turn your thoughts thither and you will be no more in the desert. Is your skin rough and scaly because you no longer bathe? He that is once washed in Christ needeth not to wash again.

From *The Joys of Asceticism in Historical Selections*, ed. by Hutton Webster (Boston: D.C. Health, 1929).

CHAPTER 3

Law, Government, and War—2000 BCE–500 CE

When the first hunter-gatherers developed stable sources of food and founded permanent settlements, the need arose for some kind of government and legal system. The earliest of these legal codes date back thousands of years and were unwritten, allowing for flexibility of interpretation on the part of rulers. Hammurabi's *Code* was one of the earliest written law codes. A thousand years later, Roman citizens finally gained a written legal code. Although Roman civil law would become a model for many Western states, its development was a difficult and painful process. In India, the Pillar Edicts of Asoka and the *Laws of Manu* governed the people and preserved social order. As emerging societies expanded and claimed more territory, war became commonplace in the ancient world, although on a much smaller scale than today. Rulers competed for the most desirable land and for the power that went with it. The documents that follow provide a glimpse into the needs and motivations of various peoples in the ancient world to develop governments, make laws, and go to war.

Do you see some similarities between the various law codes in this section? Which seem the most restrictive? Why?

What values emerge when you compare the three battle accounts? What role does religion or the gods play in each?

Military leaders were not admired as much in Chinese society as they were in other cultures at this time. Do you see any evidence of this in the excerpt from Sun-tzu's *Art of War*?

27

Code of Hammurabi—
1792–1750 BCE

When it was first discovered in the twentieth century, Hammurabi's Code was consid-
ered to be the first legal code in Western history. It was characterized by its harsh pun-
ishments similar to those found in Mosaic law based on "an eye for an eye." Hammurabi
was ruler of the Amorite or Old Babylonian dynasty from 1792 to 1750 BCE. He
was an able king with military skills who was effective in unifying Mesopotamia during
his rule. Although current scholarship regards Hammurabi's Code as a compilation of
earlier codes rather than the first legal code, it provides much insight into life in ancient
Mesopotamia. What does the type of laws found in this code tell you about
Mesopotamian society? How does the Code compare with the laws of Manu in regard to
gender and social rank?

If a seignior accused a(nother) seignior and brought a charge of murder against
him, but has not proved it, his accuser shall be put to death.

If a seignior brought a charge of sorcery against a(nother) seignior, but has
not proved it, the one against whom the charge of sorcery was brought, upon
going to the river, shall throw himself into the river, and if the river has then
overpowered him, his accuser shall take over his estate; if the river has shown
that seignior to be innocent and he has accordingly come forth safe, the one
who brought the charge of sorcery against him shall be put to death, while the
one who threw himself into the river shall take over the estate of his accuser.

If a seignior came forward with false testimony in a case, and has not proved
the word which he spoke, if that case was a case involving life, that seignior
shall be put to death.

If he came forward with (false) testimony concerning grain or money, he
shall bear the penalty of that case.

If a seignior stole the property of church or state, that seignior shall be put
to death; also the one who received the stolen goods from his hand shall be put
to death.

If a seignior has purchased or has received for safekeeping either silver or
gold or a male slave or a female slave or an ox or a sheep or an ass or any sort
of thing from the hand of a seignior's son or a seignior's slave without witnesses and contracts, since that seignior is a thief, he shall be put to death.

From *Ancient Near Eastern Texts Relating to the Old Testament* 2nd ed., ed. by James
B. Pritchard (Princeton, NJ: Princeton University Press, 1955). Reprinted by permission.

If a seignior stole either an ox or a sheep or an ass or a pig or a boat, if it belonged to the church (or) if it belonged to the state, he shall make thirtyfold restitution; if it belonged to a private citizen, he shall make good tenfold. If the thief does not have sufficient to make restitution, he shall be put to death.

If a seignior has stolen the young son of a(nother) seignior, he shall be put to death.

If a seignior has helped either a male slave of the state or a female slave of the state or a male slave of a private citizen or a female slave of a private citizen to escape through the city-gate, he shall be put to death.

If a seignior has harbored in his house either a fugitive male or female slave belonging to the state or to a private citizen and has not brought him forth at the summons of the police, that householder shall be put to death.

If a seignior committed robbery and has been caught, that seignior shall be put to death.

If the robber has not been caught, the robbed seignior shall set forth the particulars regarding his lost property in the presence of god, and the city and governor, in whose territory and district the robbery was committed, shall make good to him his lost property.

If either a sergeant or a captain has obtained a soldier by conscription or he accepted and has sent a hired substitute for a campaign of the king, that sergeant or captain shall be put to death.

If either a sergeant or a captain has appropriated the household goods of a soldier, has wronged a soldier, has let a soldier for hire, has abandoned a soldier to a superior in a lawsuit, has appropriated the grant which the king gave to a soldier, that sergeant or captain shall be put to death.

If a seignior has bought from the hand of a soldier the cattle or sheep which the king gave to the soldier, he shall forfeit his money.

When a seignior borrowed money from a merchant and pledged to the merchant a field prepared for grain or sesame, if he said to him, "Cultivate the field, then harvest (and) take the grain or sesame that is produced," if the tenant has produced grain or sesame in the field, the owner of the field at harvest-time shall himself take the grain or sesame that was produced in the field and he shall give to the merchant grain for his money, which he borrowed from the merchant, together with its interest, and also for the cost of cultivation.

If he pledged a field planted with (grain) or a field planted with sesame, the owner of the field shall himself take the grain or sesame that was produced in the field and he shall pay back the money with its interest to the merchant.

If he does not have the money to pay back, (grain or) sesame at their market value in accordance with the ratio fixed by the king he shall give to the merchant for his money, which he borrowed from the merchant, together with its interest.

If the tenant has not produced grain or sesame in the field, he may not change his contract.

If a seignior was too lazy to make [the dike of] his field strong and did not make his dike strong and a break has opened up in his dike and he has accordingly let the water ravage the farmland, the seignior in whose dike the break was opened shall make good the grain that he let get destroyed.

If he is not able to make good the grain, they shall sell him and his goods, and the farmers whose grain the water carried off shall divide (the proceeds).

If a seignior, upon opening his canal for irrigation, became so lazy that he has let the water ravage a field adjoining his, he shall measure out grain on the basis of those adjoining his.

If a seignior pointed the finger at a nun or the wife of a(nother) seignior, but has proved nothing, they shall drag that seignior into the presence of the judges and also cut off half his (hair).

If a seignior acquired a wife, but did not draw up the contracts for her, that woman is no wife.

If the wife of a seignior has been caught while lying with another man, they shall bind them and throw them into the water. If the husband of the woman wishes to spare his wife, then the king in turn may spare his subject.

If a seignior bound the (betrothed) wife of a(nother) seignior, who had had no intercourse with a male and was still living in her father's house, and he has lain in her bosom and they have caught him, that seignior shall be put to death, while that woman shall go free.

If a seignior's wife was accused by her husband, but she was not caught while lying with another man, she shall make affirmation by god and return to her house.

If the finger was pointed at the wife of a seignior because of another man, but she has not been caught while lying with the other man, she shall throw herself into the river for the sake of her husband.

If a seignior was taken captive, but there was sufficient to live on in his house, his wife [shall not leave her house, but she shall take care of her person by not] entering [the house of another].

If that woman did not take care of her person, but has entered the house of another, they shall prove it against that woman and throw her into the water.

If the seignior was taken captive and there was not sufficient to live on in his house, his wife may enter the house of another, with that woman incurring no blame at all.

If, when a seignior was taken captive and there was not sufficient to live on in his house, his wife has then entered the house of another before his (return) and has borne children, (and) later her husband has returned and has reached his city, that woman shall return to her first husband, while the children shall go with their father.

If, when a seignior deserted his city and then ran away, his wife has entered the house of another after his (departure), if that seignior has returned and wishes to take back his wife, the wife of the fugitive shall not return to her husband because he scorned his city and ran away.

If a seignior wishes to divorce his wife who did not bear him children, he shall give her money to the full amount of her marriage-price and he shall also make good to her the dowry which she brought from her father's house and then he may divorce her.

If there was no marriage-price, he shall give her one mina of silver as the divorce-settlement.

If he is a peasant, he shall give her one-third mina of silver.

If a seignior's wife, who was living in the house of the seignior, has made up her mind to leave in order that she may engage in business, thus neglecting her house (and) humiliating her husband, they shall prove it against her; and if her husband has then decided on her divorce, he may divorce her, with nothing to be given her as her divorce-settlement upon her departure. If her husband has not decided on her divorce, her husband may marry another woman, with the former woman living in the house of her husband like a maidservant.

If a woman so hated her husband that she has declared, "You may not have me," her record shall be investigated at her city council, and if she was careful and was not at fault, even though her husband has been going out and disparaging her greatly, that woman, without incurring any blame at all, may take her dowry and go off to her father's house.

If she was not careful, but was a gadabout, thus neglecting her house (and) humiliating her husband, they shall throw that woman into the water.

If a seignior's wife has brought about the death of her husband because of another man, they shall impale that woman on stakes.

If a seignior has had intercourse with his daughter, they shall make that seignior leave the city.

If a seignior chose a bride for his son and his son had intercourse with her, but later he himself has lain in her bosom and they have caught him, they shall bind that seignior and throw him into the water.

If a seignior chose a bride for his son and his son did not have intercourse with her, but he himself has lain in her bosom, he shall pay to her one-half mina of silver and he shall also make good to her whatever she brought from her father's house in order that the man of her choice may marry her.

If a seignior has lain in the bosom of his mother after (the death of) his father, they shall burn both of them.

If a son has struck his father, they shall cut off his hand.

If a seignior has destroyed the eye of a member of the aristocracy, they shall destroy his eye.

If he has broken a(nother) seignior's bone, they shall break his bone.

If he has destroyed the eye of a commoner or broken the bone of a commoner, he shall pay one mina of silver.

If he has destroyed the eye of a seignior's slave or broken the bone of a seignior's slave, he shall pay one-half his value.

28

The Twelve Tables—451–450 BCE

This code was the first effort by the Romans to create a legal system; it is also the earliest surviving piece of Roman literature. Because of the constant struggle between patricians and plebians (rich and poor Romans) for legal and social protections as well as civil rights, a commission of ten was appointed to draw up a legal code that would be binding on both groups. Because the first effort of ten tables was not entirely satisfactory to the plebians, two more tables were added in 450 BCE. This law code was the basis of what would later become Roman civil law (Ius Civile). What aspects of Roman society did the creators of this code address? Who might have benefited most from these new laws?

Cicero, *De Oratore*, I.44: Though all the world exclaim against me, I will say what I think: that single little book of the Twelve Tables, if anyone look to the fountains and sources of laws, seems to me, assuredly, to surpass the libraries of all the philosophers, both in weight of authority, and in plenitude of utility.

TABLE I.

1. If anyone summons a man before the magistrate, he must go. If the man summoned does not go, let the one summoning him call the bystanders to witness and then take him by force.

2. If he shirks or runs away, let the summoner lay hands on him.

3. If illness or old age is the hindrance, let the summoner provide a team. He need not provide a covered carriage with a pallet unless he chooses.

4. Let the protector of a landholder be a landholder; for one of the proletariat, let anyone that cares, be protector.

6-9. When the litigants settle their case by compromise, let the magistrate announce it. If they do not compromise, let them state each his own side of the case, in the *comitium* of the forum before noon. Afterwards let them talk it out together, while both are present. After noon, in case either party has failed to appear, let the magistrate pronounce judgment in favor of the one who is present. If both are present the trial may last until sunset but no later.

From *The Library of Original Sources*, ed. by Oliver J. Thatcher (Milwaukee, WI: University Research Extension Co., 1901) Vol. III, p. 9–11.

TABLE II.

2. He whose witness has failed to appear may summon him by loud calls before his house every third day.

TABLE III.

1. One who has confessed a debt, or against whom judgment has been pronounced, shall have thirty days to pay it in. After that forcible seizure of his person is allowed. The creditor shall bring him before the magistrate. Unless he pays the amount of the judgment or some one in the presence of the magistrate interferes in his behalf as protector the creditor so shall take him home and fasten him in stocks or fetters. He shall fasten him with not less than fifteen pounds of weight or, if he choose, with more. If the prisoner choose, he may furnish his own food. If he does not, the creditor must give him a pound of meal daily; if he choose he may give him more.

2. On the third market day let them divide his body among them. If they cut more or less than each one's share it shall be no crime.

3. Against a foreigner the right in property shall be valid forever.

TABLE IV.

1. A dreadfully deformed child shall be quickly killed.

2. If a father sell his son three times, the son shall be free from his father.

3. As a man has provided in his will in regard to his money and the care of his property, so let it be binding. If he has no heir and dies intestate, let the nearest agnate have the inheritance. If there is no agnate, let the members of his gens have the inheritance.

4. If one is mad but has no guardian, the power over him and his money shall belong to his agnates and the members of his *gens*.

5. A child born after ten months since the father's death will not be admitted into a legal inheritance.

TABLE V.

1. Females should remain in guardianship even when they have attained their majority.

TABLE VI.

1. When one makes a bond and a conveyance of property, as he has made formal declaration so let it be binding.

3. A beam that is built into a house or a vineyard trellis one may not take from its place.

5. *Usucapio* of movable things requires one year's possession for its completion; but *usucapio* of an estate and buildings two years.

6. Any woman who does not wish to be subjected in this manner to the hand of her husband should be absent three nights in succession every year, and so interrupt the *usucapio* of each year.

TABLE VII.

1. Let them keep the road in order. If they have not paved it, a man may drive his team where he likes.

9. Should a tree on a neighbor's farm be bent crooked by the wind and lean over your farm, you may take legal action for removal of that tree.

10. A man might gather up fruit that was falling down onto another man's farm.

TABLE VIII.

2. If one has maimed a limb and does not compromise with the injured person, let there be retaliation. If one has broken a bone of a freeman with his hand or with a cudgel, let him pay a penalty of three hundred coins If he has broken the bone of a slave, let him have one hundred and fifty coins. If one is guilty of insult, the penalty shall be twenty-five coins.

3. If one is slain while committing theft by night, he is rightly slain.

4. If a patron shall have devised any deceit against his client, let him be accursed.

5. If one shall permit himself to be summoned as a witness, or has been a weigher, if he does not give his testimony, let him be noted as dishonest and incapable of acting again as witness.

10. Any person who destroys by burning any building or heap of corn deposited alongside a house shall be bound, scourged, and put to death by burning at the stake provided that he has committed the said misdeed with malice aforethought; but if he shall have committed it by accident, that is, by negligence, it is ordained that he repair the damage or, if he be too poor to be competent for such punishment, he shall receive a lighter punishment.

12. If the theft has been done by night, if the owner kills the thief, the thief shall be held to be lawfully killed.

13. It is unlawful for a thief to be killed by day. . . .unless he defends himself with a weapon; even though he has come with a weapon, unless he shall use the weapon and fight back, you shall not kill him. And even if he resists, first call out so that someone may hear and come up.

23. A person who had been found guilty of giving false witness shall be hurled down from the Tarpeian Rock.

26. No person shall hold meetings by night in the city.

TABLE IX.

4. The penalty shall be capital for a judge or arbiter legally appointed who has been found guilty of receiving a bribe for giving a decision.

5. Treason: he who shall have roused up a public enemy or handed over a citizen to a public enemy must suffer capital punishment.

6. Putting to death of any man, whosoever he might be unconvicted is forbidden.

TABLE X.

1. None is to bury or burn a corpse in the city.

3. The women shall not tear their faces nor wail on account of the funeral.

5. If one obtains a crown himself, or if his chattel does so because of his honor and valor, if it is placed on his head, or the head of his parents, it shall be no crime.

TABLE XI.

1. Marriages should not take place between plebeians and patricians.

TABLE XII.

2. If a slave shall have committed theft or done damage with his master's knowledge, the action for damages is in the slave's name.

5. Whatever the people had last ordained should be held as binding by law.

29

The Rock and Pillar Edicts of Asoka—ca. 300–232 BCE

The greatest of the Mauryan rulers in India after the death of Alexander the Great, Ashoka initiated a policy of religious tolerance after his conversion to Buddhism. He also supported the widespread teaching of Buddhist ethics, which he called Dharma, through a series of edicts. These were inscribed on rocks and pillars that were placed throughout his kingdom. Although many of the edicts may have been carved by Buddhist monks, it is likely that they conveyed Asoka's desire to be an ethical ruler and to live by Buddhist precepts. How does the following document support the Buddhist teachings found in the Benares sermon of Buddha? How do these edicts compare with other laws of the period?

REMORSE FOR AGGRESSION

1 Kalinga was conquered by King Asoka after he had been crowned for eight years. One hundred and fifty thousand persons were thence carried away captive, one hundred thousand were there slain, and many times that number perished.

Directly after the annexation of Kalinga, began King Asoka's zealous protection of the Dharma [the teachings of Buddha], his love of that law, and his giving instruction in that law. Thus arose King Asoka's remorse for having conquered Kalinga, because the conquest of a country previously unconquered involves the slaughter, death and carrying away of people as captives. This is a matter of profound sorrow and regret to his majesty.

Rock Edict XIII

2 There is, however, further reason for King Asoka feeling still more regret, inasmuch as in such a country dwell priests, men of various denominations, and householders, upon whom is laid the duty of listening attentively to superiors, to father and mother, and to teachers, and of proper treatment of friends, acquaintances, comrades, relatives, slaves, and servants, with enduring concern. To such people in a country at war befalls violence, or slaughter, or separation from their loved ones. Or misfortune befalls the friends, acquaintances, comrades and relatives of those who are themselves well protected while their affection is undiminished. Thus for them also this is a mode of violence. And the share of this that falls on all men is matter of regret to King Asoka. . .

Rock Edict XIII

Adapted from *Asoka* by James M. MacPhail, edict trans. by V.A. Smith (Calcutta: The Association Press, 1910).

CONQUEST BY TEACHING

3 Thus of all the people who were slain, done to death, or carried away captive in Kalinga, if the hundredth or the thousandth part were to suffer again the same fate, it would now be matter of regret to King Asoka. Moreover, should any one do him wrong, that, too, must be borne with by his majesty, if it can possibly be borne with. Even upon the native people of the forests in his dominions King Asoka looks kindly and he seeks their conversion, for if he did not, repentance would come to his majesty. They are bidden to turn from evil ways that they be not chastised. For King Asoka desires that all animate things should have security, self-control, peace of mind and joyousness.

And this is the highest form of conquest, in the opinion of King Asoka— the conquest by teaching the Dharma. And this, again, has been achieved by his majesty both in his own dominions and in all the neighboring realms as far as 1500 km. . .

Rock Edict XIII

4 And for this purpose has this pious Edict been written, in order that my sons and descendants should not regard it as their duty to achieve a new conquest. If, by chance, they become engaged in a conquest by arms, they should take pleasure in patience and gentleness, and regard the conquest won by the Dharma as the only true conquest.

Rock Edict XIII

THE DHARMA

5 There is no gift like the giving of the Dharma—friendship in Dharma, liberality in Dharma, association in Dharma. Herein does it consist—in proper treatment of slaves and servants, listening attentively to father and mother, gifts to friends, relatives, priests, and ascetics, and abstaining from slaughter of animals. .

Rock Edict XI

6 Father and mother must be obeyed; similarly respect for living creatures must be firmly established; truth must be spoken. These are the virtues of the Dharma which must be practiced. Similarly, the teacher must be reverenced by the pupil, and proper courtesy must be shown to relatives.

Minor Rock Edict II

7 The Dharma is excellent. But wherein consists the Dharma. In these things: little impiety, many good deeds, compassion, liberality, truthfulness, and purity

Pillar Edict II

8 My ministers of the Dharma are engaged in the prevention of wrongful imprisonment or chastisement, in the work of removing hindrances to the release from prison, and helping cases where a man has a large family, has been smitten by calamity, or is advanced in years.

Rock Edict V

WELFARE OF THE PEOPLE

9 All men are my children. Just as, in regard to my own children, I desire that they may be provided with all kinds of welfare and happiness in this world and in the next, the same I desire also in regard to all men.

Rock Edict II

10 Work I must for the welfare of all, and the root of the matter is in effort and the dispatch of business, for nothing is more efficacious to secure the welfare of all. And for what do I toil? For no other end than this, that I may discharge my debt to animate beings . . .

Rock Edict VI

11 On the roads I have had banyan trees planted to give shade for animals and men; I have had groves of mango trees planted. At every half mile I have had wells dug; rest-houses have been built; and numerous watering places have been provided by me here and there for the enjoyment of man and beast.

Pillar Edict VII

12 Everywhere King Asoka has made arrangement for two kinds of medical treatment, namely, medical treatment for men and medical treatment for animals.

Rock Edict II

RELIGIOUS TOLERANCE

13 A man must not do reverence to his own sect or disparage that of another sect without reason. Depreciation should be for specific reason only, because the sects of other people all deserve reverence for one reason or another. By thus acting, a man exalts his own sect, and at the same time does services to the sects of other people. By acting contrariwise, a man hurts his own sect and does disservice to the sects of other people.

Rock Edict XII

14 King Asoka does reverence to men of all sects, whether ascetics or householders by gifts and various forms of reverence.

30

The *Laws of Manu*—
ca. 4th century CE

This Hindu law code is one of the oldest available sources of information about early Indian society. Though probably transcribed in the first or second century CE, the Laws of Manu *are the roots of Vedic culture. These laws governed the everyday life of the Indian people, from male/female relations to the caste system. According to Brahmin lore, Manu was a survivor of the flood and the father of the human race. What kind of social control was provided by the* Laws of Manu?

MANU THE LAWGIVER

The great sages approached Manu,* who was seated with a collected mind, and, having duly worshipped him, spoke as follows:

"Deign, divine one, to declare to us precisely and in due order the sacred laws of each of the four chief castes and of the intermediate ones.

"For thou, O Lord, alone knowest the purport, the rites, and the knowledge of the soul, taught in this whole ordinance of the Self-existent, which is unknowable and unfathomable."

He, whose power is measureless, being thus asked by the high-minded great sages, duly honored them, and answered, "Listen!"

THE FOUR CASTES

For the sake of the prosperity of the worlds, he caused the Brahmana, the Kshatriya, the Vaisya, and the Sudra to proceed from his mouth, his arms, his thighs, and his feet.

The Brahmana, the Kshatriya, and the Vaisya castes are the twice-born ones, but the fourth, the Sudra, has one birth only; there is no fifth caste.

To Brahmanas he assigned teaching and studying the Veda, sacrificing for their own benefit and for others, giving and accepting of alms. The Kshatriya he commanded to protect the people, to bestow gifts, to offer sacrifices, to study the Veda, and to abstain from attaching himself to sensual pleasures; the

---

"*The Laws of Manu*," as printed in Sources of World Civilization, ed. by Oliver and Johnson, Prentice Hall, 1994.

* Manu in Hindu mythology is a being who is both divine and human.

Vaisya to tend cattle, to bestow gifts, to offer sacrifices, to study the Veda, to trade, to lend money, and to cultivate land. One occupation only the lord prescribed to the Sudra, to serve meekly even these other three castes.

The seniority of Brahmanas is from sacred knowledge, that of Kshatriyas from valor, that of Vaisyas from wealth in grain and other goods, but that of Sudras from age alone.

A twice-born man who knowingly eats mushrooms, a village pig, garlic, a village cock, onions or leeks, will become an outcast.

Some wealthy Brahmana shall compassionately support both a Kshatriya and a Vaisya if they are distressed for a livelihood, employing them on work which is suitable for their castes. But a Brahmana who, because he is powerful, out of greed makes initiated men of the twice-born castes against their will do the work of slaves shall be fined by the king. But a Sudra, whether bought or unbought, he may compel to do servile work; for he was created by the Self-existent to be the slave of a Brahmana. A Sudra, though emancipated by his master, is not released from servitude; since that is innate in him, who can set him free from it?

With whatever limb a man of a low caste does hurt to a man of the three highest castes, even that limb shall be cut off; that is the teaching of Manu. He who raises his hand or a stick shall have his hand cut off; he who in anger kicks with his foot shall have his foot cut off.

A low-caste man who tries to place himself on the same seat with a man of a high caste shall be branded on his hip and be banished, or the king shall cause his buttock to be gashed. If out of arrogance he spits on a superior the king shall cause both his lips to be cut off; if he urines on him, the penis; if he breaks wind against him, the anus.

A man of low caste who through covetousness lives by the occupations of a higher one the king shall deprive of his property and banish.

Abstention from injuring creatures, veracity, abstention from unlawfully appropriating the goods of others, purity, and control of the organs, Manu has declared to be the summary of the law for the four castes.

. . . In childhood a female must be subject to her father, in youth to her husband, and when her lord is dead, to her sons; a woman must never be independent [Manu, V, 184].

Though destitute of virtue, or seeking pleasure (elsewhere), or devoid of good qualities, (yet) a husband must be constantly worshipped as a god by a faithful wife [Manu, V, 154].

A virtuous wife who after the death of her husband constantly remains chaste, reaches heaven, though she have no son, just like those chaste men [Manu, V, 160].

But a woman who from a desire to have offspring violates her duty towards her dead husband, brings on herself disgrace in this world, and loses her place with her husband in heaven [Manu V, 161].

A wife, a son and a slave, these three are declared to have no property: the wealth which they earn is (acquired) for him to whom they belong [Manu, VIII, 416].

(When creating them) Manu allotted to women (a love of their) bed, (of their) seat and (of) ornament, impure desires, wrath, dishonesty, malice, and bad conduct [Manu, IX, 17].

In the sacred texts which refer to marriage the appointment (of widows) is nowhere mentioned, nor is the remarriage of widows prescribed in the rules concerning marriage [Manu, IX, 65].

A man, aged thirty years, shall marry a maiden of twelve who pleases him, or a man of twenty-four a girl eight years of age; if the performance of his duties would otherwise be impeded, he must marry sooner [Manu, IX, 94].

31

The Fall of Jericho—ca. 1000 BCE

Jericho is one of the world's oldest cities, with a history extending back 8,000 years. Although there is no archaeological evidence to support this account from the Book of Joshua, it tells us much about the relationship between desert-dwelling Nomads and the inhabitants of cities. When the Jews reached the promised land of Canaan under the leadership of Joshua, who was Moses' successor, they found it occupied by the Canaanites. They claimed the land for their own by besieging and conquering the city. How did the Jews treat the residents of Jericho after they conquered it? Why might they have acted as they did?

Now Jericho was shut up from within and from without because of the people of Israel: none went out, and none came in. And the Lord said to Joshua, "See, I have given into your hand Jericho, with its king and mighty men of valor. You shall march around the city, all the men of war going around the city once. Thus shall you do for six days. And seven priests shall bear seven trumpets of rams' horns before the ark; and on the seventh day you shall march around the city seven times, the priests blowing the trumpets. And when they make a long blast with the ram's horn, as soon as you hear the sound of the trumpet, then all the people shall shout with a great shout; and the wall of the city will fall down flat, and the people shall go up every man straight before him." So Joshua the son of Nun called the priests and said to them,

"Take up the ark of the covenant, and let seven priests bear seven trumpets of rams' horns before the ark of the Lord." And he said to the people, "Go forward: march around the city, and let the armed men pass on before the ark of the Lord."

And as Joshua had commanded the people, the seven priests bearing the seven trumpets of rams' horns before the Lord went forward, blowing the trumpets, with the ark of the covenant of the Lord following them. And the armed men went before the priests who blew the trumpets, and the rear guard came after the ark, while the trumpets blew continually. But Joshua commanded the people, "You shall not shout or let your voice be heard, neither shall any word go out of your mouth until the day I bid you shout; then you shall shout." So he caused the ark of the Lord to compass the city, going about it once; and they came into the camp, and spent the night in the camp.

Then Joshua rose early in the morning, and the priests took up the ark of the Lord. And the seven priests bearing the seven trumpets of rams' horns before the ark of the Lord, while the trumpets blew continually. And the second day they marched around the city once, and returned into the camp. So they did for six days.

On the seventh day they rose early at the dawn of day, and marched around the city in the same manner seven times: it was only on that day that they marched around the city seven times. And at the seventh time, when the priests had blown the trumpets, Joshua said to the people, "Shout; for the Lord has given you the city. And the city and all that is within it shall be devoted to the Lord for destruction; only Rahab the harlot and all who are with her in her house shall live, because she hid the messengers that we sent. But you, keep yourselves from the things devoted to destruction, lest when you have devoted them you take any of the devoted things and make the camp of Israel a thing for destruction, and bring trouble upon it. But all silver and gold, and vessels of bronze and iron, are sacred to the Lord; they shall go into the treasury of the Lord." So the people shouted, and the trumpets were blown. As soon as the people heard the sound of the trumpet, the people raised a great shout, and the wall fell down flat, so that the people went up into the city, every man straight before him, and they took the city. Then they utterly destroyed all in the city, both men and women, young and old, oxen, sheep, and asses, with the edge of the sword.

And Joshua said to the two men who had spied out the land, "Go into the harlot's house, and bring out from it the woman, and all who belong to her, as you swore to her." So the young men who had been spies went in, and brought out Rahab, and her father and mother and brothers and all who belonged to her; and they brought all her kindred, and set them outside the camp of Israel. And they burned the city with fire, and all within it; only the silver and gold, and the vessels of bronze and of iron, they put into the treasury of the house of the Lord. But Rahab the harlot, and her father's household, and all who belonged to her, Joshua saved alive; and she dwelt in Israel to this day, because she hid the messengers whom Joshua sent to spy out Jericho.

Joshua laid an oath upon them at that time, saying, "Cursed before the Lord be the man that rises up and rebuilds this city, Jericho. At the cost of his first-born shall he lay its foundation, and at the cost of his youngest son shall he set up its gates."

32

The Ramayana—ca. 400 BCE

The Ramayana *is the epic story of Prince Rama of India; it was recorded by an unknown author, Valmiki, about 400-200 BCE. The Bollywood film studios in Delhi have made many films based on this epic, which relates the stories of Rama and Sita. Rama is considered to be the seventh incarnation of the god Vishnu. Krishna, the hero of the* Mahabharata, *is thought to be the eighth incarnation of Vishnu. The* Mahabharata *is one of the main scriptures of the Hindu religion (the Bhagavad Gita is one section of this poem). Many scholars believe that* The Ramayana *actually tells the story of the Aryan conquest of India. Why does the dying Vali question Rama about the morality of his action in killing him, and how does he defend the morality of his society?*

Rama drew an arrow elegantly from his quiver, poised it on the bow-string, and let it go. It sped along and pierced Vali's chest like a needle passing through a fruit.

Overcome with astonishment, Vali paused for a moment to take stock of the situation. His grip around his brother's neck relaxed involuntarily. With one hand he had held on to the arrow's shaft and arrested its passage through his chest. Now he clung to it with his hands, his feet, and the coils of his tail, and broke and retarded its motion with such stubborn strength that even Yama, the god of death, stood back, nodding his head in admiration.

Vali had never thought, even as a possibility, that there was any power on earth or in the heavens which could subdue him with any weapon or stand up before him in a fight. All this was an accepted fact, but here he was like a mis-erable worm, not even able to understand what it was that had laid him low. Could it be the "Trisula" of Shiva or could it be the "Chakra" of Vishnu or Indra's "Vajrayudha"? He laughed ironically. At the same moment he felt an admiration for his unknown assailant. Who could it be? he speculated, forgetting

From R.K. Narayan, *The Ramayana* (New York: Viking Press, 1974), p. 107–113.
Reprinted by permission of Penguin Group (USA), Inc.

his pain. He was invulnerable according to the promise of the gods, yet here was the reality, the arrow in his heart. He laughed bitterly at the cocksureness of these years; what could it be, who could it be? Why speculate? Let me find out. So saying he exercised all his remaining strength in pulling the arrow from his chest, to look at the mark on its handle. The might of Vali was applauded by the gods watching from high heavens, as he succeeded in drawing out the shaft. Blood gushed from the wound like a spring. At the sight of it, Sugreeva was grief-stricken and wept aloud. He forgot his animosity. With his ebbing strength, Vali held the arrow close to his eyes and spelt the name "Rama" engraved on it. Vali looked at the name on the arrow and almost was blinded with shock. The shock of the physical injury was not so agonizing as the spiritual shock of reading the name of Rama on the arrow. He looked at it and brooded over his own recklessness in castigating his wife for mentioning Rama's name. That poor creature showed better judgement than he.

"Rama, the Lord of culture, breeding, discrimination, and justice. How could you do this? You have destroyed the firm basis of your own virtues. Is it because of the separation from your wife [Sita] that you have lost all sense of fairness and act recklessly? If some demon like Ravana has acted treacherously, is that any justification for you to come here, slaughter the head of a monkey clan, entirely unconnected with the affair? Has your code of ethics taught you only this? What mistake have you seen in me, young man, that you should destroy me thus? Who will wear the badge of virtue in this world or others, when you have thrown it away so lightly? Is the foretaste of the *yuga* of *Kali** to be had only by us, the creatures who crawl and are called monkeys? So, Kind One, are virtues intended to be practiced only on weaker creatures? When strong men commit crimes, they become heroic deeds? Oh, incomparable one, the treasure and kingdom given to you, you handed over to the younger brother. That you performed in the city; do you wish to repeat a similar act in these forests too by depriving an older brother of his life and kingdom? When two persons are opposed to each other, how can you in support of one, hide and attack the other? What you have done to me is not heroic or an act conducted within the laws of warfare. Surely, you do not consider me a burden on this weighty earth nor are you my enemy. Pray, tell me what drove you to this terrible decision? Ravana entrapped your wife and carried her off. To redeem her and to wreak your vengeance on him, you probably seek the support of Sugreeva, which is like courting a rabbit, when you can summon a lion to serve you. Pray what judgement is this? A word from you and I'd have plucked Ravana from his citadel and flung him at your feet.

"You have done a thing which has ended my life. If someone has carried away your wife, instead of battling with him face to face, you stand aside, hide, and use all your accomplishment as an archer against an unarmed stranger. Has all your training as warrior been only for this end? Creatures like us test our

---

*In the yuga of Kali, a period far in the future, the editor states that, "righteousness, virtue, and goodness completely disappear" and "Anger, distress, hunger, and fear prevail. . . ."

worth and strength with our sinews and muscles and always fight barehanded, and never hold a weapon as you do."

Rama softly came out of his hiding, approached the dying Vali, and said with the utmost calmness, "When you disappeared into the subterranean world pursuing Mayavi, your brother waited in anxiety for a very long time, and then on a sudden resolve, started to follow your path into the tunnel since he feared that you might need help. But he was held back by the army chiefs and advisers in your court, who pressed him to rule as a trustee for the time being. But the moment you came back, you misunderstood everything and before he could even express his relief and joy on seeing you, you belaboured him mercilessly in the presence of others and attempted to take his life. When he still struggled to explain and sought your pardon for any mistake on his part, you rejected his appeal. And then after fully realizing that he had committed no wrong, you let your temper carry you on and on; you could afford, through your sense of power, to indulge your anger luxuriously, however unwarranted; and you assaulted and pursued him with the intention of killing him. After he fled, you left him alone, not because he had admitted his error and sought your pardon and asylum, and not even because it was wrong to pursue one whose back is turned in flight, not because he was your brother, but only because you dare not step on Matanga's Hill [where Sugreeva had fled]-merely self-preservation. And you bided your time. Even now you would have squeezed his life out but for my arrow. Beyond all this, you violated his wife's honor and made her your own. Guarding a woman's honor is the first duty laid on any intelligent being. But because you are conscious of your limitless strength, you act dishonorably and carry it off without any compunction as you feel no one can question you. You are well versed in the laws of conduct and morality and yet instead of affording protection to a helpless woman, life partner of a brother at that, you have molested her.

"Since Sugreeva sought my friendship and asked for help, I felt it my duty to help him by destroying you."

Vali replied, "You are judging us all wrongly, your basis is mistaken. You make too much of my acquiring my brother's wife. It's legitimate in our society. Although my brother was an enemy, I wanted to protect and help his wife while he was gone. I could not leave her to her fate."

"It is my primary duty to help the weak and destroy evil wherever I see it. Whether known or unknown, I help those that seek my help."

Vali replied, "Marriage and all its restraints on the relationship of men and women are of your human society and not known to us. Brahma has decreed for us absolute freedom in our sexual pursuits, habits, and life. In our society there is no such thing as wedlock. We are not a human society, we are monkeys and your laws and ethical codes are not applicable to us."

"I am not misled either by your explanation or appearance of being a monkey," Rama said. "I am aware that you are begotten by the chief of gods. You possess enough intelligence to know right from wrong and to argue your case even at this stage. You are fully aware of the eternal verities [truths]. You have erred and know it and how can you say now you are innocent? Could

Gajendra, who prayed for Vishnu's help when a crocodile held him in its jaws, be classed as an ordinary elephant? Could Jatayu be called a common bird? An ordinary animal has no discrimination between right and wrong. But you display in your speech deep knowledge of life's values. Creatures in human shape may be called animals but if they display profundity cease to be animals and will have to be judged by the highest standards. There can be no escape from it. It was through your steadfast meditation and prayer to Shiva that you were endowed with strength superior to even the five elements. One who is capable of such achievement cannot but be judged by the highest standards of conduct."

"Very well," said Vali," I'll accept what you say; but how could you, protector of all creatures, aim your shaft from your hiding place, like some mean hunter tracking a wild beast, instead of facing me in a fight—if you felt that I deserved that honor?"

Lakshmana [Rama's brother and companion] gave the answer. "Rama had made a vow to support your brother Sugreeva when he came seeking refuge. This was a prior promise and had to be fulfilled, while if Rama had come before you face to face you might have made a similar appeal, which would have created confusion of purpose. That's the reason why he shot unseen by you."

Vali saw the inner purport of this explanation and said, "Now I understand your words differently from the way they sound. They are simple to hear but have inner strength and I feel assured that Rama has not committed an unrighteous act. Simple-minded ones like me can never realize eternal truths without constantly blundering and failing. Pray, forgive my errors and my rude speech. Instead of treating me as a mere monkey by birth, as I myself was content to think, you have elevated my status, and honoured me. After piercing my body with your arrow, and when I am about to die—you are touching my understanding with a supreme illumination, which I consider the greatest blessing ever conferred on me. In spite of my obstinacy you have helped me attain a profound understanding and opened my mind with your magic. While other gods confer boons after being asked, you confer them on the mere utterance of your name. Great sages have attempted, after aeons of austerities, to obtain a vision of God, but you have bestowed it on me unasked. I feel proud and happy at this moment. I have only one request. I hope my brother will prove worthy of your trust in him. But at any time if any weakness seizes him and you find him in the wrong, please do not send your arrow in his direction. Treat him kindly.

"Another thing. If your brothers, at any time, blame Sugreeva as one who had engineered the death of his brother, please explain to them that Sugreeva has only engineered my salvation."

33

The Illiad—ca. 8th century BCE

The Illiad *tells the story of war between two warrior societies. Attributed the blind poet* Homer, *this epic poem was written during the dark ages of Greece. Epics like* The Illiad *were sung from memory at male gatherings. They were very popular because they seemed to contain the very essence of what it meant to be a Greek.* The Illiad *relates an event that occurred in the ninth year of the war between Greece and Troy, which ended in a fateful battle between Achilles, the Greek hero, and the Trojan warrior Hector. What values seems to be most important to the Greek warriors in this poem?*

> Then bright-plum's Hector spake . . .
> "Lady mother . . .
> Go thou to the shrine
> Of Athena, driver of spoil; take offerings with thee,
> Assembling the aged wives, and the robe thou accountest most graceful
>   and large of those in thy hall, and the dearest
> To thine own self; on the knees of fair-hair'd Athena
> Lay it, and vow thou wilt offer her there in her shrine
> Twelve yearling kine that have toil'd not, if she will but pity
> Troy town and the Trojan wives and their little children . . .

> ★ ★ ★

> Then with wailing cries all [women] lifted their hands to Athena;
> Then took the fair-cheeked Theano [Athena's priestess] the border'd robe
> And upon the knees of the fair-hair'd Athena she laid it.
> And with prayer besought the daughter of mighty Zeus;
> "O Lady Athena, who keepest guard on our city,
> Fairest of Goddesses, break now this Diomed's spear;
> Made him headlong to fall in front of the Scaean gates
> That we twelve yearling kine that never have toil'd
> May sacrifice in they shrine, if thou wilt but pity
> Troy town and the Trojan wives and their little children."

> ★ ★ ★

> Away went bright-plum'd Hector, and came
> With speed to his well-builded house; but there in his halls

---

From Homer, *The Illiad*, trans. by S.O. Andrew and M.J. Oakley (London: Everyman's Library, 1963).

He found not white-arm'd Andromache. She with her child
And a serving-woman clad in a beauteous robe,
Weeping and wailing had taken her stand on the wall,
So Hector, not finding his peerless wife within doors,
Went and stood on the threshold . . .
He came to the gate . . .
Andromache came to his side

 And she clasp'd his hand in her own and spake to him thus:
"Dear heart, this valour of thine will be thy undoing.
No pity thou hast for thy little one her, nor for me, Poor wretch that
 I am, and
that soon thy widow shall be. . .
Then Hector the great . . . spake to her thus:
"I were strangely asham'd
The Trojans to meet, and their wives in their trailing robes,
If here like a coward I skulked aloof from the fray.
My own heart will not let me; for aye have I learn'd
To be brave, and amid the foremost Trojans to fight,
In quest of my father's great glory and eke of mine own."

34

The Art of War by Sun-tzu— ca. 5th century BCE

Little is known about Sun-tzu's life except that he was military advisor to an emperor during the golden age of China. Nevertheless, Sun-tzu's small book, The Art of War, *is read globally by students of military science; it is also popular in the corporate world. A work of pragmatic philosophy, Sun-tzu's book did much to reshape the borders of China, and it eventually helped lead to the country's unification and near elimination of civil war. How do you think* The Art of War *could be useful in eliminating violent conflict?*

Sun Tzu, *The Art of War*, ed. with a forward by James Clavell, Delacorte Press, 1983.

LAYING PLANS

Sun-tzu said:

The art of war is of vital importance to the state. It is a matter of life and death, a road either to safety or to ruin. Hence under no circumstances can it be neglected.

The art of war is governed by five constant factors, all of which need to be taken into account. They are: the Moral Law; Heaven; Earth; the Commander; Method and discipline.

The Moral Law causes the people to be in complete accord with their ruler, so that they will follow him regardless of their lives, undismayed by any danger.

Heaven signifies night and day, cold and heat, times and seasons.

Earth comprises distances, great and small; danger and security; open ground and narrow passes; the chances of life and death.

The Commander stands for the virtues of wisdom, sincerity, benevolence, courage, and strictness.

By *Method and discipline* are to be understood the marshaling of the army in its proper subdivisions, the gradations of rank among the officers, the maintenance of roads by which supplies may reach the army, and the control of military expenditure.

These five factors should be familiar to every general. He who knows them will be victorious; he who knows them not will fail.

Therefore, when seeking to determine your military conditions, make your decisions on the basis of a comparison in this wise:

Which of the two sovereigns is imbued with the Moral Law?

Which of the two generals has the most ability?

With whom lie the advantages derived from Heaven and Earth?

On which side is discipline most rigorously enforced?

Which army is the stronger?

On which side are officers and men more highly trained?

In which army is there the most absolute certainty that merit will be properly rewarded and misdeeds summarily punished?

By means of these seven considerations I can forecast victory or defeat. . . . But remember: While heeding the profit of my counsel, avail yourself also of any helpful circumstances over and beyond the ordinary rules and modify your plans accordingly.

All warfare is based on deception. Hence, when able to attack, we must seem unable; when using our forces, we must seem inactive; when we are near, we must make the enemy believe we are far away; when far away, we must make him believe we are near. Hold out baits to entice the enemy. Feign disorder, and crush him. If he is secure at all points, be prepared for him. If he is in superior strength, evade him. If your opponent is of choleric temper, seek to irritate him. Pretend to be weak, that he may grow arrogant. If he is taking his ease, give him no rest. If his forces are united, separate them. Attack him where he is unprepared, appear where you are not expected.

ON WAGING WAR

When you engage in actual fighting, if victory is long in coming, the men's weapons will grow dull and their ardor will be dampened. If you lay siege to a town, you will exhaust your strength, and if the campaign is protracted, the resources of the state will not be equal to the strain. Never forget: When your weapons are dulled, your ardor dampened, your strength exhausted, and your treasure spent, other chieftains will spring up to take advantage of your extremity. Then no man, however wise, will be able to avert the consequences that must ensue.

Thus, though we have heard of stupid haste in war, cleverness has never been seen associated with long delays. In all history, there is no instance of a country having benefited from prolonged warfare. Only one who knows the disastrous effects of a long war can realize the supreme importance of rapidity in bringing it to a close. It is only one who is thoroughly acquainted with the evils of war who can thoroughly understand the profitable way of carrying it on.

The skillful general does not raise a second levy, neither are his supply wagons loaded more than twice. Once war is declared, he will not waste precious time in waiting for reinforcements, nor will he turn his army back for fresh supplies, but crosses the enemy's frontier without delay. The value of time—that is, being a little ahead of your opponent—has counted for more than either numerical superiority or the nicest calculations with regard to commissariat.

In war, then, let your great object be victory, not lengthy campaigns. Thus it may be known that the leader of armies is the arbiter of the people's fate, the man on whom it depends whether the nation shall be in peace or in peril.

THE SHEATHED SWORD

To fight and conquer in all your battles is not supreme excellence; supreme excellence consists in breaking the enemy's resistance without fighting. In the practical art of war, the best thing of all is to take the enemy's country whole and intact; to shatter and destroy it is not so good. So, too, it is better to capture an army entire than to destroy it, to capture a regiment, a detachment, or a company entire than to destroy them.

Thus the highest form of generalship is to balk the enemy's plans; the next best is to prevent the junction of the enemy's forces; the next in order is to attack the enemy's army in the field; and the worst policy of all is to besiege walled cities, because the preparation of mantlets, movable shelters, and various implements of war will take up three whole months: and the piling up of mounds over against the walls will take three months more. The general, unable to control his irritation, will launch his men to the assault like swarming ants, with the result that one third of his men are slain, while the town still remains untaken. Such are the disastrous effects of a siege.

The skillful leader subdues the enemy's troops without any fighting; he captures their cities without laying siege to them; he overthrows their kingdom without lengthy operations in the field. With his forces intact he disputes the mastery of the empire, and thus, without losing a man, his triumph is complete.

This is the method of attacking by stratagem of using the sheathed sword.

It is the rule in war: If our forces are ten to the enemy's one, to surround him; if five to one, to attack him; if twice as numerous, to divide our army into two, one to meet the enemy in front, and one to fall upon his rear; if he replies to the frontal attack, he may be crushed from behind; if to the rearward attack, he may be crushed in front.

If equally matched, we can offer battle; if slightly inferior in numbers, we can avoid the enemy; if quite unequal in every way, we can flee from him. Though an obstinate fight may be made by a small force, in the end it must be captured by the larger force.

The general is the bulwark of the state: if the bulwark is strong at all points, the state will be strong; if the bulwark is defective, the state will be weak.

There are three ways in which a sovereign can bring misfortune upon his army:

By commanding the army to advance or to retreat, being ignorant of the fact that it cannot obey. This is called hobbling the army.

By attempting to govern an army in the same way as he administers a kingdom, being ignorant of the conditions that obtain in an army. This causes restlessness in the soldiers' minds. Humanity and justice are the principles on which to govern a state, but not an army; opportunism and flexibility, on the other hand, are military rather than civic virtues.

He will win who knows when to fight and when not to fight.

He will win who knows how to handle both superior and inferior forces.

He will win whose army is animated by the same spirit throughout all its ranks.

He will win who, prepared himself, waits to take the enemy unprepared.

He will win who has military capacity and is not interfered with by the sovereign.

If you know the enemy and know yourself, you need not fear the result of a hundred battles. If you know yourself but not the enemy, for every victory gained you will also suffer a defeat. If you know neither the enemy nor yourself, you will succumb in every battle.

TACTICS

The good fighters of old first put themselves beyond the possibility of defeat, and then waited for an opportunity of defeating the enemy.

To secure ourselves against defeat lies in our own hands, but the opportunity of defeating the enemy is provided by the enemy himself. Hence the saying: One may *know* how to conquer without being able to *do* it.

Security against defeat implies defensive tactics; ability to defeat the enemy means taking the offensive. Standing on the defensive indicates insufficient strength; attacking, a superabundance of strength.

The general who is skilled in defense hides in the most secret recesses of the earth; he who is skilled in attack flashes forth from the topmost heights of heaven. Thus, on the one hand, we have ability to protect ourselves; on the other, to gain a victory that is complete.

To see victory only when it is within the ken of the common herd is not the acme of excellence. Nor is it the acme of excellence if you fight and conquer and the whole empire says, "Well done!" True excellence is to plan secretly, to move surreptitiously, to foil the enemy's intentions and balk his schemes, so that at last the day may be won without shedding a drop of blood. . . .

What the ancients called a clever fighter is one who not only wins, but excels in winning with ease. But his victories bring him neither reputation for wisdom nor credit for courage. For inasmuch as they are gained over circumstances that have not come to light, the world at large knows nothing of them, and he therefore wins no reputation for wisdom; and inasmuch as the hostile state submits before there has been any blood-shed, he receives no credit for courage.

He wins his battles by making no mistakes. Making no mistakes is what establishes the certainty of victory, for it means conquering an enemy that is already defeated.

Hence the skillful fighter puts himself into a position that makes defeat impossible and does not miss the moment for defeating the enemy. Thus it is that in war the victorious strategist only seeks battle after the victory has been won, whereas he who is destined to defeat first fights and afterward looks for victory. A victorious army opposed to a routed one is as a pound's weight placed in the scale against a single grain. The onrush of a conquering force is like the bursting of pent-up waters into a chasm a thousand fathoms deep.

The consummate leader cultivates the Moral Law and strictly adheres to method and discipline; thus it is in his power to control success.

CHAPTER 4

Science, Medicine, and Technology— 2000 BCE–500 CE

In the ancient world, science was part philosophical speculation and part pragmatic invention. sometimes both were combined in one person such as Archimedes. Technology in the ancient world was directed mainly at producing more food, distributing water, geographical studies and creating better weapons, depending on the greatest need of the rulers at that time. Medicine and the search for an understanding of the human body has always been present in highly developed societies like Egypt and India, and the simplest tribal groups. In the ancient world, the role of the healer gradually evolved from mainly relying on home remedies and magic to a more sophisticated approach which produced textbooks for the use of physicians skilled in surgery. Nevertheless, the use of magic has not entirely been discarded in healing a patient even today.

Do you see any similarities between medical practices in Egypt, China, and Greece?

Why do you think the Egyptians spent so much effort learning how to preserve the bodies of the dead? Do you think this might have helped to advance their medical knowledge?

Archimedes' use of a burning glass at the siege of Syracuse is mentioned in two medieval accounts, as well as by Pliny. Do you feel the accounts are truthful or merely imaginary?

Why was water supply important to the Mesopotamians and the Romans?

35

Egyptian Book of Surgery—
ca. 1700 BCE

This surgical treatise was found on an Egyptian papyrus dating from 1700 BCE, but scholars believe that the unknown physician-author wrote the first draft of the manuscript perhaps 1,000 years earlier. The author describes 48 cases and suggests treatment for a variety of wounds, infections, and fractures. How do these ancient treatments compare with what you know of modern medical practice?

CASE 1

A Wound in the Head Penetrating to the Bone

Examination

If thou examinist a man having a wound in his head, penetrating to the bone of his skull, (but) not having a gash, thou shouldst palpate his wound (or thou should lay thy hand upon it); shouldst thou find his skull uninjured, not having a perforation, a split or a smash in it,

Diagnosis

Thou shouldst say regarding him: "One having a wound in his head, while his wound does (not) have two lips . . . nor a gash, although it penetrates to the bone of his head, An ailment which I will treat."

Treatment

Thou shouldst bind it with (fresh) meat (the first day) and treat afterward with grease, honey and lint every day until he recovers.

CASE 14

Flesh Wound in the side of the Nose, penetrating to the nostril

From *The Edwin Smith Surgical Papyrus*, Vol. I, ed. and trans. by James Henry Breasted, University of Chicago Press, 1930.

Examination

If thou examinest a man having a wound in his nostril, piercing through, should thou find the two lips of that wound separated from each other, thou shouldst draw together for him that wound with stitching.

Diagnosis

Thou shouldst say concerning him: "One having a wound in his nostril, piercing through. An ailment which I will treat.

Treatment

Thou shouldst make for him two swabs of linen, and thou shouldst clean out every worn of blood with has coagulated in the inside of his nostril. Thou shouldst bind it with fresh meat the first day. When its stitching loosens, thou shouldst take off for him the fresh meat, and thou shouldst bind it with grease, honey and lint every day until he recovers.

CASE 33

A Crushed Cervical Vertebra

Diagnosis

If thou examinest a man having a crushed vertebra in his neck and thou findest that one vertebra has fallen into the next one, while hi is voiceless and can not speak; his falling head downward has caused that one vertebra crush into the next one: and shouldst thou find that his is unconscious of his two arms and his two legs because it, thou shouldlst say concerning him: "One having a crushed vertebra in his neck; his is unconscious of his two arms and his two legs, and his is speechless. An ailment not to be treated."

CASE 41

An Infected or possibly necrotic wound in the breast

Examination

If thou examinest a man having a diseased wound in his breast, while that wound is inflamed and a whirl of inflammation continually issues from the mouth of that wound at thy touch: the two lips of that wound are ruddy, while that man continues to be feverish from it; his flesh cannot receive a bandage, that wound cannot take a margin of skin; the granulation which is in the mouth of that wound is watery, their surface is hot and secretions drop therefrom in an oily state.

Diagnosis

Thou shouldst say concerning him: "One having a diseased wound in his breast, it being inflamed, and he continues to have fever from it. An ailment which I will treat."

Treatment

Thou shalt make for him cool applications for drawing out the inflammation from the mouth of the wound: leaves of willow, apply to it. Leaves of an (unknown) tree and dung, apply to it. Thou shouldst make for him applications for drying up the wound: Powder of green pigment, grease, triturate; bind upon it. Northern salt, ibex grease, Triturate; bind upon it. Thou shalt make for him poultices of (unknown) ingredients and bind upon it. If the like befalls in any (other) member, thou shalt treat him according to these instructions.

36

Egyptian Magic and Medicine— ca. 1500 BCE

Although ancient Egyptian physicians were skilled medical practitioners, magic spells were often used to speed the healing process and give added potency to medicine. The following documents include a spell with a series of recipes to cure common complaints such as balding. How can you reconcile the advanced techniques related in the Egyptian Book of Surgery with Egyptians' use of magic and potions?

RECITAL ON DRINKING A REMEDY*

Here is the great remedy. Come thou who expellest evil things in this my stomach and drives them out from these my limbs! Horus and Seth have been conducted to the big palace at Heliopolis, where they consulted over the connection between Seth's testicles with Horus, and Horus shall get well like one who is on earth. He who drinks this shall be cured like these gods who are

From *Sources of Medical History*, ed. by Logan Clendening (New York: Dover Publications, 1960).

* Translation based on Ebers' transcript, Joachim's translation, and Ebbell's English translation, made under the supervision of the editor.

above. . . . These words should be said when drinking a remedy. Really excellent, proven many times!

Internal Medical Diseases

The beginning of a compilation of remedies.

To expel *diseases in the belly*: thwj mixed with beer, is drunk by the man.

Another [remedy] for the belly, when it is ill: cumin 1/2 ro, goosefat 4 ro, are boiled, strained and taken.

Another: figs 4 ro, sebesten 4 ro, sweet beer 20 ro likewise.

Remedy to *open the bowels*: milk 25 ro, sycamore-fruit 8 ro, honey 8 ro, are boiled, strained and taken for four days.

Another to cause evacuation: Honey—are made into suppository.

Remedy for dejection: colocynth 4 ro, are mixed together, eaten and swallowed with beer 10 ro or wine 5 ro.

Another: colocynth 4 ro, honey 1 ro, are mixed together and eaten by the man in one day.

To kill *roundworm* [Ascaris Lumbriocoides] root of pomegranate 5 ro, water 10 ro, remains during the night in the dew, is strained and taken in 1 day.

Another to expel *the rose* [? erysipelas] in the belly: sory, wax, turpentine, are ground, mixed together and [it] is anointed herewith. Then thou shalt prepare remedy for evacuation after obstruction of his bowels: colocynth, senna, fruit of sycamore, are ground, mixed together and shaped into 4 cakes and let him eat it.

DISEASES OF THE EYE

The beginning of a compilation on the eye.

This is to be done for the accumulation of *purulency* in the blood of the eye: honey, balm of Mecca, gum ammoniac [?]. To treat its discharge: frankincense, myrrh, yellow ochre. To treat the growth [?] red ochre, malachite, honey. Afterwards thou shalt prepare for him: oil, sagapen hntt in frankincense, yellow ochre, frankincense, goose-fat, atibium, oil, herewith [it] is bandaged for 4 days. Thou shalt not disturb much.

Another for *night-blindness* in the eyes: liver of ox, roasted and crushed out, is given for this trouble. Really excellent!

Another for *blindness*: pig's eyes, its humour is fetched, real stibium, red ochre, less of honey, are ground fine, mixed together and poured into the ear of the man, so that he may be cured immediately. Do [it] and thou shalt see. Really excellent! Thou shalt recite as a spell: I have brought this which was applied to the seat of yonder trouble: it will remove the horrible suffering. Twice.

DISEASES OF THE SKIN

For *bites* by men: shell of ndw-vessel, leek, are crushed, mixed together and [it] is bandaged therewith.

The beginning of remedies to expel *discharging exanthema of the scalp* [achor]: seed of ricinus, grease, balanites-oil, are mixed together and [it] is anointed therewith.

Another:—is crushed with honey and [it] is bandaged therewith.

Another to make the hair of a bald-headed person grow: fat of lion, fat of hippopotamus, fat of crocodile, fat of cat, fat of serpent, fat of ibex, are mixed together and the head of a bald person is anointed therewith.

37

Yin and Yang in Medical Theory (China)—3rd century BCE

The earliest surviving Chinese medical texts date from the third century BCE. The document that follows became the main source of Chinese medical theory. According to its author, the legendary Yellow Emperor, the principle of Yin and Yang was the foundation of the universe; everything was the result of the conflict between light and darkness. In what major way does the Chinese approach to medicine differ from that of the Greeks, Indians, and Egyptians?

The Yellow Emperor said "The principle of Yin and Yang is the foundation of the entire universe. It underlies everything in creation. It brings about the development of parenthood; it is the root and source of life and death it is found with the temples of the gods. In order to treat and cure diseases one must search for their origins.

"Heaven was created by the concentration of Yang, the force of light, earth was created by the concentration of Yin, the forces of darkness. Yang stands for peace and serenity; Yin stands for confusion and turmoil. Yang stands for destruction; Yin stands for conservation. Yang brings about disintegration; Yin gives shape to things. . . .

The pure and lucid element of light is manifested in the upper artifices and the turbid element of darkness is manifested in the lower orifices. Yang, the element of light, originates in the pores. Yin, the element of darkness, moves

From Patricia Ebrey, *Chinese Civilization: A Sourcebook* 2nd ed. (New York: Free Press, 1993), p. 77-79. Reprinted by permission of Free Press, a division of Simon & Schuster Adult Publishing.

within the five viscera. Yang the lucid force of light truly is represented by the four extremities— and Yin the turbid force of darkness stores the power of the six treasures of nature. Water is an embodiment of Yin as fire is an embodiment of Yang. Yang creates the air, while Yin creates the senses, which belong to the physical body When the physical body dies, the spirit is restored to the air, its natural environment. The spirit receives its nourishment through the air, and the body receives its nourishment through the senses.

"If Yang is overly powerful, then Yin may be too weak. If Yin is particularly strong, then Yang is apt to be defective If the male force is overwhelming, then there will be excessive heat. If the female force is overwhelming, then there will be excessive cold. Exposure to repeated and severe heat will induce chills. Cold injures the body while heat injures the spirit When the spirit is hurt, severe pain will ensue. When the body is hurt, there will be swelling. Thus, when severe pain occurs first and swelling comes on later, one may infer that a disharmony in the spirit has done harm to the body. Likewise, when swelling appears first and severe pain is felt later on, one can say that a dysfunction in the body has injured the spirit. . . .

"Nature has four seasons and five elements. To grant long life, these seasons and elements must store up the power of creation in cold, heat, dryness, moisture, and wind. Man has five viscera in which these five climates are transformed into joy, anger, sympathy, grief. and fear. The emotions of joy and anger are injurious to the spirit just as cold and heat are injurious to the body. Violent anger depletes Yin; violent joy depletes Yang. When rebellious emotions rise to Heaven the pulse expires and leaves the body When joy and anger are without moderation, then cold and heat exceed all measure, and life is no longer secure. Yin and Yang should be respected to an equal extent.

The Yellow Emperor asked, "Is there any alternative to the law of Yin and Yang?"

Qi Bo answered: "When Yang is the stronger, the body is hot, the pores are closed, and people begin to pant; they become boisterous and coarse and do not perspire. They become feverish, their mouths are dry and sore, their stomachs feel tight, and they die of constipation. When Yang is the stronger, people can endure winter but not summer. When Yin is the stronger, the body is cold and covered with perspiration. People realize they are ill; they tremble and feel chilly. When they feel chilled, their spirits become rebellious. Their stomachs can no long digest food and they die. When Yin is stronger, people can endure summer but not winter. Thus Yin and Yang alternate. Their ebbs and surges vary, and so does the character of the diseases."

The Yellow Emperor asked, "Can anything be done to harmonize and adjust these two principles of nature?"

Qi Bo answered: "If one has the ability to know the seven injuries and the eight advantages, one can bring the two principles into harmony. If one does not know how to use this knowledge, his life will be doomed to early decay. By the age of forty the Yin force in the body has been reduced to one-half of its natural vigor and an individual's youthful prowess has deteriorated. By the age of fifty the body has grown heavy. The ears no longer hear well. The eyes no longer see clearly By the age of sixty the life producing power of Yin has declined to a very low level. Impotence sets in. The nine orifices no longer benefit each other. . . .

Those who seek wisdom beyond the natural limits will retain good hearing and clear vision. Their bodies will remain light and strong. Although they grow old in years, they will stay able-bodied and vigorous and be capable of governing to great advantage. For this reason the ancient sages did not rush into the affairs of the world. In their pleasures and joys they were dignified and tranquil. They did what they thought best and did not bend their will or ambition to the achievement of empty ends Thus their allotted span of life was without limit, like that of Heaven and earth. This is the way the ancient sages controlled and conducted themselves.

"By observing myself I learn about others, and their diseases become apparent to me. By observing the external symptoms, I gather knowledge about the internal diseases One should watch for things out of the ordinary One should observe minute and trifling things and treat them as if the were big and important. When they are treated the danger they pose will be dissipated. Experts in examining patients judge their general appearance; they feel their pulse and determine whether it is Yin or Yang that causes the disease. . . . To determine whether Yin or Yang predominates, one must be able to distinguish a light pulse of low tension from a hard pounding one With a disease of Yang, Yin predominates With a disease of Yin, Yang predominates When one is filled with vigor and strength, Yin and Yang are in proper harmony.

38

The Hippocratic Oath (Greece)— ca. 5th century BCE

The Greek physician Hippocrates (460–377 BCE) is considered the father of Western medicine. Rejecting the prevalent view that disease was caused by evil spirits and the gods' disfavor, Hippocrates believed there was a rational cause for illness. He diagnosed by observation and was the first to recognize the symptoms of pneumonia and epilepsy in children. As the founder of a medical school, he was concerned with ethical practice. The following oath, which is still administered in some form at medical school graduations, is

From *A History of Medicine* by Douglas Guthrie (Philadelphia: Lippincott, 1946).

attributed to Hippocrates, although modern scholars believe that the part concerning abortion was added later. What parts of this oath are appropriate for modern medical practitioners? What seems to be the main purpose of the first part of the oath, which deals with a student's relationship to his teacher?

I swear by Apollo the Physician, by Aesculapius, by Hygeia, by Panacea, and by all the gods and goddesses, making them my witnesses, that I will carry out according to my ability and judgment, this oath and this indenture. To hold my teacher in this art equal to my own parents; to make him partner in my livelihood; when he is need of money to share mine with him; to consider his family as my own brothers, and to teach them this art, if they want to learn it, without fee or indenture; to impart precept, oral instruction, and all other instruction to my own sons, the sons of my teacher, and to pupils who have taken the physicians' Oath, but to nobody else. I will use treatment to help the sick according to my ability and judgment, but never with a view to injury and wrongdoing. Neither will I administer a poison to anybody when asked to do so, nor will I suggest such a course. Similarly I will not give to a woman a pessary to cause abortion. But I will keep pure and holy both my life and my art. I will not use the knife, not even, verily, on sufferers from stone, but I will give place to such as are craftsmen therein. Into whatsoever houses I enter, I will enter to help the sick, and I will abstain from all intentional wrongdoing and harm, especially from abusing the bodies of man or woman, bond or free. And whatsoever I shall see or hear in the course of my profession, as well as outside my profession in my intercourse with men, if it be what should not be published abroad, I will never divulge, holding such things to be holy secrets. Now if I carry out this oath, and break it not, may I gain for ever reputation among all men for my life and for my art; but if I transgress it and forswear myself, may the opposite befall me.

39

Herodotus on Mummification,
From *The Histories*—
5th century BCE

Herodotus (ca. 480–425 BCE) was born at Halicarnassus in Asia Minor and traveled throughout the ancient world as a young man. He later wrote about his travels in a way that suggests a lively sense of curiosity and history. Herodutus also wrote an account of the Persian invasion of Greece. He was the first of the Greeks to write seriously about the world around him and about past events; he is thus regarded in the West as the "father of history." This account of the Egyptian process of mummification provides a good example of Herodotus' intellectual curiosity and attention to detail. Why do you think Herodotus was so interested in the mummification process?

The mode of embalming, according to the most perfect process, is the following:- They take first a crooked piece of iron, and with it draw out the brain through the nostrils, thus getting rid of a portion, while the skull is cleared of the rest by rinsing with drugs; next they make a cut along the flank with a sharp Ethiopian stone, and take out the whole contents of the abdomen, which they then cleanse, washing it thoroughly with palm wine, and again frequently with an infusion of pounded aromatics. After this they fill the cavity with the purest bruised myrrh, with cassia, and every other sort of spicery except frankincense, and sew up the opening. Then the body is placed in natrum for seventy days, and covered entirely over. After the expiration of that space of time, which must not be exceeded, the body is washed, and wrapped round, from head to foot, with bandages of fine linen cloth, smeared over with gum, which is used generally by the Egyptians in the place of glue, and in this state it is given back to the relations, who enclose it in a wooden case which they have had made for the purpose, shaped into the figure of a man. Then fastening the case, they place it in a sepulchral chamber, upright against the wall. Such is the most costly way of embalming the dead.

If persons wish to avoid expense, and choose the second process, the following is the method pursued:- Syringes are filled with oil made from the cedar-tree, which is then, without any incision or disembowelling, injected into the abdomen. The passage by which it might be likely to return is stopped, and the body laid in natrum the prescribed number of days. At the

From Herodotus, *The Histories*.

end of the time the cedar-oil is allowed to make its escape; and such is its power that it brings with it the whole stomach and intestines in a liquid state. The natrum meanwhile has dissolved the flesh, and so nothing is left of the dead body but the skin and the bones. It is returned in this condition to the relatives, without any further trouble being bestowed upon it.

The third method of embalming, which is practised in the case of the poorer classes, is to clear out the intestines with a clyster, and let the body lie in natrum the seventy days, after which it is at once given to those who come to fetch it away.

40–42

Archimedes Use of a Burning Glass at the Siege of Syracuse, From the *Universal History* by Polybius—3rd century BCE

Archimedes (217–212 BCE) is considered one of the greatest mathematicians and scientists of all time and an equal of Issac Newton. Except for a sojourn at Euclid's school in Alexandria, Archimedes lived his entire life in the Greek seaport colony of Syracuse on the island of Sicily. There, he was often involved in solving problems for the king, Illiero, who became his good friend. Although he never traveled, Archimedes was well known for his scientific achievements during his lifetime. When the Romans moved to conquer Syracuse, Archimedes developed some unique weapons to defend the colony. The most storied of these was the burning glass. The first document (44) is the earliest account of the weapons Archimedes developed to protect Syracuse; the two brief excerpts that follow (45, 46) are medieval accounts of the same event. Which seems the most believable to you? Which of Archimedes' weapons seems most likely to have actually existed?

40

The Technology of War

4. Meanwhile Marcellus was attacking the quarter of Arcradina from the sea with sixty quinqueremes, each vessel being filled with archers, slingers and javelin-throwers, whose task was to drive the defenders from the battlements. Besides these vessels he had eight quinqueremes grouped in pairs. Each pair had had half of their oars removed, the starboard bank for the one and the port for the other, and on these sides the vessels were lashed together. They were then rowed by the remaining oars of their outer sides, and brought up to the walls the siege engines known as *sambucae*. These are constructed as follows. A ladder is made, four feet in width and high enough to reach the top of the wall from the place where its feet are to rest. Each side is fenced in with a high protective breastwork, and the machine is also shielded by a wicker covering high overhead. It is then laid flat over the two sides of the ships where are lashed together, the top protruding a considerable distance beyond the bows. To the tops of the ships' masts are fixed pulleys with ropes, and when the *sambuca* is about to be used, the ropes are attached to the top of the ladder, and men standing in the stern haul up the machine by means of the pulleys, while others stand in the bows to support it with long poles and make sure that it is safely raised. After this the oarsmen on the two outer sides of the ships row the vessels close inshore, and the crews then attempt to prop the sambuca against the wall. At the top of the ladder there is a wooden platform which is protected on three sides by wicker screens; four men are stationed on this to engage the defenders, who in the meanwhile are struggling to prevent the *sambuca* from being lodged against the battlements. As soon as the attackers have got it into position, and are thus standing on a higher level that the wall, they pull down the wicker screens on each side of the platform and rush out on to the battlements or towers. Their comrades climb up the *sambuca* after them, the ladder being held firm by ropes which are attached to both ships. This device is aptly named, because when it is raised the combination of the ship and the ladder looks remarkably like the musical instrument in question.

5. This was the siege equipment with which the Romans planned to assault the city's towers. But Archimedes had constructed artillery which could cover a whole variety of ranges, so that while the attacking ships were still at a distance he scored so many hits with his catapults and stone-throwers that he was able to cause them severe damage and harass their approach. Then, as the distance decreased and these weapons began to carry over the enemy's heads, he

From *The Rise of the Roman Empire*, trans. by Ian Scott-Kilvert, 1979. Reprinted by permission of Penguin Group (USA), Inc.

resorted to smaller and smaller machines, and so demoralized the Romans that their advance was brought to a standstill. In the end Marcellus was reduced in despair to bringing up his ships secretly under cover of darkness. But when they had almost reached the shore, and were therefore too close to be struck by the catapults, Archimedes had devised yet another weapon to repel the marines, who were fighting from the decks. He had had the walls pierced with large numbers of loopholes at the height of a man, which were about a palm's breadth wide at the outer surface of the walls. Behind each of these and inside the walls were stationed archers with rows of so-called 'scorpions', a small catapult which discharged iron darts, and by shooting through these embrasures they put many of the marines out of action. Through these tactics he not only foiled all the enemy's attacks, both those made at long range and any attempt at hand-to-hand fighting, but also caused them heavy losses.

Then, whenever the enemy tried to work their *sambucae,* he had other engines ready all along the walls. At normal times these were kept out of sight, but as soon as they were needed they were hoisted above the walls, with their beams projecting far over the battlements, some of them carrying stones weighing as much as ten talents, and others large lumps of lead. As soon as the *sambucae* approached, these beams were swung round on a universal joint and by means of a release mechanism or trigger dropped the weight on the *sambuca;* the effect was not only to smash the ladder but to endanger the safety of the ships and of their crews.

6. Other machines invented by Archimedes were directed against the assault parties as they advanced under the shelter of screens which protected them against the missiles shot through the walls. Against these attackers the machines could discharge stones heavy enough to drive back the marines from the bows of the ships; at the same time a grappling-iron attached to a chain would be let down, and with this the man controlling the beam would clutch at the ship. As soon as the prow was securely gripped, the lever of the machine inside the wall would be pressed down. When the operator had lifted up the ship's prow in this way and made her stand on her stern, he made fast the lower parts of the machine, so that they would not move, and finally by means of a rope and pulley suddenly slackened the grappling-iron and the chain. The result was that some of the vessels heeled over and fell on the sides, and others capsized, while the majority when their bows were let fall from a height plunged under water and filled, and thus threw all into confusion. Marcellus' operations were thus completely frustrated by these inventions of Archimedes, and when he saw that the garrison not only repulsed his attacks with heavy losses but also laughed at his efforts, he took his defeat hard. At the same time he could not refrain from making a joke against himself when he said: 'Archimedes uses my ships to ladle sea-water into his wine-cups, but my *sambuca* band have been whipped out of the wine-party as intruders!' So ended the efforts to capture Syracuse from the sea.

41

The Book of Histories
(CHILIADES)

BY JOHN TZETZES

Book II. Lines 118-128

When Marcellus withdrew them [his ships] a bow-shot, the old man [Archimedes] constructed a kind of hexagonal mirror, and at an interval proportionate to the size of the mirror he set similar small mirrors with four edges, moved by links and by a form of hinge, and made it the centre of the sun's beams-its noon-tide beam, whether in summer or in mid-winter. Afterwards, when the beams were reflected in the mirror, a fearful kindling of fire was raised in the ships, and at the distance of a bow-shot he turned them into ashes. In this way did the old man prevail over Marcellus with his weapons.

42

Epitome ton Istorion

BY JOHN ZONARAS

9.4

At last in an incredible manner he [Archimedes] burned up the whole Roman fleet. For by tilting a kind of mirror toward the sun he concentrated the sun's beam upon it; and owing to the thickness and smoothness of the mirror he ignited the air from this beam and kindled a great flame, the whole of which he directed upon the ships that lay at anchor in the path of the fire, until he consumed them all.

From *Greek Mathematical Works*, trans. by Ivor Thomas, Loeb Classical Library (Cambridge: Harvard University Press, 1941), Vol. II, p. 19.

From *Dio's Roman History*, trans. by Earnest Cary, Loeb Classical Library (Cambridge: Harvard University Press, 1914), Vol. II, p. 171.

43

Pliny's *Natural History*—
1st century CE

Gaius Plinius Secundus (23–73 CE), or Pliny the Elder, was a Roman of the equestrian class. He received a classical education in Rome and then served as an officer in the Roman army. Later in life, he became a government official. During this time, he began to write Natural History, *in which he attempted to collect the knowledge of the age. Pliny was an eyewitness to the eruption of Mount Vesuvius and wrote an account of his experience. The idea of an encyclopedic collection of information dates to ancient times. Why might information gathering have been so important to an educated Roman such as Pliny?*

The world, and whatever that be which we otherwise call the heavens, by the vault of which all things are enclosed, we must conceive to be a deity, to be eternal, without bounds, neither created nor subject, at any time, to destruction. To inquire what is beyond it is no concern of man . . .

It is madness to harass the mind, as some have done, with attempts to measure the world, and to publish these attempts . . . It is madness, perfect madness, to go out of this world and to search for what is beyond it, as if one who is ignorant of his own dimensions could ascertain the measure of anything else, or as if the human mind could see what the world itself cannot contain.

That it has the form of a perfect globe we learn from the name which has been uniformly given to it, as well as from numerous natural arguments. . .

The rising and the setting of the sun clearly prove, that this globe is carried round in the space of twenty-four hours, in an eternal and never-ceasing circuit, and with incredible swiftness. I am not able to say, whether the sound caused by the whirling about of so great a mass be excessive, and, therefore, far beyond what our ears can perceive, nor, indeed, whether the resounding of so many stars, all carried along at the same time and revolving in their orbits, may not produce a kind of delightful harmony of incredible sweetness. To us, who are in the interior, the world appears to glide silently along, both by day and by night. . . .

I do not find that any one has doubted that there are four elements. The highest of these is supposed to be fire, and hence proceed the eyes of so many glittering stars. The next is that spirit, which both the Greeks and ourselves call by the same name, air. It is by the force of this vital principle, pervading all things and mingling with all, that the earth, together with the fourth element,

From Pliny's Natural History in *The Ideas that Have Influenced Civilization*, Vol. III, ed. by Oliver J. Thatcher (Milwaukee, WI: Roberts-Manchester, 1901).

water, is balanced in the middle of space. These are mutually bound together, the lighter being restrained by the heavier, so that they cannot fly off; while, on the contrary, from the lighter tending upwards, the heavier are so suspended, that they cannot fall down. . . .

I consider it, therefore, an indication of human weakness to inquire into the figure and form of God. For whatever God be, if there be any other god, and wherever he exists, he is all sense, all sight, all hearing, all life, all mind, and all within himself. To believe that there are a number of gods, derived from the virtues and vices of man, as Chastity, Concord, Understanding, Hope, Honor, Clemency, and Fidelity; or, according to the opinion of Democritus, that there are only two, Punishment and Reward, indicates still greater folly. . . . And there are nations who make gods of certain animals, and even certain obscene things, which are not to be spoken of, swearing by stinking meats and such like. . . . To assist man is to be a god; this is the path to eternal glory. . . .

Before we quit the consideration of the nature of man, it appears only proper to point out those persons who have been the authors of different inventions. Father Liber was the first to establish the practice of buying and selling; he also invented the diadem, the emblem of royalty, and the triumphal procession. . . . I have always been of opinion that letters were of Assyrian origin, but other writers . . . suppose that they were invented in Egypt by Mercury; others, again, will have it that they were discovered by the Syrians; and that Cadmus brought from Phoenicia sixteen letters into Greece. . . .

On the other hand, Epigenes, a writer of very great authority, informs us that the Babylonians have a series of observations on the stars, for a period of seven hundred and twenty thousand years, inscribed on baked bricks. Berosus and Critedemus, who make the period the shortest, give it as four hundred and ninety thousand years. From this statement, it would appear that letters have been in use from all eternity. The Pelasgi were the first to introduce them into Latium.

The brothers Euryalus and Hyperbius were the first who constructed brick kilns and houses at Athens; before which, caves in the ground served for houses. Gellius is inclined to think that Toxius, the son of Caelus, was the first inventor of mortar, it having been suggested to him by the nest of the swallow. . . . Cinyra, the son of Agriopas, invented tiles and discovered copper-mines, both of them in the island of Cyprus; he also invented the tongs, the hammer, the lever, and the anvil. Wells were invented by Danaus, who came from Egypt into that part of Greece which had previously been known as Argos Dipsion. . . .

Daedalus was the first person who worked in wood; it was he who invented the saw, the axe, the plummet, the gimlet, glue, and isinglass; the square, the level, the turner's lathe, and the key, were invented by Theodorus, of Samos. . . .

The Egyptians were the first who established a monarchical government, and the Athenians . . . a democracy. Phalaris, of Agrigentum, was the first tyrant that existed; the Lacedaemonians were the introducers of slavery; and the first capital punishment inflicted was ordered by the Areiopagus.

44

Water Regulation in Ancient Mesopotamia, From *The Code of Hammurabi*—1750 BCE

Water was an important commodity in the ancient world. In Babylon, the Tigris and the Euphrates rivers were controlled by dikes and ditches. Water use was regulated by the Code of Hammurabi. *What does the following document reveal about ancient Babylonians' main concern regarding the use of water?*

53. If a man neglects to maintain his dike and does not strengthen it, and a break is made in his dike and the water carries away the farmland, the man in whose dike the break has been made shall replace the grain which has been damaged.

54. If he is not able to replace the grain, they shall sell him and his goods and the farmers whose grain the water has carried away shall divide (the results of the sale).

55. If a man opens his canal for irrigation and neglects it and the water carries away an adjacent field, he shall pay out grain on the basis of the adjacent field.

56. If a man opens up the water and the water carries away the improvements of an adjacent field, he shall pay out ten *gur* of grain per *bur* [of damaged land]. . . .

66. If a man has stolen a watering-machine from the meadow, he shall pay five shekels of silver to the owner of the watering-machine.

From Robert F. Harper, *The Code of Hammurabi* (Chicago: University of Chicago Press, 1904).

45

Water Regulation in Rome by Vitruvius—1st century BCE

Water was also very important to the Romans; the baths were perhaps their most favored place for recreation. Traveling through Western Europe today, one sees the remains of many aqueducts constructed during the golden age of the Roman Empire. In the following document, the Roman engineer Vitruvius discusses the engineering developments that provided an ample supply of water to Roman cities.

The supply of water is made by three methods: by channels through walled conduits, or by lead pipes, or by earthenware pipes. And they are arranged as follows. In the case of conduits, the structure must be very solid; the bed of the channel must be leveled with a fall of not less than half a foot in 100 feet. The walled conduits are to be arched over so that the minimum amount of sun may strike the water. When it comes to the city walls, a reservoir is to be made. To this reservoir a triple distribution tank is to be joined to receive the water; and three pipes of equal size are to be placed in the reservoir, leading to the adjoining tanks, so that when there is an overflow from the two outer tanks, it may deliver into the middle tank. From the middle tank pipes will be laid to all basins and fountains; from the second tank to the baths, in order to furnish an annual revenue to the treasury; to avoid a deficiency in the public supply, private houses are to be supplied from the third, for private persons will not be able to divert the water, since they have their own limited supply from the distribution sources. Another reason why I have made these divisions is that those who take private supplies into their houses may by their taxes paid through tax farmers contribute to the maintenance of the water supply.

If, however, there are hills between the city and the source, we must proceed as follows: underground channels are to be dug and leveled to the fall mentioned above. If the bed is of tufa or stone, the channel may be cut in it; but if it is of soil or sand, the bed of the channel and the walls with the vaulting must be constructed, and the water should be thus conducted. Air shafts are to be so constructed that they are 120 feet apart.

But if the supply is to be by lead pipes, first of all a reservoir is to be built at the source. Then the opening of the pipe is to be determined in accordance with the amount of water, and these pipes are to be laid from the source reservoir to a reservoir which is inside the city.

From "*Water Regulation in Rome*" by Vitruvius.

When an aqueduct is to be made with lead pipes it is to have the following arrangement. If there is a fall from the source to the city and the intervening hills are not high enough to interrupt the supply, then if there are valleys, we must build substructures to bring it up to a level, as in the case of channels and conduits. If the way round the valley is not long, a circuit should be used; but if the valleys are expansive, the course will be directed down the hill, and when it reaches the bottom it is carried on a low substructure so that the level there may continue as far as possible. This will form a "belly," which the Greeks call *koilia*. When the "belly" comes to the hill opposite, and the long distance of the "belly" makes the water slow in welling up, the water is to be forced to the height of the top of the hill. . . .

Again, it is not without advantage to put reservoirs at intervals of 24,000 feet, so that if a break occurs anywhere neither the whole load of water nor the whole structure need be disturbed, and the place where it has occurred may be more easily found. But these reservoirs are to be neither in the descent nor on the level portion of the "belly," nor at risings, nor anywhere in a valley, but on unbroken level ground.

But if we wish to employ a less expensive method, we must proceed as follows. Earthenware pipes are to be made not less than two inches thick, but these pipes should be so tongued at one end that they can fit into and join one another. The joints are to be coated with quicklime mixed with oil. . . . Everything also is to be fixed as for lead pipes. Further, when the water is first let in from the source, ashes are to be put in beforehand, so that if any joints are not sufficiently coated they may be lined with the ashes.

Water supply by earthenware pipes has these advantages. First, in the construction: if a break occurs, anybody can repair it. Again, water is much more wholesome from earthenware pipes than from lead pipes. For it seems to be made injurious by lead, because white lead is produced by it; and this is said to be harmful to the human body. So if what is produced by anything is injurious, there is no doubt that the thing itself is not wholesome. We can take an example from the workers in lead who have complexions affected by pallor. For when lead is smelted in casting, the fumes from it settle on the members of the body and, burning them, rob the limbs of the virtues of the blood. Therefore it seems that water should by no means be brought in lead pipes if we desire to have it wholesome. Everyday life can be used to show that the flavor from earthenware pipes is better, because everybody (even those who load their table with silver vessels) uses earthenware to preserve the purity of water.

But if we are to create springs from which the water supplies come, we must dig wells.

But if the soil is hard, or if the veins of water lie too deep, then supplies of water are to be collected from the roofs or higher ground in concrete cisterns. . . . If the cisterns are made double or triple, so that they can be changed by percolation, they will make the supply of water much more wholesome. For when the sediment has a place to settle in, the water will be more limpid and will keep its taste without any smell. If not, salt must be added to purify it.

CHAPTER 5

Daily Life in the Ancient World

There was little or no interest in recording the daily lives of ordinary people until well into the twentieth century; however, that does not mean that there is no information available. Details of the lives of ordinary people can be found in letters, diaries, and even in tales and poems from the ancient world. In reading the following selections, you will find that those who lived in the ancient world have much in common with people living in the modern world. They suffered loneliness, worked hard, dealt with discrimination, and even looked askance at the customs of strangers.

Both in China and in the West, there has been considerable writing about farming and the role of women in society. What similarities do you find between the Chinese agricultural calendar, Cato's writing on agriculture, and the selection on Spartan life? What role did women play in ancient China? Did they have any more rights in ancient Greece or India?

Tacitus commented on the lives of the German barbarians in Germania. Did he find anything to admire about their society?

46

The Chinese Agricultural
Calendar—6th century BCE

A collection of poems, songs, and speeches, The Book of Songs *comes from the Zhou dynasty of the sixth century BCE. The oldest Chinese calendars revolved around the times for planting and harvesting, because China had a large population to feed. From these excerpts, can you determine the time of the year to which the author refers? What do you learn about the activities and attitudes of Chinese peasants during the Zhou dynasty?*

In the seventh month the Fire ebbs;
In the ninth month I hand out the coats.
In the days of the First, sharp frosts;
In the days of the Second, keen winds.
Without coats, without serge,
How should they finish the year?
In the days of the Third they plough;
In the days of the Fourth out I step
With my wife and children,
Bringing hampers to the southern acre
Where the field-hands come to take good cheer.

In the fourth month the milkwort is in spike,
In the fifth month the cicada cries.
In the eight month the harvest is gathered,
In the tenth month the boughs fall.
In the days of the first we hunt the raccoon,
And take those foxes and wild-cats
To make furs for our Lord.
In the days of the Second is the great Meet;
Practice for deeds of war.
The one year-old [boar] we keep;
The three year-old we offer to our Lord.

In the sixth month we eat wild plums and cherries,
In the seventh month we boil mallows and beans.

From *The Book of Songs: The Ancient Chinese Classic of Poetry,* trans. by Arthur Waley, 1987, p. 164–167, 244–246. Reprinted by permission of Grove/Atlantic, Inc.

In the eighth month we dry the dates,
In the tenth month we take the rice
To make with it the spring wine,
So that we may be granted long life.
In the seventh month we eat melons,
In the eighth month we cut the gourds,
In the ninth month we take the seeding hemp,
We gather bitter herbs, we cut ailanto for firewood,
That our husbandmen may eat.

In the ninth month we make ready the stackyards,
In the tenth month we bring in the harvest,
Millet for wine, millet for cooking, the early and the late,
Paddy and hemp, beans and wheat.
Come, my husbandmen,
My harvesting is over,
Go up and begin your work in the house,
In the morning gather thatch-reeds,
In the evening twist rope;
Go quickly on to the roofs.
Soon you will be beginning to sow many grains.

In the days of the Second they cut the ice with tingling blows;
In the days of the Third they bring it into the cold shed.
In the days of the Fourth very early
They offer lambs and garlic.
In the ninth month are shrewd frosts;
In the tenth month they clear the stackgrounds.
With twin pitchers they hold the village feast,
Killing for it a young lamb.
Up they go into their lord's hall,
Raise the drinking-cup of the buffalo-horn:
'Hurray for our lord; may he live for ever and ever!'

47

On Agriculture by Cato—
2nd century BCE

Marcus Portius Cato (234–149 BCE) or Cato the Elder, came from an old plebian family. He grew up on his father's farm near Rome, where he learned the quintessential Roman virtues of simplicity, frugality, honesty, austerity, and patriotism. His love of the soil, which he gained as a youth, remained with him all his life. Cato had a distinguished military career and perhaps an even more distinguished career as a public official. He championed the common people as a relentless foe of the aristocracy. The selection that follows, from De Agri Culture*, is considered the earliest existing example of Roman prose. It provides practical directions for a farm manager, but it also paints a picture of Roman life during the golden days of the Republic. Which of the Roman virtues that Cato exemplified are present in this account?*

I t is true that business and banking sometimes are more profitable than farming, but farming is less hazardous than the former and more honorable than the latter. Our ancestors had the idea and put it into law that a thief should be fined twofold and a money lender fourfold. From this fact you may gather how far below the thief they rated the money lender. When they praised a good man, they called him a "good husbandman" and a "good farmer." A man so praised was supposed to have received the highest compliments. I look upon the merchant as an active man, devoted to making money, but, as I have just said, it is a hazardous and risky occupation. From the farmers, on the other hand, come the bravest men and the most vigorous soldiers; they are highly respected, have an assured livelihood, are looked upon with least envy, and are least inclined to plot evil . . .

When you contemplate buying a farm, bear the following points in mind: you should not buy eagerly nor spare your efforts in examining, nor regard it enough to go over it once. The more you visit a good farm, the more it will please you. Observe the condition of the neighboring places; in a good locality they ought to be well kept . . . The climate should be right and free from storms; the soil should be naturally rich. If possible, it should be located at the base of a mountain and face south; it should lie in a healthful district, have an abundance of help, be well supplied with water and be situated near a prosperous town, the sea or a navigable river or near a good, busy highway. It should lie among those

From *On Agriculture by Cato*, trans. A.P. Dorjahn, ed. by Guinagh and Dorjahn in Latin Literature in Translation (Green, NY: Longmans), 1942.

fields, which do not often have new owners, and where those who have sold their land are distressed at having done so. There should be plenty of farm buildings. You should not heedlessly reject another man's way of doing things. It will prove an advantage to buy from an owner who is himself a good farmer or builder. When you come to the farmhouse, see whether or not there are many oil presses and wine vats; if there are not many, infer that the yield is proportionate . . . See to it that the equipment be modest and the land frugal. Bear in mind that a field is like a man: however great the return may be, little remains, if there are lavish expenditures. If you should ask me, what constitutes the best kind of farm, I should say: about sixty acres of every type of soil, and in a good location. Most important is the vineyard, if it supplies much good wine; second in importance is an irrigated garden; third, a willow bed; fourth, an olive grove; fifth, a meadow; sixth, a grain field; seventh, woodland; eighth, trees with vines trained to them; ninth, feed for live-stock . . .

Do the following things during winter evenings: trim the wood which was brought indoors the day before and hew it into vine supports and stakes; cut firewood; clean the stables. Do not touch timber except in a dark or waning moon. For the removal of timber by digging or cutting, the best time is the week after the full moon. If possible, refrain from hewing, cutting, or touching timber, unless it is dry and free from frost and dew . . .

Clothing allotment for the domestics: an undergarment a meter long and a woolen mantle biennially. As often as you give an undergarment or a mantle to someone, take back the old one first for patch-pieces. You ought to issue a good pair of work-shoes every two years.

If an ox begins to grow sick, give him one hen's egg raw straightway and make the animal swallow it whole. On the next day prepare a trituration consisting of a head of leek and a small measure of wine and make the ox drink it. Prepare the mixture while standing and administer it in a vessel of wood. The ox and the man who administers the remedy should stand; likewise, both should be fasting . . .

48

Lessons for Women by Pan Chao—1st–2nd century CE

Education in the Confucian classics was an important avenue for gaining high social status and political power. However, Confucian doctrine did not accord women equal status with men; women were considered inferior and unworthy or incapable of learning. Nevertheless, Confucian society did honor women as both mothers and mothers-in-law, and with status came power within the family. Despite these restrictions, a few exceptional women did gain a literary education and went on to achieve positions of influence and authority. During the Han dynasty, Pan Chao (Ban Zhao) (ca. 45-166 CE), became the outstanding female Confucian scholar at the imperial court. Her mother was the daughter of a widely respected scholar and educated Pan Chao before her marriage at age 14. Pan Chao's husband died young and she never remarried. Instead, she devoted herself to scholarship, which eventually brought her to the notice of the imperial court. Although she authored many literary works, the Lessons for Women *is the most famous. Although it seems as though it was meant for her daughters, in reality Pan Chao hoped to produce a series of guidelines for all Chinese women. What does Pan Chao suggest should be the main duty of a wife? Of a husband? What might her claim of a lack of intelligence suggest?*

INTRODUCTION

I, the unworthy writer, am unsophisticated, unenlightened, and by nature unintelligent, but I am fortunate both to have received not a little favor from my scholarly father, and to have had a (cultured) mother and instructresses upon whom to rely for a literary education as well as for training in good manners. More than forty years have passed since at the age of fourteen I took up the dustpan and the broom in the Ts'ao family. During this time with trembling heart I feared constantly that I might disgrace my parents, and that I might multiply difficulties for both the women and the men (of my husband's family). Day and night I was distressed in heart, (but) I labored without confessing weariness. Now and hereafter, however, I know how to escape (from such fears).

Being careless, and by nature stupid, I taught and trained (my children) without system. Consequently I fear that my son Ku may bring disgrace upon the Imperial Dynasty by whose Holy Grace he has unprecedentedly received

From Nancy Lee Swan, *Pan Chao: Foremost Woman Scholar of China*, The Century Company, 1932, pp. 82–90.

the extraordinary privilege of wearing the Gold and the Purple, a privilege for the attainment of which (by my son, I) a humble subject never even hoped. Nevertheless, now that he is a man and able to plan his own life, I need not again have concern for him. But I do grieve that you, my daughters, just now at the age for marriage, have not at this time had gradual training and advice; that you still have not learned the proper customs for married women. I fear that by failure in good manners in other families you will humiliate both your ancestors and your clan. I am now seriously ill, life is uncertain. As I have thought of you all in so untrained a state, I have been uneasy many a time for you. At hours of leisure I have composed in seven chapters these instructions under the title, "Lessons for Women." In order that you may have something wherewith to benefit your persons, I wish every one of you, my daughters, each to write out a copy for yourself.

From this time on every one of you strive to practise these (lessons).

CHAPTER I

Humility

On the third day after the birth of a girl the ancients observed three customs: (first) to place the baby below the bed; (second) to give her a potsherd with which to play; and (third) to announce her birth to her ancestors by an offering. Now to lay the baby below the bed plainly indicated that she is lowly and weak, and should regard it as her primary duty to humble herself before others. To give her potsherds with which to play indubitably signified that she should practise labor and consider it her primary duty to be industrious. To announce her birth before her ancestors clearly meant that she ought to esteem as her primary duty the continuation of the observance of worship in the home.

These three ancient customs epitomize a woman's ordinary way of life and the teachings of the traditional ceremonial rites and regulations. Let a woman modestly yield to others; let her respect others; let her put others first, herself last. Should she do something good, let her not mention it; should she do something bad, let her not deny it. Let her bear disgrace; let her even endure when others speak or do evil to her. Always let her seem to tremble and to fear. (When a woman follows maxims such as these,) then she may be said to humble herself before others.

Let a woman retire late to bed, but rise early to duties; let her not dread tasks by day or by night. Let her not refuse to perform domestic duties whether easy or difficult. That which must be done, let her finish completely, tidily, and systematically. (When a woman follows such rules as these,) then she may be said to be industrious.

Let a woman be correct in manner and upright in character in order to serve her husband. Let her live in purity and quietness (of spirit), and attend to her own affairs. Let her love not gossip and silly laughter. Let her cleanse and purify and arrange in order the wine and the food for the offerings to the ancestors. (When a woman observes such principles as these,) then she may be said to continue ancestral worship.

No woman who observes these three (fundamentals of life) has ever had a bad reputation or has fallen into disgrace. If a woman fail to observe them, how can her name be honored; how can she but bring disgrace upon herself?

CHAPTER II

Husband and Wife

The Way of husband and wife is intimately connected with *Yin* and *Yang*, and relates the individual to gods and ancestors. Truly it is the great principle of Heaven and Earth, and the great basis of human relationships. Therefore the "Rites" honor union of man and woman; and in the "Book of Poetry" the "First Ode" manifests the principle of marriage. For these reasons the relationship cannot but be an important one.

If a husband be unworthy then he possesses nothing by which to control his wife. If a wife be unworthy, then she possesses nothing with which to serve her husband. If a husband does not control his wife, then the rules of conduct manifesting his authority are abandoned and broken. If a wife does not serve her husband, then the proper relationship (between men and women) and the natural order of things are neglected and destroyed. As a matter of fact the purpose of these two (the controlling of women by men, and the serving of men by women) is the same.

Now examine the gentlemen of the present age. They only know that wives must be controlled, and that the husband's rules of conduct manifesting his authority must be established. They therefore teach their boys to read books and (study) histories. But they do not in the least understand that husbands and masters must (also) be served, and that the proper relationship and the rites should be maintained.

Yet only to teach men and not to teach women,—is that not ignoring the essential relation between them? According to the "Rites," it is the rule to begin to teach children to read at the age of eight years, and by the age of fifteen years they ought then to be ready for cultural training. Only why should it not be (that girls' education as well as boys' be) according to this principle?

CHAPTER III

Respect and Caution

As *Yin* and *Yang* are not of the same nature, so man and woman have different characteristics. The distinctive quality of the *Yang* is rigidity; the function of the *Yin* is yielding. Man is honored for strength; a woman is beautiful on account of her gentleness. Hence there arose the common saying: "A man though born like a wolf may, it is feared, become a weak monstrosity; a woman though born like a mouse may, it is feared, become a tiger."

Now for self-culture nothing equals respect for others. To counteract firmness nothing equals compliance. Consequently it can be said that the WAY of respect and acquiescence is woman's most important principle of conduct. So respect may be defined as nothing other than holding on to that which is permanent; and acquiescence nothing other than being liberal and generous. Those who are steadfast in devotion know that they should stay in their proper places; those who are liberal and generous esteem others, and honor and serve (them).

If husband and wife have the habit of staying together, never leaving one another, and following each other around within the limited space of their own rooms, then they will lust after and take liberties with one another. From such action improper language will arise between the two. This kind of discussion may lead to licentiousness. Out of licentiousness will be born a heart of disrespect to the husband. Such a result comes from not knowing that one should stay in one's proper place.

Furthermore, affairs may be either crooked or straight; words may be either right or wrong. Straightforwardness cannot but lead to quarreling; crookedness cannot but lead to accusation. If there are really accusations and quarrels, then undoubtedly there will be angry affairs. Such a result comes from not esteeming others, and not honoring and serving (them).

(If wives) suppress not contempt for husbands, then it follows (that such wives) rebuke and scold (their husbands). (If husbands) stop not short of anger, then they are certain to beat (their wives). The correct relationship between husband and wife is based upon harmony and intimacy, and (conjugal) love is grounded in proper union. Should actual blows be dealt, how could matrimonial relationship be preserved? Should sharp words be spoken, how could (conjugal) love exist? If love and proper relationship both be destroyed, then husband and wife are divided.

CHAPTER IV

Womanly Qualifications

A woman (ought to) have four qualifications: (1) womanly virtue; (2) womanly words; (3) womanly bearing; and (4) womanly work. Now what is called womanly virtue need not be brilliant ability, exceptionally different from others. Womanly words need be neither clever in debate nor keen in conversation. Womanly appearance requires neither a pretty nor a perfect face and form. Womanly work need not be work done more skilfully than that of others.

To guard carefully her chastity; to control circumspectly her behavior; in every motion to exhibit modesty; and to model each act on the best usage, this is womanly virtue.

To choose her words with care; to avoid vulgar language; to speak at appropriate times; and not to weary others (with much conversation), may be called the characteristics of womanly words.

To wash and scrub filth away; to keep clothes and ornaments fresh and clean; to wash the head and bathe the body regularly, and to keep the person free from disgraceful filth, may be called the characteristics of womanly bearing.

With whole-hearted devotion to sew and to weave; to love not gossip and silly laughter; in cleanliness and order (to prepare) the wine and food for serving guests, may be called the characteristics of womanly work.

These four qualifications characterize the greatest virtue of a woman. No woman can afford to be without them. In fact they are very easy to possess if a woman only treasure them in her heart. The ancients had a saying: "Is Love afar off? If I desire love, then love is at hand!" So can it be said of these qualifications.

CHAPTER V

Whole-hearted Devotion

Now in the "Rites" is written the principle that a husband may marry again, but there is no Canon that authorizes a woman to be married the second time. Therefore it is said of husbands as of Heaven, that as certainly as people cannot run away from Heaven, so surely a wife cannot leave (a husband's home).

If people in action or character disobey the spirits of Heaven and of Earth, then Heaven punishes them. Likewise if a woman errs in the rites and in the proper mode of conduct, then her husband esteems her lightly. The ancient book, "A Pattern for Women," says: "To obtain the love of one man is the crown of a woman's life; to lose the love of one man is to miss the aim in woman's life." For these reasons a woman cannot but seek to win her husband's heart. Nevertheless, the beseeching wife need not use flattery, coaxing words, and cheap methods to gain intimacy.

Decidedly nothing is better (to gain the heart of a husband) than whole-hearted devotion and correct manners. In accordance with the rites and the proper mode of conduct, (let a woman) live a pure life. Let her have ears that hear not licentiousness; and eyes that see not depravity. When she goes outside her own home, let her not be conspicuous in dress and manners. When at home let her not neglect her dress. Women should not assemble in groups, nor gather together, (for gossip and silly laughter). They should not stand watching in the gateways. (If a woman follows) these rules, she may be said to have whole-hearted devotion and correct manners.

If, in all her actions, she is frivolous, she sees and hears (only) that which pleases herself. At home her hair is dishevelled, and her dress is slovenly. Outside the home she emphasizes her femininity to attract attention; she says what ought not to be said; and she looks at what ought not to be seen. (If a woman does such as) these, (she may be) said to be without whole-hearted devotion and correct manners.

CHAPTER VI

Implicit Obedience

Now "to win the love of one man is the crown of a woman's life; to lose the love of one man is her eternal disgrace." This saying advises a fixed will and a whole-hearted devotion for a woman. Ought she then to lose the hearts of her father-and mother-in-law?

There are times when love may lead to differences of opinion (between individuals); there are times when duty may lead to disagreement. Even should the husband say that he loves something, when the parents-in-law say "no," this is called a case of duty leading to disagreement. This being so, then what about the hearts of the parents-in-law? Nothing is better than an obedience which sacrifices personal opinion.

Whenever the mother-in-law says, "Do not do that," and if what she says is right, unquestionably the daughter-in-law obeys. Whenever the mother-in-law says, "Do that," even if what she says is wrong, still the daughter-in-law submits unfailingly to the command.

Let a woman not act contrary to the wishes and the opinions of parents-in-law about right and wrong; let her not dispute with them what is straight and what is crooked. Such (docility) may be called obedience which sacrifices personal opinion. Therefore the ancient book, "A Pattern for Women," says: "If a daughter-in-law (who follows the wishes of her parents-in-law) is like an echo and a shadow, how could she not be praised?"

CHAPTER VII

Harmony with Younger Brothers-
and Sisters-in-law

In order for a wife to gain the love of her husband, she must win for herself the love of her parents-in-law. To win for herself the love of her parents-in-law, she must secure for herself the good will of younger brothers- and sisters-in-law. For these reasons the right and the wrong, the praise and the blame of a woman alike depend upon younger brothers- and sisters-in-law. Consequently it will not do for a woman to lose their affection.

They are stupid both who know not that they must not lose (the hearts of) younger brothers- and sisters-in-law, and who cannot be in harmony with them in order to be intimate with them. Excepting only the Holy Men, few are able to be faultless. Now Yen Tzû's greatest virtue was that he was able to reform. Confucius praised him (for not committing a misdeed) the second time. (In comparison with him) a woman is the more likely (to make mistakes).

Although a woman possesses a worthy woman's qualifications, and is wise and discerning by nature, is she able to be perfect? Yet if a woman live in harmony with her immediate family, unfavorable criticism will be silenced (within the home. But) if a man and woman disagree, then this evil will be noised abroad. Such consequences are inevitable. The "Book of Change" says:

> "Should two hearts harmonize,
> The united strength can cut gold.
> Words from hearts which agree,
> Give forth fragrance like the orchid."

This saying may be applied to (harmony in the home).

Though a daughter-in-law and her younger sisters-in-law are equal in rank, nevertheless (they should) respect (each other); though love (between them may be) sparse, their proper relationship should be intimate. Only the virtuous, the beautiful, the modest, and the respectful (young women) can accordingly rely upon the sense of duty to make their affection sincere, and magnify love to bind their relationships firmly.

Then the excellence and the beauty of such a daughter-in-law becomes generally known. Moreover, any flaws and mistakes are hidden and unrevealed. Parents-in-law boast of her good deeds; her husband is satisfied with her. Praise of her radiates, making her illustrious in district and in neighborhood; and her brightness reaches to her own father and mother.

But a stupid and foolish person as an elder sister-in-law uses her rank to exalt herself; as a younger sister-in-law, because of parents' favor, she becomes filled with arrogance. If arrogant, how can a woman live in harmony with others? If love and proper relationships be perverted, how can praise be secured? In such instances the wife's good is hidden, and her faults are declared. The mother-in-law will be angry, and the husband will be indignant. Blame will reverberate and spread in and outside the home. Disgrace will gather upon the daughter-in-law's person, on the one hand to add humiliation to her own father and mother, and on the other to increase the difficulties of her husband.

Such then is the basis for both honor and disgrace; the foundation for reputation or for ill-repute. Can a woman be too cautious? Consequently to seek the hearts of young brothers- and sisters-in-law decidedly nothing can be esteemed better than modesty and acquiescence.

Modesty is virtue's handle; acquiescence is the wife's (most refined) characteristic. All who possess these two have sufficient for harmony with others. In the "Book of Poetry" it is written that "here is no evil; there is no dart." So it may be said of (these two, modesty and acquiescence).

49

Songs Composed by Buddhist Nuns—ca. 1st century BCE

These brief poems written by Buddhist nuns are from an ancient collection of more than 500 poems called The Therigatha *(theri means "nun"). Although composed much earlier, the poems were finally transcribed around the first century BCE. What seems to be the main reason these women became nuns? Is this in agreement with Buddha's teachings?*

MUTTA

[So free am I, so gloriously free]

So free am I, so gloriously free,
Free from three petty things—
From mortar, from pestle and from my twisted lord,
Freed from rebirth and death I am,
And all that has held me down
Is hurled away.

UBBIRI

["O Ubbiri, who wails in the wood"]

"O Ubbiri, who wails in the wood
'O Jiva! Dear daughter!'
Return to your senses, in this charnel field
Innumerable daughters, once as full of life as Jiva,
Are burnt. Which of them do you mourn?"
The hidden arrow in my heart plucked out,
The dart lodged there, removed.
The anguish of my loss,
The grief that left me faint all gone,
The yearning stilled,
To the Buddha, the Dhamma [Moral Law], and the Sangha [Community
   of Buddhists]
I turn, my heart now healed.

SUMANGALAMATA

[*A woman well set free! How free I am*]

A woman well set free! How free I am,
How wonderfully free, from kitchen drudgery.
Free from the harsh grip of hunger,
And from empty cooking pots,
Free too of that unscrupulous man,
The weaver of sunshades.
Calm now, and serene I am,
All lust and hatred purged.
To the shade of the spreading trees I go
And contemplate my happiness.

METTIKA

[*Though I am weak and tired now*]

Though I am weak and tired now,
And my youthful step long gone,
Leaning on this staff,
I climb the mountain peak.
My cloak cast off, my bowl overturned,
I sit here on this rock.
And over my spirit blows
The breath
Of liberty
I've won, I've won the triple gems [the Buddha, the Dhamma and the
    Sangha]
The Buddha's way is mine.

50

Spartan Life by Lycurgus— 8th century BCE

The Greek city-states of Sparta and Athens are often compared today; Athens is usually admired and Sparta denigrated. Their final victory over the Messenians compelled the Spartans to accept a life of stern military discipline in order to control the vanquished Messenians, who in the new Spartan society became serfs, or helots. Helots outnumbered Spartans 10 to 1 and did not relish a life of constant labor; there was always a chance they would revolt. Thus, from the age of 7 until 60, each Spartan male lived a life of discipline and self-denial. They scorned luxuries, leisure time, and costly food. Spartans lived for the good of the state and were trained to be highly skilled warriors. Spartan women also were given physical training, moved freely within the community, and enjoyed domestic independence because their husbands spent most of their time in the barracks. Women too were trained to put the good of the state first in their lives. The state also determined whether children should live or die. The weak and sickly were left to die of exposure in the hills. Surprisingly, the Spartans did not often go to war, but instead maintained peace by a series of alliances. Most of the other Greek city-states, including Athens, admired the Spartans. What do you see that is good about the Spartan system? Why might the Spartans and Athenians eventually have become bitter enemies?

In order to [promote] the good education of their youth (which . . . he [Lyeurgus] thought the most important and noblest work of a lawgiver), he went so far back as to take into consideration their very conception and birth, by regulating their marriages. For Aristotle is wrong in saying, that, after he had tried all ways to reduce the women to more modesty and sobriety, he was at last forced to leave them as they were, because that, in the absence of their husbands, who spent the best part of their lives in the wars, their wives, whom they were obliged to leave absolute mistresses at home, took great liberties and assumed the superiority; and were treated with overmuch respect and called by the title of lady or queen. The truth is, he took in their case, also, all the care that was possible; he ordered the maidens to exercise themselves with wrestling, running, throwing and quoit, and casting the dart, to the end that the fruit they conceived might, in strong and healthy bodies, take firmer root and find better growth, and withal that they, with this greater vigor, might be the more able to undergo the pains of childbearing. And to the end he might

From Plutarch: The Library of Original Sources, Vol. II: The Greek World, ed. by Oliver J. Thatcher (Milkwaukee, WI: University Research Extension Co.), p. 118–119.

take away their overgreat tenderness and fear of exposure to the air, and all acquired womanishness, he ordered that the young women should go naked in the processions, as well as the young men, and dance, too, in that condition, at certain solemn feasts, singing certain songs, whilst the young men stood around, seeing and hearing them. On these occasions, they now and then made, by jests, a befitting reflection upon those who had misbehaved themselves in the wars; and again sang encomiums upon those who had done any gallant action, and by these means inspired the younger sort with an emulation of their glory. Those that were thus commended went away proud, elated, and gratified with their honor among the maidens; and those who were rallied were as sensibly touched with it as if they had been formally reprimanded; and so much the more, because the kings and the elders, as well as the rest of the city, saw and heard all that passed. Nor was there anything shameful in this nakedness of the young women; modesty attended them, and all wantonness was excluded. It taught them simplicity and a care for good health, and gave them some taste of higher feelings, admitted as they thus were to the field of noble action and glory. Hence it was natural for them to think and speak as Gorgo, for example, the wife of Leonidas, is said to have done, when some foreign lady, as it would seem, told her that the women of Lacedœmon were the only women of the world who could rule men; "With good reason," she said, "for we are the only women who bring forth men."

These public processions of the maidens, and their appearing naked in their exercises and dancings, were incitements to marriage, operating upon the young with the rigor and certainty, as Plato says, of love, if not of mathematics. But besides all this, to promote it yet more effectually, those who continued bachelors were in a degree disfranchised by law; for they were excluded from the sight of those public processions in which the young men and maidens danced naked, and, in winter-time, the officers compelled them to march naked themselves round the market-place, singing as they went a certain song to their own disgrace, that they justly suffered this punishment for disobeying the laws. Moreover, they were denied that respect and observance which the younger men paid their elders; and no man, for example, found fault with what was said to Dercyllidas, though so eminent a commander; upon whose approach one day, a young man, instead of rising, retained his seat, remarking, "No child of yours will make room for me." . . .

Nor was it lawful, indeed, for the father himself to breed up the children after his own fancy; but as soon as they were seven years old, they were to be enrolled in certain companies and classes, where they all lived under the same order and discipline, doing their exercises and taking their play together. Of these, he who showed the most conduct and courage was made captain; they had their eyes always upon him, obeyed his orders, and underwent patiently whatsoever punishment he inflicted; so that the whole course of their education was one continued exercise of a ready and perfect obedience. The old men, too, were spectators of their performances, and often raised quarrels and disputes among them, to have a good opportunity of finding out their different characters, and of seeing which would be valiant, which a coward, when they should come to more dangerous encounters. Reading and writing they gave them, just enough to serve their turn; their chief care was to make them good subjects, and to teach them to endure pain and conquer in battle. To this end, as they grew in years, their discipline was proportionately increased; their heads were close-clipped, they were accustomed to go barefoot, and for the most part to play naked.

After they were twelve years old, they were no longer allowed to wear any undergarment; they had one coat to serve them a year; their bodies were hard and dry, with but little acquaintance of baths and unguents; these human indulgences they were allowed only on some few particular days in the year. They lodged together in little bands upon beds made of the rushes which grew by the banks of the river Eurotas, which they were to break off with their hands without a knife; if it were winter, they mingled some thistle-down with their rushes, which it was thought had the property of giving warmth. By the time they were come to this age, there was not any of the more hopeful boys who had not a lover to bear him company. The old men, too, had an eye upon them, coming often to the grounds to hear and see them contend either in wit or strength with one another, and this as seriously and with as much concern as if they were their fathers, their tutors, or their magistrates; so that there scarcely was any time or place without some one present to put them in mind of their duty, and punish them if they had neglected it. . . .

Their discipline continued still after they were full-grown men. No one was allowed to live after his own fancy; but the city was a sort of camp, in which every man had his share of provisions and business set out, and looked upon himself not so much born to serve his own ends as the interest of his country. Therefore, if they were commanded nothing else, they went to see the boys perform their exercises, to teach them something useful, or to learn it themselves of those who knew better. And, indeed, one of the greatest and highest blessings Lycurgus procured his people was the abundance of leisure, which proceeded from his forbidding to them the exercise of any mean and mechanical trade. Of the money-making that depends on troublesome going about and seeing people and doing business, they had no need at all in a state where wealth obtained no honor or respect. The Helots tilled their ground for them, and paid them yearly in kind the appointed quantity, without any trouble of theirs. To this purpose there goes a story of a Lacedœmonian [Spartan] who, happening to be at Athens when the courts were sitting, was told of a citizen that had been fined for living an idle life, and was being escorted home in much distress of mind by his condoling friends; the Lacedœmonian was much surprised at it, and desired his friend to show him the man who was condemned for living like a freeman. So much beneath them did they esteem the frivolous devotion of time and attention to the mechanical arts and to money-making.

51

Periclean Athens— 5th century BCE

After the defeat of the Persians, the Athenians dominated the sea and became the richest city-state in Greece. During this period, Athens saw a flowering of art and drama—both comedy and tragedy—as well as the development of a democratic political system that is still admired today. This period is called Periclean because at this time Pericles was the leader of Athens; he created a democratic society and supported the arts. However, with success came arrogance, eventually resulting in a bitter war (the first and second Peloponnesian Wars) with Sparta that destroyed both city-states. What does Pericles say is the essence of the Athenian state? How do Athens and Sparta differ in their military systems?

Our constitution does not copy the laws of neighbouring states; we are rather a pattern to others than imitators ourselves. Its administration favours the many instead of the few; this is why it is called a democracy. If we look to the laws, they afford equal justice to all in their private differences; if to social standing, advancement in public life falls to reputation for capacity, class considerations not being allowed to interfere with merit; nor again does poverty bar the way, if a man is able to serve the state, he is not hindered by the obscurity of his condition. The freedom which we enjoy in our government extends also to our ordinary life. There, far from exercising a jealous surveillance over each other, we do not feel called upon to be angry with our neighbour for doing what he likes, or even to indulge in those injurious looks which cannot fail to be offensive, although they inflict no positive penalty. But all this ease in our private relations does not make us lawless as citizens. Against this fear is our chief safeguard, teaching us to obey the magistrates and the laws, particularly such as regard the protection of the injured, whether they are actually on the statute book, or belong to that code which, although unwritten, yet cannot be broken without acknowledged disgrace.

Further, we provide plenty of means for the mind to refresh itself from business. We celebrate games and sacrifices all the year round, and the elegance of our private establishments forms a daily source of pleasure and helps to banish the spleen; while the magnitude of our city draws the produce of the world into our harbour, so that to the Athenian the fruits of other countries are as familiar a luxury as those of his own.

From Thucydides, History of the Peloponnesian War, trans. by Richard Crawley, 1896, Book 2, p. 111–114.

If we turn to our military policy, there also we differ from our antagonists. We throw open our city to the world, and never by alien acts exclude foreigners from any opportunity of learning or observing, although the eyes of an enemy may occasionally profit by our liberality; trusting less in system and policy than to the native spirit of our citizens; while in education, where our rivals from their very cradles by a painful discipline seek after manliness, at Athens we live exactly as we please, and yet are just as ready to encounter every legitimate danger. In proof of this it may be noticed that the Lacedœmonians do not invade our country alone, but bring with them all their confederates; while we Athenians advance unsupported into the territory of a neighbour, and fighting upon a foreign soil usually vanquish with ease men who are defending their homes. Our united force was never yet encountered by an enemy, because we have at once to attend to our marine and to despatch our citizens by land upon a hundred different services; so that, wherever they engage with some such fraction of our strength, a success against a detachment is magnified into a victory over the nation, and a defeat into a reverse suffered at the hands of our entire people. And yet if with habits not of labour but of ease, and courage not of art but of nature, we are still willing to encounter danger, we have the double advantage of escaping the experience of hardships in anticipation and of facing them in the hour of need as fearlessly as those who are never free from them.

Nor are these the only points in which our city is worthy of admiration. We cultivate refinement without extravagance and knowledge without effeminacy; wealth we employ more for use than for show, and place the real disgrace of poverty not in owning to the fact but in declining the struggle against it. Our public men have, besides politics, their private affairs to attend to, and our ordinary citizens, though occupied with the pursuits of industry, are still fair judges of public matters; for, unlike any other nation, regarding him who takes no part in these duties not as unambitious but as useless, we Athenians are able to judge at all events if we cannot originate, and instead of looking on discussion as a stumbling-block in the way of action, we think it an indispensable preliminary to any wise action at all. Again, in our enterprises we present the singular spectacle of daring and deliberation, each carried to its highest point, and both united in the same persons; although usually decision is the fruit of ignorance, hesitation of reflexion. But the palm of courage will surely be adjudged most justly to those who best know the difference between hardship and pleasure and yet are never tempted to shrink from danger. In generosity we are equally singular, acquiring our friends by conferring not by receiving favours. Yet, of course, the doer of the favour is the firmer friend of the two, in order by continued kindness to keep the recipient in his debt; while the debtor feels less keenly from the very consciousness that the return he makes will be a payment, not a free gift. And it is only the Athenians who, fearless of consequences, confer their benefits not from calculations of expediency, but in the confidence of liberality.

In short, I say that as a city we are the school of Hellas; while I doubt if the world can produce a man, who where he has only himself to depend upon, is equal to so many emergencies, and graced by so happy a versatility as the

Athenian. And that this is no mere boast thrown out for the occasion, but plain matter of fact, the power of the state acquired by these habits proves. For Athens alone of her contemporaries is found when tested to be greater than her reputation, and alone gives no occasion to her assailants to blush at the antagonist by whom they have been worsted, or to her subjects to question her title by merit to rule. Rather, the admiration of the present and succeeding ages will be ours, since we have not left our power without witness, but have shown it by mighty proofs; and far from needing a Homer for our panegyrist, or others of his craft whose verses might charm for the moment only for the impression they gave to melt at the touch of fact, we have forced every sea and land to be the highway of our daring, and everywhere, whether for evil or for good, have left imperishable monuments behind us. Such is the Athens for which these men, in the assertion of their resolve not to lose her, nobly fought and died; and well may every one of their survivors be ready to suffer in her cause.

52

Aristotle on Economics— 4th century BCE

The Greek philosopher Aristotle (384-322 BCE) was known as "the brain" by his contemporaries at school, which was not surprising because he was an expert on an amazing variety of topics. Aristotle is also known for being the tutor of Alexander of Macedon. Here, he discusses the role of the wife in the home. How do the gender roles recommended by Aristotle compare with those observed in India and China?

A good wife should be the mistress of her home, having under her care all that is within it, according to the rules we have laid down. She should allow none to enter without her husband's knowledge, dreading above all things the gossip of gadding women, which tends to poison the soul. She alone should have knowledge of what happens within, whilst if any harm is wrought by those from without, her husband will bear the blame. She must exercise control of the money spent on such festivities as her husband has

---

From Aristotle, *Aristotle in 23 Volumes*, Vol. 18, trans. by G.C. Armstrong (London: William Heinemann Ltd., 1935).

approved, keeping, moreover, within the limit set by law upon expenditure, dress, and ornament; [10] and remembering that beauty depends not on costliness of raiment, nor does abundance of gold so conduce to the praise of a woman as self-control in all that she does, and her inclination towards an honorable and well-ordered life.[1] For such adornment of the soul as this is in truth ever a thing to be envied, and a far surer warrant for the payment, to the woman herself in her old age and to her children after her, of the due meed of praise.

This, then, is the province over which a woman should be minded to bear an orderly rule; for it seems not fitting that a man should know all that passes within the house. But in all other matters, let it be her aim to obey her husband; giving no heed to public affairs, nor desiring any part in arranging the marriages of her children. [20] Rather, when the time shall come to give or receive in marriage sons or daughters, let her even then hearken to her husband in all respects, and agreeing with him obey his behest; considering that it is less unseemly for him to deal with a matter within the house than it is for her to pry into those outside its walls. Nay, it is fitting that a woman of well-ordered life should consider that her husband's uses are as laws appointed for her own life by divine will, along with the marriage state and the fortune she shares. If she endures them with patience and gentleness, she will rule her home with ease; otherwise, not so easily. Wherefore not only when her husband is in prosperity [30] and good report does it beseem her to be in modest agreement with him, and to render him the service he wills, but also in times of adversity. If, through sickness or fault of judgement, his good fortune fails, then must she show her quality,[2] encouraging him ever with words of cheer and yielding him obedience in all fitting ways; only let her do nothing base or unworthy of herself, or remember any wrong her husband may have done her through distress of mind. Let her refrain from all complaint, nor charge him with the wrong, but rather attribute everything of this kind to sickness or ignorance or accidental errors. For the more sedulous her service herein, the fuller will be his gratitude [40] when he is restored, and freed from his trouble; and if she has failed to obey him when he commanded aught that is amiss, the deeper will be his recognition when health returns. Wherefore, whilst careful to avoid such, in other respects she will serve him more assiduously than if she had been a bondwoman bought and taken home. For he has indeed bought her with a great price—with partnership in his life and in the procreation of children; than which things nought could be greater or more divine. And besides all this, the wife who had only lived in company with a fortunate husband would not have had the like opportunity to show her true quality. For though there be no small merit in a right and noble use of prosperity, still the right endurance of adversity justly receives an honor greater by far. [50] For

---

1 Cf. 1 Peter 3.3.4.

2 Or (if manifestam esse represents dêlonoti) "then plainly it is her part to encourage . . . and to yield . . ."

only a great soul can live in the midst of trouble and wrong without itself committing any base act. And so, while praying that her husband may be spared adversity, if trouble should come it beseems the wife to consider that here a good woman wins her highest praise. Let her bethink herself how <u>Alcestis</u> would never have attained such renown nor <u>Penelope</u> have deserved all the high praises bestowed on her had not their husbands known adversity; whereas the troubles of <u>Admetus</u> and <u>Ulysses</u> have obtained for their wives a reputation that shall never die. For because in time of distress they proved themselves faithful and dutiful to their husbands, the gods have bestowed on them the honor they deserved. To find partners in prosperity is easy enough; [60] but only the best women are ready to share in adversity. For all these reasons it is fitting that a woman should pay her husband an honor greater by far, nor feel shame on his account even when, as <u>Orpheus</u> says, Holy health of soul, and wealth, the child of a brave spirit, companion him no more. <u>Orpheus</u> Fr.

53

Tacitus on Germania— 1st century CE

Germania, the part of Germany north of the Rhine River, was on the fringe of the Roman Empire. The Germans had a much different culture than the Romans; although the Germans were admired for their military prowess, most Romans considered them to be an inferior people. Here, the Roman orator, senator, and historian Tacitus provides us with an account of his perception of the German people. What does he admire most about the Germans? How does he show disdain for their culture?

The Germans themselves I should regard as aboriginal, and not mixed at all with other races through immigration or intercourse. For, in former times, it was not by land but on shipboard that those who sought to emigrate would arrive; and the boundless and, so to speak, hostile ocean beyond us, is seldom entered by a sail from our world. And, beside the perils of rough and unknown seas, who would leave Asia, or Africa, or Italy for

From *The Agricola and German of Tacitus, and the Dialogue on Oratory*, trans. by Alfred John Church and William Jackson Brodribb (New York: Macmillan, 1906), p. 87–107.

Germany, with its wild country, its inclement skies, its sullen manners and aspect, unless indeed it were his home? In their ancient songs, their only way of remembering or recording the past, they celebrate an earth-born god, Tuisco, and his son Mannus, as the origin of their race, as their founders. . . . Some with the freedom of conjecture permitted by antiquity, assert that the god had several descendants, and the nation several appellations. . . . The name Germany, on the other hand, they say, is modern and newly introduced, from the fact that the tribes which first crossed the Rhine and drove out the Gauls, and are now called Tungrians, were then called Germans. Thus what was the name of a tribe, and not of a race, gradually prevailed, till all called themselves by this self-invented name of Germans, which the conquerors had first employed to inspire terror.

. . .

The tribes of Germany are free from all taint of intermarriages with foreign nations, and they appear as a distinct, unmixed race, like none but themselves. Hence, too, the same physical peculiarities throughout so vast a population. All have fierce blue eyes, red hair, huge frames, fit only for a sudden exertion. They are less able to bear laborious work. Heat and thirst they cannot in the least endure; to cold and hunger their climate and their soil inure them.

. . .

They choose their kings by birth, their generals by merit. These kings have not unlimited or arbitrary power, and the generals do more by example than by authority. . . . But to reprimand, to imprison, even to flog, is permitted to the priests alone, and that not as a punishment, or at the general's bidding, but, as it were, by the mandate of the god whom they believe to inspire the warrior. . . . And what most stimulates their courage is, that their squadrons or battalions, instead of being formed by chance or by a fortuitous gathering, are composed of families and clans. Close by them too, are those dearest to them, so that they hear the shrieks of women, the cries of infants. . . .

Tradition says that armies already wavering and giving way have been rallied by women who, with earnest entreaties and bosoms laid bare, have vividly represented the horrors of captivity, which the Germans fear with such extreme dread on behalf of their women. . . . They even believe that the sex has a certain sanctity and prescience, and they do not despise their counsels, or make light of their answers. . . .

Mercury is the deity whom they chiefly worship, and on certain days they deem it right to sacrifice to him even with human victims. . . .

Augury and divination by lot no people practice more diligently. The use of lots is simple. A little bough is lopped off a fruit-bearing tree, and cut into small pieces; these are distinguished by certain marks, and thrown carelessly and at random over a white garment. In public questions the priest of the particular state, in private the father of the family invokes the gods, and, with his eyes towards heaven, takes up each piece three times, and finds in them a meaning according to the mark previously impressed on them. . . . It is peculiar to this people to seek omens and monitions from horses. Kept at the public expense, in these same woods and groves, are white horses, pure from the taint of earthly labor; these are yoked to a sacred car, and accompanied by the priest and the king, or chief of the tribe, who note their neighings and snortings.

. . .

When they go into battle, it is a disgrace for the chief to be surpassed in valor, a disgrace for his followers not to equal the valor of the chief. And it is an infamy and a reproach for life to have survived the chief, and returned from the field. To defend, to protect him, to ascribe one's own brave deeds to his renown, is the height of loyalty. The chief fights for victory; his vassals fight for their chief. . . . Feasts and entertainments, which though inelegant, are plentifully furnished, are their only pay. The means of this bounty come from war and rapine. Nor are they as easily persuaded to plough the earth and to wait for the year's produce as to challenge an enemy and earn the honor of wounds. Nay, they actually think it tame and stupid to acquire by the sweat of toil what they might win by their blood.

Whenever they are not fighting, they pass much of their time in the chase, and still more in idleness giving themselves up to sleep and to feasting, the bravest and the most warlike doing nothing, and surrendering the management of the household of the home, and of the land, to the women, the old men and all the weakest members of the family. . . . It is the custom of the states to bestow by voluntary and individual contribution on the chiefs a present of cattle or of grain, which, while accepted as a compliment, supplies their wants. They are particularly delighted by gifts from neighboring tribes . . . such as choice steeds, heavy armor, trappings, and neckchains. We have now taught them to accept money also.

It is well known that the nations of Germany have no cities, and that they do not even tolerate closely contiguous dwellings. They live scattered and apart, just as a spring, a meadow, or a wood has attracted them. Their villages they do not arrange in our fashion, . . . but every person surrounds his dwelling with an open space, either as a precaution against the disasters of fire, or because they do not know how to build. No use is made by them of stone or tile; they employ timber for all purposes, rude masses without ornament or attractiveness. . . .

They all wrap themselves in a cloak which is fastened with a clasp, or, if this is not forthcoming, with a thorn, leaving the rest of their persons bare. . . . They also wear the skins of wild beasts. . . .

Their marriage code, however, is strict, and indeed no part of their manners is more praiseworthy. Almost alone among barbarians they are content with one wife, except a very few among them. . . . Lest the woman should think herself to stand apart from aspirations after noble deeds and from the perils of war, she is reminded by the ceremony which inaugurates marriage that she is her husband's partner in toil and danger, destined to suffer and to dare with him alike both in peace and in war. . . .

Very rare for so numerous a population is adultery, the punishment for which is prompt, and in the husband's power. Having cut off the hair of the adulteress and stripped her naked, he expels her from the house in the presence of her kinfolk, and then flogs her through the whole village. The loss of chastity meets with no indulgence; neither beauty, youth nor wealth will procure the culprit a husband. No one in Germany laughs at vice, nor do they call it the fashion to corrupt and to be corrupted. . . . To limit the number of their children or to destroy any of their subsequent offspring is accounted infamous, and good habits are here more effectual than good laws elsewhere.

. . .

It is a duty among them to adopt the feuds as well as the friendships of a father or a kinsman. These feuds are not implacable; even homicide is expiated by the payment of a certain number of cattle and of sheep, and the satisfaction is accepted by the entire family, greatly to the advantage of the state, since feuds are dangerous in proportion to a people's freedom.

. . .

[S]laves are not employed after our manner with distinct domestic duties assigned to them, but each one has the management of a house and home of his own. The master requires from the slave a certain quantity of grain, of cattle, and of clothing, as he would from a tenant, and this is the limit of subjection. All other household functions are discharged by the wife and children. To strike a slave or to punish him with bonds or with hard labor is a rare occurrence. They often kill them, not in enforcing strict discipline, but on the impulse of passion, as they would an enemy, only it is done with impunity. The freedmen do not rank much above slaves, and are seldom of any weight in the family, never in the state, with the exception of those tribes which are ruled by kings. There indeed they rise above the freeborn and the noble; elsewhere the inferiority of the freedman marks the freedom of the state.

Of lending money on interest and increasing it by compound interest they know nothing,—a more effectual safeguard than if it were prohibited.

Land proportioned to the number of inhabitants is occupied by the whole community in turn, and afterwards divided among them according to rank. A wide expanse of plains makes the partition easy. They till fresh fields every year, and they have still more land than enough; . . . corn [wheat] is the only produce required from the earth; hence even the year itself is not divided by them into as many seasons as with us. Winter, spring, and summer have both a meaning and a name; the name and blessings of autumn are alike unknown.

54

Savatri and the God of Death, From the *Mahabharata*— 300–400 CE

The Mahabharata *is to India what* The Illiad *is to Greece, but it is often referred to as "the Hindu Bible." A work that is, on one hand, an epic and, on the other hand, sacred scripture, is possible in the Hindu vision, if not in the Western one. The* Mahabharata *contains almost all the lore and legends that live on today in Hindu society. Although the main part of the epic relates the story of a tragic war that ended an era, the following tale does not concern the war; it is one of the most popular in the* Mahabharata. *What virtues does Savatri display when she confronts the god of death? Does she act according to women's role as set out in the* Laws of Manu?

Ashvapati, the virtuous king of Madras, grew old without offspring to continue his royal family. Desiring a son, Ashvapati took rigid vows and observed long fasts to accumulate merit. It is said that he offered 10,000 oblations to the goddess Savatri in hopes of having a son. After eighteen years of constant devotion, Ashvapati was granted his wish for an offspring even though the baby born was a girl.

The king rejoiced at his good fortune and named the child Savatri in honor of the goddess who gave him this joy to brighten his elder years.

Savatri was both a beautiful and an intelligent child. She was her father's delight and grew in wisdom and beauty as the years passed. As the age approached for Savatri to be given in marriage as custom demanded, no suitor came forward to ask her father for her hand—so awed were all the princes by the beauty and intellect of this unusual maiden. Her father became concerned lest he not fulfill his duty as father and incur disgrace for his failure to provide a suitable husband for his daughter. At last, he instructed Savatri herself to lead a procession throughout the surrounding kingdoms and handpick a man suitable for her.

Savatri returned from her search and told her father that she had found the perfect man. Though he was poor and an ascetic of the woods, he was handsome, well educated, and of kind temperament. His name was Satyavan and he was actually a prince whose blind father had been displaced by an evil king.

From Lustrul Maidens and Ascetic Kings: Buddhist and Hindu Stories of Life, ed. by Amore and Shinn (New York: Oxford University Press, 1981).

Ashvapati asked the venerable sage Narada whether Satyavan would be a suitable spouse for Savatri. Narada responded that there was no one in the world
more worthy than Satyavan. However, Narada continued, Satyavan had one
unavoidable flaw. He was fated to live a short life and would die exactly one
year from that very day. Ashvapati then tried to dissuade Savatri from marrying
Satyavan by telling her of the impending death of her loved one. Savatri held
firm to her choice, and the king and Narada both gave their blessings to this
seemingly ill-fated bond.

After the marriage procession had retreated from the forest hermitage of
Savatri's new father-in-law, Dyumatsena, the bride removed her wedding sari
and donned the ocher robe and bark garments of her ascetic family. As the
days and weeks passed, Savatri busied herself by waiting upon the every need
of her new family. She served her husband, Satyavan, cheerfully and skillfully.
Satyavan responded with an even-tempered love which enhanced the bond of
devotion between Savatri and himself. Yet the dark cloud of Narada's prophecy
cast a shadow over this otherwise blissful life.

When the fateful time approached, Savatri began a fast to strengthen her
wifely resolve as she kept nightly vigils while her husband slept. The day
marked for the death of Satyavan began as any other day at the hermitage.
Satyavan shouldered his axe and was about to set off to cut wood for the day's
fires when Savatri stopped him to ask if she could go along saying, "I cannot
bear to be separated from you today." Satyavan responded, "You've never come
into the forest before and the paths are rough and the way very difficult.
Besides, you've been fasting and are surely weak." Savatri persisted, and
Satyavan finally agreed to take her along. Savatri went to her parents-in-law to
get their permission saying she wanted to see the spring blossoms which now
covered the forest. They too expressed concern over her health but finally
relented out of consideration for her long period of gracious service to them.

Together Satyavan and Savatri entered the tangled woods enjoying the
beauty of the flowers and animals which betoken spring in the forest. Coming
to a fallen tree, Satyavan began chopping firewood. As he worked, he began to
perspire heavily and to grow weak. Finally, he had to stop and lie down telling
Savatri to wake him after a short nap. With dread in her heart, Savatri took
Satyavan's head in her lap and kept a vigil knowing Satyavan's condition to be
more serious than rest could assuage. In a short time, Savatri saw approaching a
huge figure clad in red and carrying a small noose. Placing Satyavan's head
upon the ground, Savatri arose and asked the stranger of his mission. The lord
of death replied, "I am Yama and your husband's days are finished. I speak to
you, a mortal, only because of your extreme merit. I have come personally
instead of sending my emissaries because of your husband's righteous life."

Without a further word, Yama then pulled Satyavan's soul out of his body
with the small noose he was carrying. The lord of death then set off immediately
for the realm of the dead in the south. Grief stricken and yet filled with wifely
devotion, Savatri followed Yama at a distance. Hours passed yet hunger and
weariness could not slow Savatri's footsteps. She persisted through thorny paths
and rocky slopes to follow Yama and his precious burden. As Yama walked south

he thought he heard a woman's anklets tingling on the path behind him. He turned around to see Savatri in the distance following without pause. He called out to her to return to Satyavan's body and to perform her wifely duties of cremating the dead. Savatri approached Yama and responded, "It is said that those who walk seven steps together are friends. Certainly we have traveled farther than that together. Why should I return to a dead body when you possess the soul of my husband?"

Yama was impressed by the courage and wisdom of this beautiful young woman. He replied, "Please stop following me. Your wise words and persistent devotion for your husband deserve a boon. Ask of me anything except that your husband's life be restored, and I will grant it." Savatri asked that her blind father-in-law be granted new sight. Yama said that her wish would be granted, and then he turned to leave only to find that Savatri was about to continue following. Yama again praised her devotion and offered a second, and then a third boon. Savatri told Yama of the misfortune of her father-in-law's lost kingdom and asked that Yama assist in ousting the evil king from Dyumatsena's throne. Yama agreed. Then Savatri utilized her third boon to ask that her own father be given one hundred sons to protect his royal line, and that too was granted by Yama.

Yama then set off in a southerly direction only to discover after a short while that Savatri still relentlessly followed him. Yama was amazed at the thoroughly self-giving attitude displayed by Savatri and agreed to grant one last boon if Savatri would promise to return home. Yama again stipulated that the bereaved wife could not ask for her husband's soul. Savatri agreed to the two conditions and said, "I only ask for myself one thing, and that is that I may be granted one hundred sons to continue Satyavan's royal family." Yama agreed only to realize, upon prompting from Savatri, that the only way Satyavan's line could be continued would be for him to be restored to life. Although he had been tricked by the wise and thoughtful Savatri, Yama laughed heartily and said, "So be it! Auspicious and chaste lady, your husband's soul is freed by me." Loosening his noose Yama permitted the soul of Satyavan to return to its earthly abode and Savatri ran without stopping back to the place where Satyavan had fallen asleep. Just as Savatri arrived at the place where her husband lay, he awoke saying, "Oh, I have slept into the night, why did you not waken me?"

CHAPTER 6

Arts and Culture—
2000 BCE–500 CE

Writers in China and India produced a variety of poems, songs and tales in the ancient world. Culture for the Romans involved blood sport and satire, whereas the Hindus preferred in moralistic fables. How did the values of these societies influence their cultural pursuits?

What is the main topic of the Chinese poems?

Rome, a large sophisticated empire, produced literature by the first century that seems shockingly modern in content. What do you notice in the writings of Plutarch, Juvenal, and Ovid that seems particularly "modern"?

Much of the art of the ancient world is found in temples, pyramids and statues. Since this is a book of documents rather than photographs the amount of sources is limited. However writers in China and India produced a variety of poems, songs and tales in the ancient world. Culture for the Romans involved blood sport and satire, while the Hindus preferred in moralistic fables. How did the values of these societies influence their cultural pursuits?

55

Seneca on Gladiatorial Contests—1st century CE

The Roman playwright and philosopher Lucius Anneus Seneca (4 BCE–65 CE) served for a time as tutor to the Roman Emperor Nero. Much later, he fell out of favor with Nero and was forced to commit suicide in 65 CE. Although Seneca is better known for his plays, in the Moral Epistles *he comments on the gladiatorial shows at the Roman circus. In the following excerpt, Seneca describes a contest between criminals in which the combatants wear no armor or protective covering. What does Seneca imply about these contests?*

I chanced to stop in at a midday show, expecting fun, weight, and some relaxation, when men's eyes take respite from the slaughter of their fellow men. The preceding combats were merciful by comparison; now all trifling is put aside and it is pure murder. The men have no protective covering. Their entire bodies are exposed to the blows, and no blow is ever struck in vain. . . . In the morning men are thrown to the lions and the bears, at noon they are thrown to their spectators. The spectators call for the slayer to be thrown to those who in turn will slay him, and they detain the victor for another butchering. The outcome for the combatants is death; the fight is waged with sword and fire. This goes on while the arena is free. "But one of them was a highway robber, he killed a man!" Because he killed he deserved to suffer this punishment, granted. . . . "Kill him! Lash him! Burn him! Why does he meet the sword so timidly? Why doesn't he kill boldly? Why doesn't he die game? Whip him to meet his wounds! Let them trade blow for blow, chests bare and within reach!" And when the show stops for intermission, "Let's have men killed meanwhile! Let's not have nothing going on!"

From *Moral Epistles of Seneca* in N. Lewis and M. Reinhold, *Roman Civilization*, vol. 2 (New York: Columbia, 1955), p. 230.

56

An Aristocratic View of Roman Society, From *Lives* by Plutarch—1st century CE

Mertreus Plutarchus, or Plutarch (ca. 45–125 CE), was a Greek priest of Apollo known throughout the Roman world for his writing. His concern was always with the study and judgment of human character. That he was an acute observer of human nature is evident in this selection from the life of Pericles. Of what is Plutarch most critical in this excerpt?

PERICLES

I. On seeing certain wealthy foreigners in <u>Rome</u> carrying puppies and young monkeys about in their bosoms and fondling them, <u>Caesar</u>[1] asked, we are told, if the women in their country did not bear children, thus in right princely fashion rebuking those who squander on animals that proneness to love and loving affection which is ours by nature and which is due only to our fellow-men. [2] Since, then, our souls are by nature possessed of great fondness for learning and fondness for seeing, it is surely reasonable to chide those who abuse this fondness on objects all unworthy either of their eyes or ears, to the neglect of those which are good and serviceable. Our outward sense, since apprehends the objects which encounter it by virtue of their mere impact upon it, must the exercise of his mind every man, if he pleases, has the natural power to turn himself away in every case, and to change, without the least difficulty, [3] to that object upon which he himself determines. It is meet, therefore, that he pursue what is best, to the eye that he may not merely regard it, but also be edified by regarding it. A color is suited to the eye if its freshness, and its pleasantness as well, stimulates and nourishes the vision and so our intellectual vision must be applied to such objects as, by their very charm, invite it onward to its own proper good. [4] Such objects are to be found in virtuous deeds; these implant in those who search them out a great and zealous eagerness which leads to imitation. In other cases, admiration of the deed is not immediately accompanied

From Plutarch, *Plutarch's Lives*, trans. by Bernadotte Perrin (Cambridge, MA, Harvard University Press, 1914).

1 Caesar Augustus.

by an impulse to do it. Nay, many times, on the contrary, while we delight in the work we despise the workman, as, for instance, in the case of perfumes and dyes; we take a delight in them, but dyers and perfumers we regard as illiberal and vulgar folk. [5] Therefore it was a fine saying of <u>Antisthenes</u>, when he heard that <u>Ismenias</u> was an excellent piper: "But he's a worthless man," said he, "otherwise he wouldn't be so good a piper." And so Philip[2] once said to his son, who, as the wine went round, plucked the strings charmingly and skilfully, "Art not ashamed to pluck the strings so well?" It is enough, surely, if a king have leisure to hear others pluck the strings, and he pays great deference to the Muses if he be but a spectator of such contests.

---

2 Philip of Macedon, to Alexander.

57

On the City of Rome, From the *Third Satire* by Juvenal— 2nd century CE

Little is known about the life of the Roman satirist Juvenal. He is best remembered for coining the phrase "bread and circuses" to describe the life of the citizens of Rome. In this excerpt, he is bitterly critical of the cosmopolitan city of Rome during the second century CE. What is Juvenal's main complaint about the city? Does he have the same concerns as Plutarch? Why or why not?

Since at Rome there is no place for honest pursuits, no profit to be got by honest toil—my fortune is less to-day than it was yesterday, and to-morrow must again make that little less—we purpose emigrating to the spot where Daedalus put off his wearied wings, while my grey hairs are still but few, my old age green and erect; while something yet remains for Lachesis to spin, and I can bear myself on my own legs, without a staff to support my right hand. Let us leave our native land. There let Arturius and Catulus live. Let those

---

From *The Satires of Juvenal, Persius, Sulpicia and Lucilius*, trans. by Rev. Lewis Evans (London: Bell & Daldy, 1869).

continue in it who turn black to white; for whom it is an easy matter to get contracts for building temples, clearing rivers, constructing harbors, cleansing the sewers, the furnishing of funerals, and under the mistress-spear set up the slave to sale.

It is that the city is become Greek, Quirites, that I cannot tolerate; and yet how small the proportion even of the dregs of Greece! Syrian Orontes has long since flowed into the Tiber, and brought with it its language, morals, and the crooked harps with the flute-player, and its national tambourines, and girls made to stand for hire at the Circus. Go thither, you who fancy a barbarian harlot with embroidered turban. That rustic of yours, Quirinus, takes his Greek supper-cloak, and wears Greek prizes on his neck besmeared with Ceroma. One forsaking steep Sicyon, another Amydon, a third from Andros, another from Samos, another again from Tralles, or Alabanda, swarm to Esquiliae, and the hill called from its osiers, destined to be the very vitals, and future lords of great houses.

Besides, there is nothing that is held sacred by these fellows, or that is safe from their lust.

Difficult indeed is it for those to emerge from obscurity whose noble qualities are cramped by narrow means at home; but at Rome, for men like these, the attempt is still more hopeless; it is only at an exorbitant price they can get a wretched lodging, keep for their servants, and a frugal meal. A man is ashamed here to dine off pottery ware, which, were he suddenly transported to the Marsi and a Sabine board, contented there with a coarse bowl of blue earthenware, he would no longer deem discreditable. Here, in Rome, the splendor of dress is carried beyond men's means; here, something more than is enough, is taken occasionally from another's chest. In this fault all participate. Here we all live with a poverty that apes our betters. Why should I detain you? Everything at Rome is coupled with high price. What have you to give, that you may occasionally pay your respects to Cossus? that Veiento may give you a passing glance, though without deigning to open his mouth? One shaves the beard, another deposits the hair of a favorite; the house is full of venal cakes.

I must live in a place, where there are no fires, no nightly alarms. Already is Ucalegon shouting for water! already is he removing his chattels: the third story in the house you live in is already in a blaze. Yet you are unconscious! For if the alarm begin from the bottom of the stairs, he will be the last to be burnt whom a single tile protects from the rain, where the tame pigeons lay their eggs. Codrus had a bed too small for his Procula, six little jugs the ornament of his sideboard, and a little can besides beneath it, and a Chiron reclining under the same marble; and a chest now grown old in the service contained his Greek books, and mice gnawed poems of divine inspiration. Codrus possessed nothing at all; who denies the fact? and yet all that little nothing that he had, he lost. But the climax that crowns his misery is the fact, that though he is stark naked and begging for a few scraps, no one will lend a hand to help him to bed and board. But, if the great mansion of Asturius has fallen, the matrons appear in weeds, the senators in mourning robes, the praetor adjourns the courts.

If you can tear yourself away from the games in the circus, you can buy a capital house at Sora, or Fabrateria, or Frusino, for the price at which you are now hiring your dark hole for one year. There you will have your little garden, a well so shallow as to require no rope and bucket, whence with easy draft you may water your sprouting plants. Live there, enamored of the pitchfork, and the dresser of your trim garden, from which you could supply a feast to a hundred Pythagoreans. It is something to be able in any spot, in any retreat whatever, to have made oneself proprietor even of a single lizard. Here full many a patient dies from want of sleep; but that exhaustion is produced by the undigested food that loads the fevered stomach. For what lodging-houses allow of sleep? None but the very wealthy can sleep at Rome. Hence is the source of the disease. The passing of wagons in the narrow curves of the streets, and the mutual reviles of the team drivers brought to a standstill, would banish sleep even from Drusus and sea-calves. If duty calls him, the rich man will be borne through the yielding crowd, and pass rapidly over their heads on the shoulders of his tall Liburnian, and, as he goes, will read or write, or even sleep inside his litter, for his sedan with windows closed entices sleep. And still he will arrive before us. In front of us, as we hurry on, a tide of human beings stops the way; the mass that follows behind presses on our loins in dense concourse; one man pokes me with his elbow, another with a hard pole; one knocks a beam against my head, another a ten-gallon cask. My legs are coated thick with mud; then, anon, I am trampled upon by great heels all round me, and the hob-nail of the soldier's caliga remains imprinted on my toe.

58

Ars Amatoria, or *The Art of Love*, by Ovid—1st century CE

These excerpts from Ovid's major work on the art of love date from the beginning of the first century CE. These clever poems supposedly instruct both men and women in the art of seduction. Although written 2,000 years ago, these sophisticated verses are still both relevant and a pleasure to read. Ovid's work influenced many writers of the medieval and renaissance eras, including Chaucer and Shakespeare. What impression do you get from these verses of Roman society?

BOOK I PART XIV: LOOK PRESENTABLE

Don't delight in curling your hair with tongs,
don't smooth your legs with sharp pumice stone.
Leave that to those who celebrate Cybele the Mother,
howling wildly in the Phrygian manner.
Male beauty's better for neglect: Theseus
carried off Ariadne, without a single pin in his hair.
Phaedra loved Hippolytus: he was unsophisticated:
Adonis was dear to the goddess, and fit for the woods.
Neatness pleases, a body tanned from exercise:
a well fitting and spotless toga's good:
no stiff shoe-thongs, your buckles free of rust,
no sloppy feet for you, swimming in loose hide:
don't mar your neat hair with an evil haircut:
let an expert hand trim your head and beard.
And no long nails, and make sure they're dirt-free:
and no hairs please, sprouting from your nostrils.
No bad breath exhaled from unwholesome mouth:
don't offend the nose like a herdsman or his flock.
Leave the rest for impudent women to do,
or whoever's the sort of man who needs a man.

Ovid, *Ars Amatoria*, trans. by Tony Kline, available at http://www.tonykline.co.uk. Reprinted by permission.

BOOK II PART XVII:
DON'T MENTION HER FAULTS

Above all beware of reproaching girls for their faults,
it's useful to ignore so many things.
Andromeda's dark complexion was not criticised
by Perseus, who was borne aloft by wings on his feet.
Andromache by all was rightly thought too tall:
Hector was the only one who spoke of her as small.
Grow accustomed to what's called bad, you'll call it good:
Time heals much: new love feels everything.
While a new-grafted twig's growing in the green bark,
struck by the lightest breeze, it may fall:
Later, hardened by time, it resists the winds,
and the strong tree will bear adopted wealth.
Time itself erases all faults from the flesh,
and what was a flaw, ceases to make you pause.
A new ox-hide makes nostrils recoil:
tamed by familiarity, the odour fades.
An evil may be sweetened by its name: let her be 'dark'
whose pigment's blacker than Illyrian pitch:
if she squints, she's like Venus: if she's grey, Minerva:
let her be 'slender', who's truly emaciated:
call her 'trim', who's tiny, 'full-bodied' if she's gross,
and hide the fault behind the nearest virtue.

59, 60

Two Chinese Poems—
ca. 1st century BCE

The universality of human experience is expressed in these two brief poems. In "The Orphan," an orphaned boy laments the treatment he receives from his brother and sister-in-law. In "The Lament of Hsi-Chun," a Chinese princess sent to a distant land as a political bride laments her fate. What element in these two poems makes them relevant to modern readers?

LAMENT OF HSI-CHUN

My people have married me
In a far corner of Earth:
Sent me away to a strange land,
To the king of the Wu-sun.
A tent is my house,
Of felt are my walls;
Raw flesh my food
With mare's milk to drink.
Always thinking of my own country,
My heart sad within.
Would I were a yellow stork
And could fly to my old home!

THE ORPHAN

To be an orphan,
To be fated to be an orphan,
How bitter is this lot!
When my father and mother were alive
I used to ride in a carriage
With four fine horses.

But when they both died,
My brother and sister-in-law
Sent me out to be a merchant.
In the south I travelled to the "Nine Rivers"
And in the east as far as Ch'i and Lu.
At the end of the year when I came home
I dared not tell them what I had suffered—
Of the lice and vermin in my head,
Of the dust in my face and eyes.
My brother told me to get ready the dinner,
My sister-in-law told me to see after the horses.
I was always going up into the hall
And running down again to the parlour.
My tears fell like rain. . . .
I want to write a letter and send it
To my mother and father under the earth,
And tell them I can't go on any longer
Living with my brother and sister-in-law.

61, 62

Two Hindu Tales—
ca. 1st century CE

From the earliest times, societies have used tales or fables to teach values and morality in a simple and entertaining way. These two tales come out of the Hindu culture in India; they likely date from at least 2,000 years ago. What values illustrated in these simple stories seem most important to the ancient Hindus?

The Man in the Moon

THERE was a blacksmith once who complained: "I am not well, and my work is too warm. I want to be a stone on the mountain. There it must be cool, for

From Eva March Tappan, ed., *The World's Story: A History of the World in Story, Song and Art* (Boston: Houghton-Mifflin, 1914), Vol. II.

the wind blows and the trees give a shade." A wise man who had power over all things replied: "Go you, be a stone." And he was a stone, high up on the mountain-side. It happened that a stone-cutter came that way for a stone, and when he saw the one that had been the blacksmith, he knew that it was what he sought, and he began to cut it. The stone cried out: "This hurts! I no longer want to be a stone. A stone-cutter I want to be. That would be pleasant." The wise man, humoring him, said, "Be a cutter." Thus he became a stone-cutter, and as he went seeking suitable stone, he grew tired, and his feet were sore. He whimpered, "I no longer want to cut stone. I would be the sun; that would be pleasant." The wise man commanded, "Be the sun." And he was the sun. But the sun was warmer than the blacksmith, than a stone, than a stone-cutter, and he complained, "I do not like this. I would be the moon. It looks cool." The wise man spake yet again, "Be the moon." And he was the moon. "This is warmer than being the sun," murmured he, "for the light from the sun shines on me ever. I do not want to be the moon. I would be a smith again. That, verily, is the best life." But the wise man replied, " I am weary of your changing. You wanted to be the moon; the moon you are, and it you will remain."

And in yon high heaven lives he to this day.

The Legend of the Rice

IN the days when the earth was young and all things were better than they now are, when men and women were stronger and of greater beauty, and the fruit of the trees was larger and sweeter than that which we now eat, rice, the food of the people, was of larger grain. One grain was all a man could eat; and in those early days, such, too, was the merit of the people, they never had to toil gathering the rice, for, when ripe, it fell from the stalks and rolled into the villages, even unto the granaries. And upon a year when the rice was larger and more plentiful than ever before, a widow said to her daughter "Our granaries are too small. We will pull them down and build larger." When the old granaries were pulled down and the new one not yet ready for use, the rice was ripe in the fields. Great haste was made, but the rice came rolling in where the work was going on, and the widow, angered, struck a grain and cried, "Could you not wait in the fields until we were ready? You should not bother us now when you are not wanted." The rice broke into thousands of pieces and said "From this time forth, we will wait in the fields until we are wanted," and from that time the rice has been of small grain, and the people of the earth must gather it into the granary from the fields.

CHAPTER 7

Religion and
Philosophy—500–1500 CE

B etween 500 and 1500 CE, the great religions of the world began to
expand and their converts multiplied. In addition, the new religion of
Islam spread into territory formerly claimed by Christianity. At the same
time, the Christian religion split into two branches—Roman and Orthodox.
Christian missionaries and saints tried to spread the word of God whereas
philosophers tried to rationalize his existence.

63

The Benedictine Rule—
535–540 CE

Benedict of Nursia was born near Spoleto, Italy, and later went to Rome to complete his studies in law and rhetoric. Disgusted by the corruption of Rome, he fled the city to live a life of prayer, silence, and study with a few like-minded friends. When the miraculous restoration of an earthen sieve broken by his servant was hailed as a miracle, Benedict fled the notoriety that resulted to live as a hermit in a cave. Attracted by his visible holiness, many men came to live by the monastic rule Benedict established to maintain both sanctity and order among his community of believers. Benedict built a series of monasteries and refined the rule that would later become the standard for monasticism in the West. Why might Benedict have developed these rules for his monks? What kind of life do these rules demand?

. . . They shall sleep clothed, and girt with belts or with ropes; and they shall not have their knives at their sides while they sleep, lest perchance in a dream they should wound the sleepers. . . .

More than anything else is this special vice to be cut off root and branch from the monastery, that one should presume to give or receive anything without the order of the abbot, or should have anything of his own. He should have absolutely not anything; neither a book, nor tablets, nor a pen—nothing at all . . . All things shall be common to all. . . .

The use of baths shall be offered to the sick as often as it is necessary: to the healthy, and especially to youths, it shall not be so readily conceded. . . .

And there shall be the greatest silence at table, so that the muttering or the voice of no one shall be heard there, except that of the reader alone. . . .

Let two cooked dishes suffice for all the brothers: and, if it is possible to obtain apples or growing vegetables, a third may be added . . . But the eating of the flesh of quadrupeds shall be abstained from altogether by every one, excepting alone the weak and the sick. . . .

Indeed we read that wine is not suitable for monks at all. But because, in our day, it is not possible to persuade the monks of this, let us agree at least as to the fact that we should not drink till we are sated, but sparingly. . . .

As soon as they have risen from the table, all shall sit together and one shall read selections or lives of the Fathers, or indeed anything which will edify the

From *The Ideas that Have Influenced Civilization*, Vol. IV, ed. by Oliver J. Thatcher (Milwaukee, WI: Roberts-Manchester, 1901).

hearers. But not the Pentateuch or Kings; for, to weak intellects, it will be of no use at that hour to hear this part of Scripture; but they shall be read at other times. . . .

Idleness is the enemy of the soul. And therefore, at fixed times, the brothers ought to be occupied in manual labor; and again, at fixed times, in sacred reading. . . .

All guests who come shall be received as though they were Christ. . . .

64

The *Qur'an*—7th century CE

The Qur'an, *the Holy Book of Islam, is to Muslims what the* Bible *is to Christians. Compiled in Arabic shortly after Muhammad's death, it is believed to be the word of God revealed to Muhammad during a 20-year period that started in 610 CE and continued to shortly before his death. The* Qur'an *differs from the* Hadith *in that the* Hadith *contains the sayings of Muhammad, whereas the* Qur'an *is the word of God. In what ways is the* Qur'an *similar to the* Bible *and in what ways is it different?*

In the name of God, the most merciful and compassionate.
  Praise be to God, the Lord of the worlds;
  The most merciful, the compassionate;
  The king of the day of Judgment.
  Thee do we worship, and of Thee do we beg assistance.
  Direct us on the right way,
  The way of those to whom Thou has been gracious; not of those against whom Thou art angry, nor of those who go astray.

In the name of God, the most merciful and compassionate.
  Praise the name of thy Lord, the Most High, Who hath created and completely formed His creatures: Who determineth them to various ends, and directeth them to attain the same, Who produceth the pastures for cattle, and afterwards rendereth the same dry stubble of a dusky hue.

  God will enable thee to rehearse His revelations, and thou shall not forget any part thereof, except what God shall please, for He knoweth that which is manifest, and that which is hidden. And God will facilitate unto thee the most

From *The Short Koran*, ed. by George M. Lamsa, 1949, Ziff-Davis Publishing Company.

easy way. Therefore admonish thy people, if thy admonition shall be profitable unto them.

Whosoever feareth God, he will be admonished: but the most wretched unbeliever will turn away from it; who shall be cast to be broiled in the greater fire of hell, wherein he shall not die, neither shall he live.

Now hath he attained felicity who is purified by faith, and who remembereth the name of his Lord, and prayeth. But ye prefer this present life: yet the life to come is better, and more durable.

Verily this is written in the ancient Books, the Books of Abraham and Moses.

God! There is no god but Him, the Living, the Self-subsisting: He hath sent down unto thee the Book of the Koran with truth, confirming that which was revealed before it; For He had formerly sent down the Law and the Gospel, a guidance unto men; and He had also sent down the Salvation.

Verily those who believe not the signs of God shall suffer a grievous punishment; for God is mighty, able to revenge.

Surely nothing is hidden from God, of that which is on earth, or in the heavens; it is He who formeth you in the wombs, as He pleaseth; there is no God but Him, the Mighty, the Wise.

It is He who hath sent down unto thee the Book, wherein are some verses clear to be understood: they are the foundation of the Book; and others are parabolical. But they whose hearts are perverse will follow that which is parabolical therein, out of love of schism, and a desire of the interpretation thereof, yet none knoweth the interpretation thereof, except God. But they who are well grounded in knowledge say, We believe therein, the whole is from our Lord; and none will consider except the prudent.

The Doctrine of One God

God! There is no God but Him; the Living, the Self-subsisting: neither slumber nor sleep seizeth Him; to Him belongeth whatsoever is in the heavens, and on earth. Who is he that can intercede with Him, but through His good pleasure? He knoweth that which is past, and that which is to come unto them, and they shall not comprehend anything of His knowledge, but so far as He pleaseth. His throne is extended over the heavens and the earth; and the preservation of both is no burden unto Him. He is the High, the Mighty.

Let there be no compulsion in religion. Now is right direction manifestly distinguished from deceit: whoever therefore shall deny Tagut [Satan] and believe in God, he shall surely take hold on a strong handle, which shall not be broken; God is He who heareth and seeth.

God is the patron of those who believe; He shall lead them out of darkness into light; but as to those who believe not, their patrons are Tagut; they shall lead them from the light into darkness; they shall be the companions of hell fire, they shall remain therein forever. . . .

Wine and Gambling

O true believers! surely wine, and gambling and images, and divining arrows, are an abomination of the work of Satan; therefore avoid them, that ye may prosper.

Satan seeketh to sow dissension and hatred among you, by means of wine and gambling, and to divert you from remembering God, and from prayer; will ye not therefore abstain from them?

Obey God, and obey the Apostle, and take heed to yourselves; but if ye turn back, know that the duty of God's Apostle is only to preach publicly.

On those who believe and do good works, it is no sin that they have tasted wine or gambled before they were forbidden; if they fear God, and believe, and do good works, and shall for the future fear God, and believe, and shall persevere to fear him, and to do good, for God loveth those who do good.

Paradise

The description of Paradise, which is promised unto the pious: therein are rivers of incorruptible water; and rivers of milk, the taste whereof changeth not; and rivers of wine, pleasant unto those who drink; and rivers of clarified honey. And therein shall they have plenty of all kinds of fruits; and pardon from their Lord. Shall the man for whom these things are prepared, be as they who must dwell forever in hell fire, and will have the boiling water given them to drink, which shall burst their bowels?

They [the righteous] shall repose on couches, the linings thereof shall be of thick silk interwoven with gold: and the fruit of the two gardens shall be near at hand to gather.

Which, therefore, of your Lord's benefits will ye ungratefully deny?

Therein shall be damsels, remaining their eyes from beholding any besides their spouses: whom no man or Jinni shall have touched before them,

65

The Hadith—
ca. 8th–10th century

The Hadith, *or* Sunnal, *is the second of the twin pillars of Islamic teaching. The literal meaning of the term "hadith" is "sayings of the Prophet." The authors of the* Hadith *were Islamic scholars who collected and verified the sayings of Mohammed over several centuries beginning during his lifetime. In the* Hadith, *Mohammed explains God's message to the people, but the book also contains a history of Mohammed's actions as Allah's messenger. How does the* Hadith *differ from the* Qur'an?

ON MAKING PEACE BETWEEN PEOPLE

Allah, the Exalted, has said:

> Most of their conferrings together are devoid of good, except such as enjoin charity, or the promotion of public welfare or of public peace (4.115).
> Reconciliation is best (4.129).
> Be mindful of your duty to Allah and try to promote accord between yourselves (8.2).
> All believers are brothers; so make peace between your brothers (49.11).

Abu Hurairah relates that the Holy Prophet said: Charity is incumbent upon every human limb every day on which the sun rises. To bring about just reconciliation between two contestants is charity. Helping a person to mount his animal, or to load his baggage on to it is charity. A good word is charity. Every step taken towards the mosque for *salat*[1] is charity. To remove anything from the street that causes inconvenience is charity (Bokhari and Muslim).

Umm Kulthum relates that she heard the Holy Prophet say: He who brings about peace between people and attains good or says that which is good is not a liar (Bokhari and Muslim). Muslim's version adds: I did not hear him let people have a latitude in what they said except in three situations: war, making peace, and talk between husband and wife.

From "*The Hadith.*"

[1] Ritual prayer. Muslims pray five times daily and on Friday attend community prayer services at a mosque.

ON THE SUPERIORITY OF THE POOR
AND WEAK AMONG MUSLIMS

Allah, the Exalted, has said:

Continue thy companionship with those who call on their Lord, morning
and evening, seeking His pleasure, and look not beyond them (18.29).

Haritha ibn Wahb relates that he heard the Holy Prophet say: Shall I tell
you who are the dwellers of Paradise? It is every weak one who is accounted
weak and is looked down upon, who if he takes an oath relying upon Allah He
would fulfill it. Now shall I tell you who are the denizens of the Fire? It is every
ignorant, impertinent, prideful and arrogant one (Bokhari and Muslim). . . .

Abu Sa'id Khudri relates that the Holy Prophet said: There was a contest
between Paradise and the Fire. The Fire said: I shall compass the tyrants and
the arrogant ones; and Paradise said: My dwellers will be the weak and the
lowly. Allah decided between them, saying: Thou art Paradise, My mercy,
through thee I shall have mercy on whomsoever I determine; and thou art the
Fire. My torment, through thee I shall chastise whomsoever I determine. It is
for Me to fill both of you (Muslim). . . .

Abu Hurairah relates that a dark-skinned woman (or perhaps young man)
used to take care of the mosque. The Holy Prophet missed her (or him) and
inquired about her (or him) and was told that she (or he) had died. He said:
Why did you not let me know? as if they had not considered the matter of any
importance. He then said: Show me the grave, and on being shown it he prayed
over it and said: These graves cover those in them with darkness and Allah
illumines them for the denizens in consequence of my prayers for them
(Bokhari and Muslim). . . .

Usamah relates that the Holy Prophet said: I stood at the gate of Paradise
and observed that the generality of those who entered it were the lowly. The
wealthy had been held back from it. Then those condemned to the Fire were
ordered to it and I stood at the gate of the Fire and observed that the generality of those who entered it were women (Bokhari and Muslim).

ON KIND TREATMENT OF ORPHANS,
GIRLS, THE WEAK, THE POOR,
AND THE LOWLY

Allah, the Exalted, has said:

Continue to be kindly gracious towards the believers (15.89).
   Continue thy companionship with those who call on their Lord, morning and evening, seeking His pleasure, and look not beyond them, for if
thou dost that thou wouldst be seeking the values of this life (18.29).

Oppress not the orphan and chide not him who asks (93.10–11).

Knowest thou him who rejects the faith? That is the one who drives away the orphan and urges not the feeding of the poor (107.2–4). . . .

Abu Hurairah relates that the Holy Prophet said: He who exerts himself on behalf of widows and the indigent is like one who strives[2] in the cause of Allah; and the narrator thinks he added: and like the guardian who never retreats, and like one who observes the fast and does not break it (Bokhari and Muslim). . . .

Anas relates that the Holy Prophet said: He who brings up two girls through their childhood will appear on the Day of Judgment attached to me like two fingers of a hand (Muslim). . . .

Ayesha[3] relates: A poor woman came to me with her two daughters. I gave her three dates. She gave one to each girl and raised the third to her own mouth to eat. The girls asked her for it. So she broke it into two parts and gave one to each of the girls. I was much struck by her action and mentioned what she had done to the Holy Prophet. He said: Allah appointed Paradise for her in consequence of it; or he said: Allah freed her from the Fire on account of it.

Abu Shuraih Khuwailad ibn Amr Khuza'i relates that the Holy Prophet said: Allah, I declare sinful any failure to safeguard the rights of two weak ones; orphans and women (Nisai).

ON A HUSBAND'S RIGHT
CONCERNING HIS WIFE

Allah, the Exalted, has said:

Men are appointed guardians over women, because of that in respect of which Allah has made some of them excel others, and because the men spend their wealth. So virtuous women are obedient and safeguard, with Allah's help, matters the knowledge of which is shared by them with their husbands (4.35). . . .

Ibn Umar relates that the Holy Prophet said: Every one of you is a steward and is accountable for that which is committed to his charge. The ruler is a steward and is accountable for his charge, a man is a steward in respect of his household, a woman is a steward in respect of her husband's house and his children. Thus everyone of you is a steward and is accountable for that which is committed to his charge (Bokhari and Muslim).

Abu Ali Talq ibn Ali relates that the Holy Prophet said: When a man calls his wife for his need, she should go to him even if she is occupied in baking bread (Tirmidhi and Nisai). . . .

---

[2] Jihad. See question 6.

[3] One of the Prophet's wives and a chief source of hadith.

Umm Salamah relates that the Holy Prophet said: If a woman dies and her husband is pleased with her she will enter Paradise (Tirmidhi).

Mu'az ibn Jabal relates that the Holy Prophet said: Whenever a woman distresses her husband his mate from among the *houris*[4] of Paradise says to her: Allah ruin thee, do not cause him distress for he is only thy guest and will soon part from thee to come to us (Tirmidhi).

Usamah ibn Zaid relates that the Holy Prophet said: I am not leaving a more harmful trial for men than woman (Bokhari and Muslim).

ON STRIVING IN THE CAUSE OF ALLAH

Allah, the Exalted, has said:

Fight the idolators all together, as they fight you all together, and know that Allah is with the righteous (9.36). . . .

Allah has purchased of the believers their persons and their belongings in return for the promise that they shall have Paradise, for they fight in the cause of Allah and they slay the enemy or are themselves slain. This is a promise that He has made incumbent upon Himself as set out in the Torah, and the Gospel and the Qur'an; and who is more faithful to his promises than Allah?

---

[4] Beautiful virgins who serve the saved in Paradise.

66

Deliverance from Error
by al Ghazzali—1058–1111 CE

The Muslim philosopher, jurist, and teacher Abu Hamid Muhammad al Ghazzali was a prolific author who wrote dozens of books on philosophical and religious themes. The following document comes from his autobiography, Deliverance from Error. *Here, al Ghazzali relates his struggles to attain truth. Compare this document with the writing of Thomas Aquinas. What are they both seeking? What do they both conclude is the answer?*

The different religious observances and religious communities of the human race, and likewise the different theological systems of the religious leaders, with all the multiplicity of sects and variety of practices, constitute ocean depths in which the majority drown and only a minority reach safety. From my early youth, since I attained the age of puberty before I was twenty, until the present time when I am over fifty, I have ever recklessly launched out into the midst of these ocean depths; I have ever bravely embarked on this open sea, throwing aside all craven caution; I have poked into every dark recess; I have made an assault on every problem; I have plunged into every abyss; I have scrutinized the creed of every sect; I have tried to lay bare the inmost doctrines of every community. All this have I done that I might distinguish between true and false, between sound tradition and heretical innovation.

To thirst after a comprehension of things as they really are was my habit and custom from a very early age. It was instinctive with me, a part of my God-given nature, a matter of temperament and not of my choice or contriving. Consequently as I drew near the age of adolescence the bonds of mere authority (*taqlid*) ceased to hold me, and inherited beliefs lost their trip upon me, for I saw that Christian youths always grew up to be Christians, Jewish youths to be Jews, and Muslim youths to be Muslims.

I therefore said within myself: "To begin with, what I am looking for is knowledge of what things really are, so I must undoubtedly try to find what knowledge really is." It was plain to me that sure and certain knowledge is that knowledge in which the object is disclosed in such a fashion that no doubt remains along with it, that no possibility of error or illusion accompanies it, and that the mind cannot even entertain such a supposition. Certain knowledge must

From *Anthology of Islamic Literature*, ed., James Kritzeck, 1987, trans. by W. Montgomery Watt. Reprinted by permission of Penguin Books (USA), Inc.

also be infallible; and this infallibility or security from error is such that no attempt to show the falsity of the knowledge can occasion doubt or denial, even though the attempt is made by someone who turns stones into gold or a rod into a serpent. Thus I know that ten is more than three. Let us suppose that someone says to me: "No, three is more than ten, and in proof of that I shall change this rod into a serpent"; and let us suppose that he actually changes the rod into a serpent and that I witness him doing so. No doubts about what I know are raised in me because of this. The only result is that I wonder precisely how he is able to produce this change. Of doubt about my knowledge there is no trace.

After these reflections I knew that whatever I do not know in this fashion and with this mode of certainty is not reliable and infallible knowledge; and knowledge that is not infallible is not certain knowledge.

Thereupon I investigated the various kinds of knowledge I had, and found myself destitute of all knowledge with this characteristic of infallibility except in the case of sense-perception and necessary truths. So I said: "Now that despair has come over me, there is no point in studying any problems except on the basis of what is self-evident, namely, necessary truths and the affirmations of the senses. I must first bring these to be judged in order that I may be certain on this matter. Is my reliance on sense-perception and my trust in the soundness of necessary truths of the same kind as my previous trust in the beliefs I had merely taken over from others, and as the trust most men have in the results of thinking? Or is it a justified trust that is in no danger of being betrayed or destroyed?"

I proceeded therefore with extreme earnestness to reflect on sense-perception and on necessary truths, to see whether I could make myself doubt them. The outcome of this protracted effort to induce doubt was that I could no longer trust sense-perception either. Doubt began to spread here and say: "From where does this reliance on sense-perception come? The most powerful sense is that of sight. Yet when it looks at the shadow (e.g., of a stick or the gnomon of a sundial), it sees it standing still, and judges that there is no motion. Then by experiment and observation, after an hour it knows that the shadow is moving and, moreover, that it is moving not by fits and starts but gradually and steadily by infinitely small distances in such a way that it is never in a state of rest. Again, it looks at the heavenly body (sc. the sun) and sees it small, the size of a shilling;[1] yet geometrical computations show that it is greater than the earth in size."

In this and similar cases of sense-perception the sense as judge forms his judgments, but another judge, the intellect, shows him repeatedly to be wrong; and the charge of falsity cannot be rebutted.

To this I said: "My reliance on sense-perception also has been destroyed. Perhaps only those intellectual truths which are first principles (or derived from first principles) are to be relied upon, such as the assertion that ten are more than three, that the same thing cannot be both affirmed and denied at one time, that one thing is not both generated in time and eternal, nor both existent and nonexistent, nor both necessary and impossible."

---

[1] Literally *dīnār*

Sense-perception replied: "Do you not expect that your reliance on intellectual truths will fare like your reliance on sense-perception? You used to trust in me; then along came the intellect-judge and proved me wrong; if it were not for the intellect-judge you would have continued to regard me as true. Perhaps behind intellectual apprehension there is another judge who, if he manifests himself, will show the falsity of intellect in its judging, just as, when intellect manifested itself, it showed the falsity of sense in its judging. The fact that such a supraintellectual apprehension has not manifested itself is no proof that it is impossible."

My ego hesitated a little about the reply to that, and sense-perception heightened the difficulty by referring to dreams. "Do you not see," it said, "how, when you are asleep, you believe things and imagine circumstances, holding them to be stable and enduring, and, so long as you are in that dream-condition, have no doubts about them? And is it not the case that when you awake you know that all you have imagined and believed is unfounded and ineffectual? Why then are you confident that all your waking beliefs, whether from sense or intellect, are genuine? They are true in respect of your present state; but it is possible that a state will come upon you whose relation to your waking consciousness is analogous to the relation of the latter to dreaming. In comparison with this state your waking consciousness would be like dreaming! When you have entered into this state, you will be certain that all the suppositions of your intellect are empty imaginings. It may be that that state is what the Sufis claim as their special 'state' (*sc.* mystical union or ecstasy), for they consider that in their 'states' (or ecstasies), which occur when they have withdrawn into themselves and are absent from their senses, they witness states (or circumstances) which do not tally with these principles of the intellect. Perhaps that 'state' is death; for the Messenger of God (God bless and preserve him) says: 'The people are dreaming; when they die, they become awake.' So perhaps life in this world is a dream by comparison with the world to come; and when a man dies, things come to appear differently to him from what he now beholds, and at the same time the words are addressed to him: 'We have taken off thee thy covering, and thy sight today is sharp (Koran 50:21).'"

When these thoughts had occurred to me and penetrated my being, I tried to find some way of treating my unhealthy condition; but it was not easy. Such ideas can only be repelled by demonstration; but a demonstration requires a knowledge of first principles; since this is not admitted, however, it is impossible to make the demonstration. The disease was baffling, and lasted almost two months, during which I was a sceptic in fact though not in theory nor in outward expression. At length God cured me of the malady; my being was restored to health and an even balance; the necessary truths of the intellect became once more accepted, as I regained confidence in their certain and trustworthy character.

This did not come about by systematic demonstration or marshalled argument, but by a light which God most high cast into my breast. That light is the key to the greater part of knowledge. Whoever thinks that the understanding of things divine rests upon strict proofs has in his thought narrowed down the wideness of God's mercy.

67

Christianity Meets Aristotle, From *The Summa Theologica* by Thomas Aquinas—1223–1274 CE

Perhaps the greatest medieval theologian was the Dominican monk Thomas Aquinas. A professor of theology at the University of Paris, he attempted to reconcile Christian tradition and Aristotelian principles in The Summa Theologica, *his major work. The medieval intellectual rationale of Aquinas and others, called Scholasticism, provided a framework for understanding the universe. How does Aquinas use reason to prove the existence of God? When does he believe faith is necessary?*

THE EXISTENCE OF GOD

. . . A thing can be self-evident in either of two ways: on the one hand, self-evident in itself, though not to us; on the other, self-evident in itself, and to us. A proposition is self-evident because the predicate is included in the essence of the subject: *e.g., Man is an animal*, for animal is contained in the essence of man. If, therefore, the essence of the predicate and subject be known to all, the proposition will be self-evident to all; as is clear with regard to the first principles of demonstration, the terms of which are certain common notions that no one is ignorant of, such as being and non-being, whole and part, and the like. If, however, there are some to whom the essence of the predicate and subject is unknown, the proposition will be self-evident in itself, but not to those who do not know the meaning of the predicate and subject of the proposition. Therefore, it happens, as Boethius says, that there are some notions of the mind which are common and self-evident only to the learned, as that incorporeal substances are not in space. Therefore I say that this proposition, *God exists*, of itself is self-evident, for the predicate is the same as the subject, because God is His own existence as will be hereafter shown. Now because we do not know the essence of God, the proposition is not self-evident to us, but needs to be demonstrated by things that are more known to us, though less known in their nature—namely, by His effects. . . .

From Thomas Aquinas, *The Summa Theologica* in *Basic Writing of Saint Thomas Aquinas*, ed. by Anton C. Pegis, 1945, Vol. I, p. 19-23, 92-25, 97, 101-102. Reprinted by permission of Random House, Inc.

Demonstration can be made in two ways: One is through the cause, and is called *propter quid*, and this is to argue from what is prior absolutely. The other is through the effect, and is called a demonstration *quia;* this is to argue from what is prior relatively only to us. When an effect is better known to us than its cause, from the effect we proceed to the knowledge of the cause. And from every effect the existence of its proper cause can be demonstrated, so long as its effects are better known to us; because, since every effect depends upon its cause, if the effect exists, the cause must preexist. Hence the existence of God, in so far as it is not self-evident to us, can be demonstrated from those of His effects which are known to us. . . .

The existence of God can be proved in five ways. The first and more manifest way is the argument from motion. It is certain, and evident to our senses, that in the world some things are in motion. Now whatever is moved is moved by another, for nothing can be moved except it is in potentiality to that towards which it is moved; whereas a thing moves inasmuch as it is in act. For motion is nothing else than the reduction of something from potentiality to actuality. But nothing can be reduced from potentiality to actuality, except by something in a state of actuality. Thus that which is actually hot, as fire, makes wood, which is potentially hot, to be actually hot, and thereby moves and changes it. Now it is not possible that the same thing should be at once in actuality and potentiality in the same respect, but only in different respects. For what is actually hot cannot simultaneously be potentially hot; but it is simultaneously potentially cold. It is therefore impossible that in the same respect and in the same way a thing should be both mover and moved, *i.e.,* that it should move itself. Therefore, whatever is moved must be moved by another. If that by which it is moved be itself moved, then this also must needs be moved by another, and that by another again. But this cannot go on to infinity, because then there would be no first mover, and, consequently, no other mover, seeing that subsequent movers move only inasmuch as they are moved by the first mover; as the staff moves only because it is moved by the hand. Therefore it is necessary to arrive at a first mover, moved by no other; and this everyone understands to be God.

The second way is from the nature of efficient cause. In the world of sensible things we find there is an order of efficient causes. There is no case known (neither is it, indeed, possible) in which a thing is found to be the efficient cause of itself; for so it would be prior to itself, which is impossible. Now in efficient causes it is not possible to go on to infinity, because in all efficient causes following in order, the first is the cause of the intermediate cause, and the intermediate is the cause of the ultimate cause, whether the intermediate cause be several, or one only. Now to take away the cause is to take away the effect. Therefore, if there be no first cause among efficient causes, there will be no ultimate, nor any intermediate, cause. But if in efficient causes it is possible to go on to infinitely, there will be no first efficient cause, neither will there be an ultimate effect, nor any intermediate efficient causes; all of which is plainly false. Therefore it is necessary to admit a first efficient cause, to which everyone gives the name of God.

The third way is taken from possibility and necessity, and runs thus. We find in nature things that are possible to be and not to be, since they are found to be generated, and to be corrupted, and consequently, it is possible for them to be and not to be. But it is impossible for these always to exist, for that which can not-be at some time is not. Therefore, if everything can not-be, then at one time there was nothing in existence. Now if this were true, even now there would be nothing in existence, because that which does not exist begins to exist only through something already existing. Therefore, if at one time nothing was in existence, it would have been impossible for anything to have begun to exist; and thus even now nothing would be in existence—which is absurd. Therefore, not all beings are merely possible, but there must exist something the existence of which is necessary. But every necessary thing either has its necessity caused by another, or not. Now it is impossible to go on to infinity in necessary things which have their necessity caused by another, as has been already proved in regard to efficient causes. Therefore we cannot but admit the existence of some being having of itself its own necessity, and not receiving it from another, but rather causing in others their necessity. This all men speak of as God.

The fourth way is taken from the gradation to be found in things. Among beings there are some more and some less good, true, noble, and the like. But *more* and *less* are predicated of different things according as they resemble in their different ways something which is the maximum, as a thing is said to be hotter according as it more nearly resembles that which is hottest: so that there is something which is truest, something best, something noblest, and, consequently, something which is most being, for those things that are greatest in truth are greatest in being, as it is written in [Aristotle's] *Metaph*. ii. Now the maximum in any genus is the cause of all in that genus, as fire, which is the maximum of heat, is the cause of all hot things, as is said in the same book. Therefore there must also be something which is to all beings the cause of their being, goodness, and every other perfection; and this we call God.

The fifth way is taken from the governance of the world. We see that things which lack knowledge, such as natural bodies, act for an end, and this is evident from their acting always, or nearly always, in the same way, so as to obtain the best result. Hence it is plain that they achieve their end, not fortuitously, but designedly. Now whatever lacks knowledge cannot move towards an end, unless it be directed by some being endowed with knowledge and intelligence; as the arrow is directed by the archer. Therefore some intelligent being exists by whom all natural things are directed to their end; and this being we call God. . . .

HOW GOD IS KNOWN BY US

Since everything is knowable according as it is actual, God, Who is pure act without any admixture of potentiality, is in Himself supremely knowable. But what is supremely knowable in itself may not be knowable to a particular intellect, because of the excess of the intelligible object above the intellect; as, for example, the sun, which is supremely visible, cannot be seen by the bat by reason of its excess of light.

Therefore, some who considered this held that no created intellect can see the essence of God. This opinion, however, is not tenable. For the ultimate beatitude of man consists in the use of his highest function, which is the operation of the intellect. Hence, if we suppose that a created intellect could never see God, it would either never attain to beatitude, or its beatitude would consist in something else beside God; which is opposed to faith. For the ultimate perfection of the rational creature is to be found in that which is the source of its being; since a thing is perfect so far as it attains to its source. Further, the same opinion is also against reason. For there resides in every man a natural desire to know the cause of any effect which he sees. Thence arises wonder in men. But if the intellect of the rational creature could not attain to the first cause of things, the natural desire would remain vain.

Hence it must be granted absolutely that the blessed see the essence of God. . . .

Two things are required both for sensible and for intellectual vision—*viz.*, power of sight, and union of the thing seen with the sight. For vision is made actual only when the thing seen is in a certain way in the seer. Now in corporeal things it is clear that the thing seen cannot be by its essence in the seer, but only by its likeness: as the likeness of a stone is in the eye, whereby the vision is made actual, whereas the substance of the stone is not there. But if the source of the visual power and the thing seen were one and the same thing, it would necessarily follow that the seen would possess both the visual power, and the form whereby it sees, from that one same thing.

Now it is manifest both that God is the author of the intellectual power and that He can be seen by the intellect. And since the intellectual power of the creature is not the essence of God, it follows that it is some kind of participated likeness of Him Who is the first intellect. Hence also the intellectual power of the creature is called an intelligible light, as it were, deprived from the first light, whether this be understood of the natural power, or of some superadded perfection of grace or of glory. Therefore, in order to see God, there is needed some likeness of God on the part of the visual power, whereby the intellect is made capable of seeing God. But on the part of the thing seen, which must in some way be united to the seer, the essence of God cannot be seen through any created likeness. First, because, as Dionysius says, *by the likenesses of the inferior order of things, the superior can in no way be known;* as by the likeness of a body the essence of an incorporeal thing cannot be known. Much less therefore can the essence of God be seen through any created species whatever. Secondly, because the essence of God is His very being, as was shown above, which cannot be said of any created form. Hence, no created form can be the likeness representing the essence of God to the seer. Thirdly, because the divine essence is uncircumscribed, and contains in itself supereminently whatever can be signified or understood by a created intellect. Now this cannot in any way be represented by any created species, for every created form is determined according to some aspect of wisdom, or of power, or of being itself, or of some like thing. Hence, to say that God is seen through some likeness is to say that the divine essence is not seen at all; which is false.

Therefore it must be said that to see the essence of God there is required some likeness in the visual power, namely, the light of glory strengthening the intellect to see God, which is spoken of in the *Psalm* (xxxv. 10): *In Thy light we shall see light.* The essence of God, however, cannot be seen by any created likeness representing the divine essence as it is in itself. . . .

. . . It is impossible for God to be seen by the sense of sight, or by any other sense or power of the sensitive part of the soul. For every such power is the act of a corporeal organ, as will be shown later. Now act is proportioned to the being whose act it is. Hence no power of that kind can go beyond corporeal things. But God is incorporeal, as was shown above. Hence, He cannot be seen by the sense or the imagination, but only by the intellect. . . .

. . . It is impossible for any created intellect to see the essence of God by its own natural power. For knowledge takes place according as the thing known is in the knower. But the thing known is in the knower according to the mode of the knower. Hence the knowledge of every knower is according to the mode of its own nature. If therefore the mode of being of a given thing exceeds the mode of the knower, it must result that the knowledge of that thing is above the nature of the knower. Now the mode of being of things is manifold. For some things have being only in this individual matter; such are all bodies. There are other beings whose natures are themselves subsisting, not residing in matter at all, which, however, are not their own being, but receive it: and these are the incorporeal substances called angels. But to God alone does it belong to be His own subsistent being.

Therefore, what exists only in individual matter we know naturally, since our soul, through which we know, is the form of some particular matter. Now our soul possesses two cognitive powers. One is the act of a corporeal organ, which naturally knows things existing in individual matter; hence sense knows only the singular. But there is another kind of cognitive power in the soul, called the intellect; and this is not the act of any corporeal organ. Therefore the intellect naturally knows natures which exist only in individual matter; not indeed as they are in such individual matter, but according as they are abstracted therefrom by the consideration of the intellect. Hence it follows that through the intellect we can understand these things in a universal way; and this is beyond the power of sense. Now the angelic intellect naturally knows natures that are not in matter; but this is beyond the power of the intellect of the human soul in the state of its present life, united as it is to the body.

It follows, therefore, that to know self-subsisting being is natural to the divine intellect alone, and that it is beyond the natural power of any created intellect: for no creature is its own being, since its being is participated. Therefore, a created intellect cannot see the essence of God unless God by His grace unites Himself to the created intellect, as an object made intelligible to it. . . .

. . . It is impossible for any created intellect to comprehend God; but *to attain to God with the mind in some degree is great beatitude*, as Augustine says.

In proof of this we must consider that what is comprehended is perfectly known; and that is perfectly known which is known so far as it can be known. Thus if anything which is capable of scientific demonstration is held only by an opinion resting on a probable proof, it is not comprehended. For instance, if anyone knows by scientific demonstration that a triangle has three angles equal to two right angles, he comprehends that truth; whereas if anyone accepts it as a probable opinion because wise men or most men teach it, he does not comprehend the thing itself because he does not attain to that perfect mode of knowledge of which it is intrinsically capable. But no created intellect can attain to that perfect mode of the knowledge of the divine intellect whereof it is intrinsically capable. Here is the proof. Everything is knowable according to its actuality. But God, Whose being is infinite as was shown above, is infinitely knowable. Now no created intellect can know God infinitely. For a created intellect knows the divine essence more or less perfectly in proportion as it receives a greater or lesser light of glory. Since therefore the created light of glory received into any created intellect cannot be infinite it is clearly impossible for any created intellect to know God in an infinite degree. Hence it is impossible that it should comprehend God. . . .

68

A Woman's Faith, From *Letters* by Catherine of Siena— 14th century CE

Born in Siena, Italy, Catharine lived in a dangerous age that was fraught with war, famine, and plague. Much to the dismay of her parents, Catherine from an early age wanted to become a nun. Finally, her parents gave their consent and she joined the Dominican Order at the age of 16. Catharine was a mystic who had many visions, but she is best known for her writings, even though she didn't learn to write until the end of her life. Catharine dictated her work to secretaries and was known for her blunt words. She feared not prelate, pope, or king, and spoke to them with the authority of the handmaiden of God. Why might high-ranking nobles and church officials have been willing to receive criticism from this relatively humble nun? What strikes you as most important about her comments?

From Letters of St. Catherine of Siena, Vol. 1, trans. by Suzanne Noffke (Arizona Center for Medieval and Renaissance Studies, 2001), p. 224–227. Reprinted by permission.

TO LOUIS, DUKE OF ANJOU

In the name of Jesus Christ crucified and of gentle Mary.

Dearest lord and brother in Christ gentle Jesus,

I Caterina, servant and slave of the servants of Jesus Christ, am writing to you in his precious blood. I long to see your heart nailed fast to the cross, to see your desire so grow that soon you will be ready and eager to raise the standard of the most holy cross against the unbelievers. If you look at the Lamb slain and consumed with love on the cross to free you from death and give you the life of grace, I am certain this holy memory will fire you with longing to do it soon, and will curb any unruly pleasure and earthly vanity in your heart and soul. Such pleasure passes away like the wind and always leaves death in the souls of its possessors. Unless it is set in order it leads them at death into eternal death, for they have by their sin given up seeing God and have made themselves worthy of seeing and associating with the devils. And it is fitting that those who sin against God, the infinite Good, should suffer infinite punishment.

I am talking about those who spend their whole lives in pleasure and in sumptuous living, looking for luxuries and for great honor at huge banquets. They spend everything they have on nothing but such things. The poor are dying of hunger, but they are busy looking for plenty of big meals, elegant dishes, expensive tables, and fine fancy clothes. They don't care that their wretched souls are dying of starvation because they deprive them of their food: holy virtue, holy confession, and God's holy Word—I mean the Word incarnate, God's only-begotten Son. We should by our affection and love be following in that Word's footsteps, loving what he loves, seeking what he sought. We should be loving virtue and despising vice, seeking God's honor and our own and our neighbors' salvation. This is why Christ said we do not live on bread alone but on God's Word.

So I want you, dear lord and brother in Christ gentle Jesus, to follow this gracious Word, Christ crucified, in true virtue. Don't let yourself be deceived by the world or by the strength of your youth. For if we follow only the world, what Christ said of the Jews could be said of us: "They are like tombs, beautiful and whitened on the outside, but inside full of the bones and stench of the dead." Oh how well does gentle First Truth speak! It is indeed so, for on the outside they seem beautiful in all their finery, but their heart and affection are filled with these dead transitory things that give off the disgusting stench of bodily and spiritual corruption. But I trust that by God's goodness you will make such an effort to amend your life that those words will not apply to you. No, with tremendously blazing love you will take up the cross, where the death of deadly sin was spent and destroyed, where we won life. And here is what it will do for you: when you take up the cross, all your past sins against God will be taken away. And then God will say to you, "Come, my beloved son. You have worked hard for me. Now I will relieve you; I will lead you to the wedding feast of everlasting life, where there is satiety without boredom, hunger without pain, pleasure without discord." Earthly wedding feasts and banquets are not like this. They are costly, but we gain nothing from them, and the more we stuff ourselves at them, the more empty we become, and our enjoyment becomes a source of sadness.

You had a good example of that yesterday, when you gave a banquet that was so festive yet turned out to be such a great sorrow for you. God permitted this because of his very great love for your soul. He wanted to show you and the others who were there what sort of thing our empty revelry is. And God showed how little he liked what was going on—the words, the actions, the manners, the plottings.

Ah, but I'm very much afraid our obtuseness is such that it doesn't even let us think about divine judgment! I'm telling you in the name of Christ crucified never to forget yesterday, so that your affairs will always be conducted in good order, with virtue and fear of God, rather than with no fear of God. Take heart, take heart, for I trust that he in his goodness will do this for you. Let your grief over what happened not be crippling; rather let it be the healing pain of a holy self-knowledge. Let it be a holy restraint to hold in check any disordered vanity in you—just as you do to your running horse when you pull in the reins to keep him on course.

Up now, my dear son in Christ our gentle Jesus! Embrace the most holy cross. Answer God, who is using this cross to call you. This is how you will fulfill his will and my desire. And this is why I said I long to see your heart and your desire nailed fast to the cross. Before the holy father leaves, see that you reaffirm your holy desire by taking the holy cross in his holiness' presence, and the sooner the better, for the Christian people as well and for the unbelievers. Be sure to do it soon; don't put it off any longer. Be willing to do without material things rather than lose the spiritual, especially in this dear holy work that God has put into your hands. He is making you worthy of what he in his goodness usually does for his great servants.

I'll say no more. Remember, my lord, that you will surely die, and you don't know when. Keep living in God's holy and tender love. Forgive my presumption.

Jesus, gentle Jesus!

CHAPTER 8

Law, Government and War—500–1500 CE

A s nations and empires grew, legal codes were refined by rules to better govern their subjects. This era also witnessed a series of wars over religion as well as a new world-conquering group, the Mongols. Several documents in this section contain law codes and constitutions from both Eastern and Western societies. What, if anything, do they have in common? The remaining documents deal with the conduct and motivation of warriors and their reasons for fighting. Why was religion such an important factor in many of the wars of the Middle Ages? What motivated conquerors such as the Mongols and Seljuk Turks?

69

Justinian's *Code*—529–565 CE

Justinian (483-565 BCE) was born a peasant but became the heir of his childless uncle, a Byzantine general who became emperor of the eastern Roman Empire in 518. As a result, Justinian inherited the throne in 527, a few months after his uncle died. As emperor, he wanted to reform the legal code as well as gain territory. His main accomplishments were in governmental reform and the codification of Byzantine law. The following excerpt from Justinian's Code *deals with family law, including marriage, divorce, and parental responsibility. The code would later form the basis of European law for hundreds of years. What does this legal code tell you about the status of women in this society?*

FORMATION OF MARRIAGE

Marriage is the union of a man and a woman, a partnership for life involving divine as well as human law.

Marriage cannot take place unless everyone involved consents, that is, those who are being united and those in whose power they are.

According to Pomponius, if I have a grandson by one son and a granddaughter by another who are both in my power, my authority alone will be enough to allow them to marry, and this is correct.

A girl who was less than twelve years old when she married will not be a lawful wife until she reaches that age while living with her husband.

Where a grandson marries, his father must also consent; but if a granddaughter gets married, the consent and authority of the grandfather will suffice. Insanity prevents marriage being contracted, because consent is required; but once validly contracted, it does not invalidate the marriage.

When the relationship of brother and sister arises because of adoption, it is an impediment to marriage while the adoption lasts. So I will be able to marry a girl whom my father adopted and then emancipated. Similarly, if she is kept in his power and I am emancipated, we can be married. It is advisable, then, for someone who wishes to adopt his son-in-law to emancipate his daughter-in-law and for someone who wished to adopt his daughter-in-law to emancipate his son. We are not allowed to marry our paternal or maternal aunts or paternal or maternal great-aunts although paternal and maternal great-aunts are related in the fourth degree. Again, we are not allowed to marry a paternal aunt or great-aunt, even though they are related to us by adoption.

From "The Digest of Justinian," Latin text ed. by T. Mommsen with the aid of Paul Krueger, English translation edited by Alan Watson, Vol. II. Copyright © 1985 by the University of Pennsylvania Press. Reprinted by permission.

People who wrongfully prevent children in their power from marrying, or who refuse to provide a dowry for them can be forced by proconsuls and provincial governors to arrange marriages and provide dowries for them. Those who do not try to arrange marriages are held to prevent them.

Where he marries someone because his father forces him to do so and he would not have married her if the choice had been his, the marriage will nevertheless be valid, because marriage cannot take place without the consent of the parties; he is held to have chosen this course of action.

The *lex Papia* provides that all freeborn men, apart from senators and their children, can marry freedwomen.

Living with a freewoman implies marriage, not concubinage, as long as she does not make money out of prostitution.

An emancipated son can marry without his father's consent, and any son he has will be his heir.

Women accused of adultery cannot marry during the lifetime of their husbands, even before conviction.

Women who live in a shameful way and make money out of prostitution, even where it is not done openly, are held in disgrace. If a woman lives as a concubine with anyone other than her patron, I would say that she lacks the character of the mother of a household.

As far as marriages are concerned, it is always necessary to consider not just what is lawful but also what is decent. If the daughter, granddaughter, or great-granddaughter of a senator marries a freedman or someone who was an actor, or whose father or mother were actors, the marriage will be void.

DIVORCES AND REPUDIATIONS

Marriage is dissolved by the divorce, death, captivity, or other kind of slavery of either of the parties.

The word "divorce" derives from either the diversity of views it involves or because people who dissolve their marriage go in different directions. Where repudiation, that is, renunciation, is involved, these words are used: "Keep your things to yourself"; or "Look after your own things." It is agreed that in order to end betrothals a renunciation must be made. Here the established words are: "I do not accept your conditions." It makes no difference whether the repudiation is made in the presence of the other party.

A true divorce does not take place unless an intention to remain apart permanently is present. So things said or done in anger are not effective until the parties show by their persistence that they are an indication of their considered opinion. So where repudiation takes place in anger and the wife returns shortly afterward, she is not held to have divorced her husband.

Julian asks in the eighteenth book of his *Digest* whether an insane woman can repudiate her husband or be repudiated by him. He writes that an insane woman can be repudiated, because she is in the same position as a person who does not know of the repudiation. But she could not repudiate her husband because of her madness, and her curator cannot do this either but her father can repudiate for her. He would not have dealt with repudiation here unless it was established that the marriage was to continue. This opinion seems to me to be correct.

The wives of people who fall into enemy hands can still be considered married women only in that other men cannot marry them hastily. Generally, as long as it is certain that a husband who is in captivity is still alive, his wife does not have the right to contract another marriage, unless she herself has given some ground for repudiation. But if it is not certain whether the husband in captivity is alive or has died, then if five years have passed since his capture, his wife has the right to marry again so that the first marriage will be held to have been dissolved with the consent of the parties and each of the parties will have their rights withdrawn. The same rule applies where a husband stays at home and his wife is captured.

Where someone who has given the other party written notice of divorce regrets having done this and the notice is served in ignorance of the change of mind, the marriage is held to remain valid, unless the person who receives the notice is aware of the change of mind and wants to end the marriage himself. Then the marriage will be dissolved by the person who received the notice.

THE RECOGNITION OF CHILDREN

It is not just a person who smothers a child who is held to kill it but also the person who abandons it, denies it food, or puts it on show in public places to excite pity which he himself does not have.

If anyone asks his children to support him or children seek support from their father, a judge should look into the question. Should a father be forced to support only children in his power or should he also support children who have been emancipated or have become independent in some other way? I think it is better to say that even where children are not in power, they must be supported by their parents and they, on the other hand, must support their parents. Must we support only our fathers, our paternal grandfathers, paternal great-grandfathers, and other relatives of the male sex, or are we compelled to support our mothers and other relatives in the maternal line? It is better to say that in each case the judge should intervene so as to give relief to the necessities of some of them and the infirmity of others. Since this obligation is based on justice and affection between blood relations, the judge should balance the claims of each person involved. The same is true in the maintenance of children by their parents. So we force a mother to support her illegitimate children and them to support her. The deified Pius also says that a maternal grandfather is compelled to support his grandchildren. He also stated in a rescript that a father must support his daughter, if it is proved in court that he was really her father. But where a son can support himself, judges should decide not to compel the provision of maintenance for him. So the Emperor Pius stated: "The appropriate judges before whom you will appear must order you to be supported by your father according to his means, provided that where you claim you are a tradesman, it is your ill health which makes you incapable of supporting yourself by your own labor." If a father denies that the person seeking support is his son and so maintains that he need not provide it, or where a son denies that the person seeking support is his father, the judges must decide this summarily. If it is established that the person is a son or a father, they must order him to be supported. But if this is not proved, they should not award maintenance. Remember if the judges declare that support must be provided, this does not affect the truth of the matter; for they did not declare that the person was the man's son, but only that he must be supported. If anyone refuses to provide support, the judges must determine the maintenance according to his means. If he fails to provide this, he can be forced to comply with the judgment by the seizing of his property in execution and selling it. The judge must also decide whether a relative or a father has any good reason for not supporting his children.

70

The Seventeen Article Constitution by Prince Shotoku—604 CE

The author of this document, Prince Shotoku, is one of the heroes of ancient Japan. A Buddhist, one-time envoy to China, and later regent, Shotoku was concerned with the spread of Chinese Buddhism and with conforming Japanese society to the Chinese model. The following document borrows from Confucianism and Buddhism to promote proper behavior in Japan. What Buddhist and Confucian ideals are incorporated into this document?

"The Seventeen Article Constitution," in Japan: A Documentary History, Vol. I: The Dawn of History to the Late Tokugawa Period, ed. David J. Lu (Armonk, NY: M. E. Sharpe, 1997), p. 23–26. English translation copyright © 1997 by David J. Lu. Reprinted by permission of M. E. Sharpe, Inc. All rights reserved. Not for reproduction.

S ummer, 4th month, 3rd day [12th year of Empress Suiko, 604 A.D.] The Crown Prince personally drafted and promulgated a constitution consisting of seventeen articles, which are as follows:

I. Harmony is to be cherished, and opposition for opposition's sake must be avoided as a matter of principle. Men are often influenced by partisan feelings, except a few sagacious ones. Hence there are some who disobey their lords and fathers, or who dispute with their neighboring villages. If those above are harmonious and those below are cordial, their discussion will be guided by a spirit of conciliation, and reason shall naturally prevail. There will be nothing that cannot be accomplished.

II. With all our heart, revere the three treasures. The three treasures, consisting of Buddha, the Doctrine, and the Monastic Order, are the final refuge of the four generated beings, and are the supreme objects of worship in all countries. Can any man in any age ever fail to respect these teachings? Few men are utterly devoid of goodness, and men can be taught to follow the teachings. Unless they take refuge in the three treasures, there is no way of rectifying their misdeeds.

III. When an imperial command is given, obey it with reverence. The sovereign is likened to heaven, and his subjects are likened to earth. With heaven providing the cover and earth supporting it, the four seasons proceed in orderly fashion, giving sustenance to all that which is in nature. If earth attempts to overtake the functions of heaven, it destroys everything. Therefore when the sovereign speaks, his subjects must listen; when the superior acts, the inferior must follow his examples. When an imperial command is given, carry it out with diligence. If there is no reverence shown to the imperial command ruin will automatically result.

IV. The ministers and functionaries must act on the basis of decorum, for the basis of governing the people consists in decorum. If the superiors do not behave with decorum, offenses will ensue. If the ministers behave with decorum, there will be no confusion about ranks. If the people behave with decorum, the nation will be governed well of its own.

V. Cast away your ravenous desire for food and abandon your covetousness for material possessions. If a suit is brought before you, render a clear-cut judgment. . . . Nowadays, those who are in the position of pronouncing judgment are motivated by making private gains, and as a rule, receive bribes. Thus the plaints of the rich are like a stone flung into water, while those of the poor are like water poured over a stone. Under these circumstances, the poor will be denied recourses to justice, which constitutes a dereliction of duty of the minister.

VI. Punish that which is evil and encourage that which is good. This is an excellent rule from antiquity. Do not conceal the good qualities of others, and always correct that which is evil which comes to your attention. Consider those flatterers and tricksters as constituting a superb weapon for the overthrow of the state, and a sharp sword for the destruction of people. Smooth-tongued adulators love to report to their superiors the errors of their inferiors; and to their inferiors, castigate the errors of their superiors. Men of this type lack loyalty to the sovereign and have no compassion for the people. They are the ones who can cause great civil disorders.

VII. Every man must be given his clearly delineated responsibility. If a wise man is entrusted with office, the sound of praise arises. If a wicked man holds office, disturbances become frequent. . . . In all things, great or small, find the right man, and the country will be well governed. On all occasions, in an emergency or otherwise, seek out a wise man, which in itself is an enriching experience. In this manner, the state will be lasting and its sacerdotal functions will be free from danger. Therefore did the sage kings of old seek the man to fill the office, not the office for the sake of the man.

VIII. The ministers and functionaries must attend the court early in the morning and retire late. The business of the state must not be taken lightly. A full day is hardly enough to complete work, and if the attendance is late, emergencies cannot be met. If the officials retire early, the work cannot be completed.

IX. Good faith is the foundation of righteousness, and everything must be guided by faith. The key to the success of the good and the failure of the bad can also be found in good faith. If the officials observe good faith with one another, everything can be accomplished. If they do not observe good faith, everything is bound to fail.

X. Discard wrath and anger from your heart and from your looks. Do not be offended when others differ with you. Everyone has his own mind, and each mind has its own leanings. Thus what is right with him is wrong with us, and what is right with us is wrong with him. We are not necessarily sages, and he is not necessarily a fool. We are all simply ordinary men, and none of us can set up a rule to determine the right from wrong. . . . Therefore, instead of giving way to anger as others do, let us fear our own mistakes. Even though we may have a point, let us follow the multitude and act like them.

XI. Observe clearly merit and demerit and assign reward and punishment accordingly. Nowadays, rewards are given in the absence of meritorious work, punishments without corresponding crimes. The ministers, who are in charge of public affairs, must therefore take upon themselves the task of administering a clear-cut system of rewards and punishments.

XII. Provincial authorities or local nobles are not permitted to levy exactions on the people. A country cannot have two sovereigns, nor the people two masters. The people of the whole country must have the sovereign as their only master. The officials who are given certain functions are all his subjects. Being the subjects of the sovereign, these officials have no more right than others to levy exactions on the people.

XIII. All persons entrusted with office must attend equally to their functions. If absent from work due to illness or being sent on missions, and work for that period is neglected, on their return, they must perform their duties conscientiously by taking into account that which transpired before and during their absence. Do not permit lack of knowledge of the intervening period as an excuse to hinder effective performance of public affairs.

XIV. Ministers and functionaries are asked not to be envious of others. If we envy others, they in turn will envy us, and there is no limit to the evil that envy can cause us. We resent others when their intelligence is superior to ours, and we envy those who surpass us in talent. This is the reason why it takes five hundred years before we can meet a wise man, and in a thousand years it is still difficult to find one sage. If we cannot find wise men and sages, how can the country be governed?

XV. The way of a minister is to turn away from private motives and to uphold public good. Private motives breed resentment, and resentful feelings cause a man to act discordantly. If he fails to act in accord with others, he sacrifices the public interests for the sake of his private feelings. When resentment arises, it goes counter to the existing order and breaks the law. Therefore it is said in the first article that superiors and inferiors must act in harmony. The purport is the same.

XVI. The people may be employed in forced labor only at seasonable times. This is an excellent rule from antiquity. Employ the people in the winter months when they are at leisure. However, from spring to autumn, when they are engaged in agriculture or sericulture, do not employ them. Without their agricultural endeavor, there is no food, and without their sericulture, there is no clothing.

XVII. Major decisions must not be made by one person alone, but must be deliberated with many. On the other hand, it is not necessary to consult many people on minor questions. If important matters are not discussed fully, there may always be a fear of committing mistakes. A thorough discussion with many can prevent it and bring about a reasonable solution.

71

Instructions to the Subjects of Charlemagne's Empire— ca. 800 CE

Charlemagne was the first ruler to attempt to centralize authority in Western Europe after the fall of the Roman Empire. As ruler, Charlemagne tried to both improve the quality of the religious life and further the spread of literacy within his domain. (Charlemagne himself only learned to read in later years.) He also required his nobles and religious leaders to field troops to support his reign. Despite his best efforts, his empire fell apart shortly after his death, leaving effective authority in place only at the local level. How does this document show that there was little separation between church and state in ninth century Europe?

Concerning going to the army; the count in his county under penalty of the ban, and each man under penalty of sixty *solidi* shall go to the army, so that they come to the appointed muster at that place where it is ordered. And the count himself shall see in what manner they are prepared, that is, each one shall have a lance, shield, bow with two strings, twelve arrows. And the bishops, counts, abbots shall oversee their own men and shall come on the day of the appointed muster and there show how they are prepared. Let them have breast-plates or helmets, and let them proceed to the army, that is, in the summer.

Be it known, therefore, to your devotion pleasing to God, that we, together with our faithful, have considered it to be useful that the bishoprics and monasteries entrusted by the favor of Christ to our control, in addition to the order of monastic life and the intercourse of holy religion, in the culture of letters also ought to be zealous in teaching those who by the gift of God are able to learn, according to the capacity of each individual, so that just as the observance of the rule imparts order and grace to honesty of morals, so also zeal in teaching and learning may do the same for sentences, so that those who desire to please God by living rightly should not neglect to please him also by speaking correctly. For it is written: "Either from thy words thou shalt be justified or from thy words thou shalt be condemned." For although correct conduct may be better than

From "Laws of Charles the Great" ed. Dana Munro in *Translations and Reprints from the Original Sources of European History*, vol. VI, no. 5, ed. by Department of History of the University of Pennsylvania (Philadelphia: University of Pennsylvania Press, 1898).

knowledge, nevertheless knowledge precedes conduct. Therefore, each one ought to study what he desires to accomplish, so that so much the more fully the mind may know what ought to be done, as the tongue hastens in the praises of omnipotent God without the hindrances of errors. For since errors should be shunned by all men, so much the more ought they to be avoided as far as possible by those who are chosen for this very purpose alone, so that they ought to be the especial servants of truth. For when in the years just passed letters were often written to us from several monasteries in which it was stated that the brethren who dwelt there offered up in our behalf sacred and pious prayers, we have recognized in most of these letters both correct thoughts and uncouth expressions; because what pious devotion dictated faithfully to the mind, the tongue, uneducated on account of the neglect of study, was not able to express in the letter without error. Whence it happened that we began to fear lest perchance, as the skill in writing was less, so also the wisdom for understanding the Holy Scriptures might be much less than it rightly ought to be. And we all know well that, although errors of speech are dangerous, far more dangerous are errors of the understanding. Therefore, we exhort you not only not to neglect the study of letters, but also with most humble mind, pleasing to God, to study earnestly in order that you may be able more easily and more correctly to penetrate the mysteries of the divine Scriptures.

72

Ordinance of Government by Al Mawardi—11th century CE

Al Mawardi was a Muslim philosopher, jurist, and expert in government who was educated in Basrah and Baghdad. He wrote a number of books of political science, including the following excerpt, in which he discusses the role of the Imam. This position replaced that of the prophet and was concerned both with defending the faith and with governance. Religious and civil authority were combined in one leader beginning with Muhammad; the office of imam, or caliph, dates from his death in 632 CE. What kind of power did the Imam have? Which of his duties seem purely religious in nature? Why?

From Islam from the Prophet Muhammed to the Capture of Constantinople, ed. and trans. by Bernard Lewis (New York: Harper & Row, 1974), Vol. I, p. 150–151, 171–179. Reprinted by permission.

The office of Imam was set up in order to replace the office of Prophet in the defense of the faith and the government of the world. By general consensus [*ijmā'*], from which only al-Asamm dissents, the investiture of whichsoever member of the community exercises the functions of Imam is obligatory. But there is disagreement as to whether this obligation derives from reason or from Holy Law. One group says it derives from reason, since it is in the nature of reasonable men to submit to a leader who will prevent them from injuring one another and who will settle quarrels and disputes, for without rulers men would live in anarchy and heedlessness like benighted savages. . . .

Another group says that the obligation derives from the Holy Law and not from reason, since the Imam deals with matters of Holy Law to which, in reason, he would be allowed not to devote himself, since reason does not make them obligatory. All that reason requires is that a reasonable man should refrain from mutual injury and conflict with his neighbor and act equitably in mutual fairness and good relations, conducting himself in accordance with his own reason, and not with someone else's. But it is the Holy Law which intervenes to entrust these affairs to its religious representative. . . .

The obligation of the Imamate, which is thus confirmed, is a collective duty, like the Holy War and the pursuit of knowledge, so that when it is performed by those whose charge it is, the general obligation of the rest of the community lapses. If no one discharges it, then two groups of people must be distinguished from the rest; first, the electors, who choose an Imam for the community; and second, those eligible for the Imamate, one of whom must be made Imam. The rest of the community, who belong neither to the one nor to the other group, commit no sin or offense if there is a delay in filling the Imamate. When these two groups are constituted and take over the collective obligation, each group must conform to the prescribed conditions. The conditions required in the electors are three:

1. Rectitude ['*adāla*] in all respects.

2. The knowledge to recognize the required qualifications for the Imamate.

3. The discernment and wisdom to choose the candidate best suited to the Imamate, the most capable and the best informed of the conduct of public affairs.

He who is in the city of the Imam has no privilege or precedence, because of this, over those in other places. That those who are present in the city of the Imam undertake the appointment of the new Imam is custom, not law; this happens because they are the first to hear of his death and because those who are best qualified to succeed him are usually to be found in his city.

The conditions of eligibility for the Imamate are seven:

1. Rectitude in all respects.

2. The knowledge to exercise personal judgment [*ijtihād*] in cases and decisions.

3. Soundness of hearing, sight, and tongue so that he may deal accurately with those matters which can only be attained by them.

4. Soundness of limb so that he has no defect which would prevent him from moving freely and rising quickly.

5. The discernment needed to govern the subjects and conduct public affairs.

6. The courage and vigor to defend the lands of Islam and to wage holy war against the enemy.

7. Descent, that is to say, he must be of the tribe of Quraysh, as is prescribed by a text and accepted by consensus. . . .

The Imamate is conferred in two ways: one is by the choice of the electors [literally, those competent to bind and to loosen], and the other is by the nomination of the previous Imam. . . .

When the electors meet, they scrutinize the qualified candidates and proceed to appoint that one among them who is the most worthy, who best meets the required conditions, and to whom the people are most willing to give obedience. They recognize him without delay. If the exercise of their judgment leads them to choose a particular person from the community, they offer him the Imamate. If he accepts, they swear allegiance to him, and the Imamate is vested in him by this procedure. Allegiance to him and obedience to him then become binding on the entire community. If he holds back and refuses the Imamate, it cannot be imposed upon him, since it is a contract by consent and choice and may not involve compulsion or constraint. In such case the Imamate is offered to another qualified candidate.

If two candidates are equally well qualified, the elder takes precedence in choice; however, seniority, where the parties are of age, is not a necessary condition, and if the younger is appointed, it is still valid. If one is wiser and the other braver, the choice should be determined by the needs of the time. If the need for courage is more urgent because of the disorder of the frontiers and the appearance of rebels, then the braver has a better claim. If the need for wisdom is more urgent because of the quiescence of the populace and the appearance of heretics, then it is the wiser who has a better claim. . . .

The duties of the Imam in the conduct of public affairs are ten:

1. To maintain the religion according to established principles and the consensus of the first generation of Muslims. If an innovator appears or if some dubious person deviates from it, the Imam must clarify the proofs of religion to him, expound that which is correct, and apply to him the proper rules and penalties so that religion may be protected from injury and the community safeguarded from error.

2. To execute judgments given between litigants and to settle disputes between contestants so that justice may prevail and so that none commit or suffer injustice.

3. To defend the lands of Islam and to protect them from intrusion so that people may earn their livelihood and travel at will without danger to life or property.

4. To enforce the legal penalties for the protection of God's commandments from violation and for the preservation of the rights of his servants from injury or destruction.

5. To maintain the frontier fortresses with adequate supplies and effective force for their defense so that the enemy may not take them by surprise, commit profanation there, or shed the blood, either of a Muslim or an ally [*mu'āhad*].

6. To wage holy war [*jihād*] against those who, after having been invited to accept Islam, persist in rejecting it, until they either become Muslims or enter the Pact [*dhimma*] so that God's truth may prevail over every religion [cf. Qur'ān, ix, 33].

7. To collect the booty and the alms [*sadaqa*] in conformity with the prescriptions of the Holy Law, as defined by explicit texts and by independent judgment [*ijtihād*], and this without terror or oppression.

8. To determine the salaries and other sums due from the treasury, without extravagance and without parsimony, and to make payment at the proper time, neither in advance nor in arrears.

9. To employ capable and trustworthy men and appoint sincere men for the tasks which he delegates to them and for the money which he entrusts to them so that the tasks may be competently discharged and the money honestly safeguarded.

10. To concern himself directly with the supervision of affairs and the scrutiny of conditions so that he may personally govern the community, safeguard the faith, and not resort to delegation in order to free himself either for pleasure or for worship, for even the trustworthy may betray and the sincere may deceive. God said, "O David, we have made you our vicegerent [*khalīfa*] on earth; therefore, judge justly among men and do not follow your caprice, which will lead you astray from God's path." [Qur'ān, xxxviii, 25]. In this, God was not content with delegation, but required a personal performance and did not excuse the following of passions, which, He says, lead astray from His path, and this, though He considered David worthy to judge in legion and to hold His viceregency [*khilāfa*]. This is one of the duties of government of any shepherd. The Prophet of God, may God bless and save him, said, "You are all shepherds, and you are all answerable for your flocks."

. . .

The rules of the Imamate and its general jurisdiction over the interests of religion and the governance of the community, as we have described them, being established, and the investiture of an Imam being duly confirmed, the authority which comes from him to his deputies is of four kinds:

1. Those who have unlimited authority of unlimited scope. These are the viziers, for they are entrusted with all public affairs without specific attribution.

2. Those who have unlimited authority of limited scope. Such are the provincial and district governors, whose authority is unlimited within the specific areas assigned to them.

3. Those who have limited authority of unlimited scope. Such are the chief qādī, the commander of the armies, the commandant of the frontier fortresses, the intendant of the land tax, and the collector of the alms, each of whom has unlimited authority in the specific functions assigned to him.

4. Those with limited authority of limited scope, such as the *qādī* of a town or district, the local intendant of the land tax, collector of tithes, the frontier commandment, or the army commander, every one of whom has limited authority of limited scope.

73

Speech at the Council of Clermont Proclaiming the First Crusade Against the Muslims—1095 CE

Religious wars were a trademark of the second millennium and continued well into the third millennium. A series of wars that had a far-reaching effect on both East and West were the Crusades. The Catholic Church, led by Pope Urban II, was determined to regain the holy city of Jerusalem, which had been taken over by the forces of Islam. Because Muslims also revered Jerusalem, the struggle for the city lasted for centuries. Here, Robert the Monk, a contemporary of Pope Urban II who later wrote a history of the Crusades, recounts the stirring speech given by the pope in 1095 at the Council of Clermont in France. What reasons does Pope Urban give for encouraging the Crusade? How do you think his words were received?

From *The First Crusade: The Chronicle of Fulcher of Chartres and Other Source Materials*, Second Edition, edited by Edward Peters. Copyright © 1998, 1971 University of Pennsylvania Press. Reproduced by permission of the publisher.

"Oh race of Franks, race from across the mountains, race chosen and beloved by God — as shines forth in very many of your works — set apart from all nations by the situation of your country, as well as by your catholic faith and the honor of the holy church! To you our discourse is addressed and for you our exhortation is intended. We wish you to know what a grievous cause has led us to your country, what peril threatening you and all the faithful has brought us.

"From the confines of Jerusalem and the city of Constantinople a horrible tale has gone forth and very frequently has been brought to our ears, namely, that a race from the kingdom of the Persians, an accursed race, a race utterly alienated from God, a generation forsooth which has not directed its heart and has not entrusted its spirit to God, has invaded the lands of those Christians and has depopulated them by the sword, pillage and fire; it has led away a part of the captives into its own country, and a part it has destroyed by cruel tortures; it has either entirely destroyed the churches of God or appropriated them for the rites of its own religion. They destroy the altars, after having defiled them with their uncleanness. They circumcise the Christians, and the blood of the circumcision they either spread upon the altars or pour into the vases of the baptismal font. When they wish to torture people by a base death, they perforate their navels, and dragging forth the extremity of the intestines, bind it to a stake; then with flogging they lead the victim around until the viscera having gushed forth the victim falls prostrate upon the ground. Others they bind to a post and pierce with arrows. Others they compel to extend their necks and then, attacking them with naked swords, attempt to cut through the neck with a single blow. What shall I say of the abominable rape of the women? To speak of it is worse than to be silent. The kingdom of the Greeks is now dismembered by them and deprived of territory so vast in extent that it cannot be traversed in a march of two months. On whom therefore is the labor of avenging these wrongs and of recovering this territory incumbent, if not upon you? You, upon whom above other nations God has conferred remarkable glory in arms, great courage, bodily activity, and strength to humble the hairy scalp of those who resist you.

"Let the deeds of your ancestors move you and incite your minds to manly achievements; the glory and greatness of king Charles the Great, and of his son Louis, and of your other kings, who have destroyed the kingdoms of the pagans, and extended in these lands the territory of the holy church. Let the holy sepulchre of the Lord our Saviour, which is possessed by unclean nations, especially incite you, and the holy places which are now treated with ignominy and irreverently polluted with their filthiness. Oh, most valiant soldiers and descendants of invincible ancestors, be not degenerate, but recall the valor of your progenitors.

"But if you are hindered by love of children, parents and wives, remember what the Lord says in the Gospel, 'He that loveth father or mother more than me, is not worthy of me.' 'Every one that hath forsaken houses, or brethren, or sisters, or father, or mother, or wife, or children, or lands for my name's sake shall receive an hundred-fold and shall inherit everlasting life.' Let none of your possessions detain you, no solicitude for your family affairs, since this land which you inhabit, shut in on all sides by the seas and surrounded by the mountain peaks, is too narrow for your large population; nor does it abound in wealth; and it furnishes scarcely food enough for its cultivators. Hence it is that you murder one another, that you wage war, and that frequently you perish by mutual wounds. Let therefore hatred depart from among you, let your quarrels end, let wars cease, and let all dissensions and controversies slumber. Enter upon the road to the Holy Sepulchre; wrest that land from the wicked race, and subject it to yourselves. That land which as the Scripture says 'floweth with milk and honey,' was given by God into the possession of the children of Israel.

"Jerusalem is the navel of the world; the land is fruitful above others, like another paradise of delights. This the Redeemer of the human race has made illustrious by His advent, has beautified by residence, has consecrated by suffering, has redeemed by death, has glorified by burial. This royal city, therefore, situated at the center of the world, is now held captive by His enemies, and is in subjection to those who do not know God, to the worship of the heathens. She seeks therefore and desires to be liberated and does not cease to implore you to come to her aid. From you especially she asks succor, because, as we have already said, God has conferred upon you above all nations great glory in arms. Accordingly undertake this journey for the remission of your sins, with the assurance of the imperishable glory of the kingdom of heaven."

When Pope Urban had said these and very many similar things in his urbane discourse, he so influenced to one purpose the desires of all who were present, that they cried out, "It is the will of God! It is the will of God!" When the venerable Roman pontiff heard that, with eyes uplifted to heaven he gave thanks to God and, with his hand commanding silence, said:

"Most beloved brethren, today is manifest in you what the Lord says in the Gospel, 'Where two or three are gathered together in my name there am I in the midst of them.' Unless the Lord God had been present in your spirits, all of you would not have uttered the same cry. For, although the cry issued from numerous mouths, yet the origin of the cry was one. Therefore I say to you that God who implanted this in your breasts, has drawn it forth from you. Let this then be your war-cry in combats, because this word is given to you by God. When an armed attack is made upon the enemy, let this one cry be raised by all the soldiers of God: It is the will of God! It is the will of God!

"And we do not command or advise that the old or feeble, or those unfit for bearing arms, undertake this journey; nor ought women to set out at all, without their husbands or brothers or legal guardians. For such are more of a hindrance than aid, more of burden than advantage. Let the rich aid the needy; and according to their wealth, let them take with them experienced soldiers. The priests and clerks of any order are not to go without the consent of their bishop; for the journey would profit them nothing if they went without permission of these. Also, it is not fitting that laymen should enter upon the pilgrimage without the blessing of their priests.

"Whoever, therefore, shall determine upon this holy pilgrimage and shall make his vow to God to that effect and shall offer himself to Him as a living sacrifice, holy, acceptable unto God, shall wear the sign of the cross of the Lord on his forehead or on his breast. When, truly, having fulfilled his vow he wishes to return, let him place the cross on his back between his shoulders. Such, indeed, by the twofold action will fulfill the precept of Lord, as He commands in the Gospel, 'He that taketh not his cross and followeth after me, is not worthy of me.'"

74

Crusader's Motives by Ekkehard of Aurach (First Crusade)— 11th century CE

In the following brief excerpt, Ekkehard of Aurach, a German historian and contemporary of Pope Urban, talks about the motives of the crusaders. What does Ekkehard say was the main motive of those who went to fight in the Crusades?

The West Franks were easily induced to leave their fields, since France had, during several years, been terribly visited now by civil war, now by famine, and again by sickness. . . . Among the other nations, the common people, as well as those of higher rank, related that, aside from the apostolic summons, they had in some instances been called to the land of promise by certain prophets who had appeared among them, or through heavenly signs and revelations. Others confessed that they had been induced to pledge themselves by some misfortune. A great part of them started forth with wife and child and laden with their entire household equipment.

From James Harvey Robinson, ed., *Readings in European History*, vol. I (Boston: Ginn, 1904), p. 318.

75

Impressions of the Franks by Usama ibn Munquidh— 12th century CE

In his memoirs, the Syrian warrior and nobleman Usama Ibn Munquidh provides a revealing account of Muslim attitudes towards the Frankish crusaders they encountered in the Middle East. The differences between their cultures are clearly revealed in this brief excerpt. What most mystified Usama regarding the conduct of the Franks? What does he admire about them?

Among the Franks—God damn them!—no quality is more highly esteemed in a man than military prowess. The knights have a monopoly of the positions of honour and importance among them, and no one else has any prestige in their eyes. They are the men who give counsel, pass judgment and command the armies. On one occasion I went to law with one of them about some herds that the Prince of Baniyas seized in a wood; this was at a time when there was a truce between us, and I was living in Damascus. I said to King Fulk, the son of Fulk. 'This man attacked and seized my herd. This is the season when the cows are in calf; their young died at birth, and he has returned the herd to me completely ruined.' The King turned to six or seven of his knights and said: 'Come, give a judgment on this man's case.' They retired from the audience chamber and discussed the matter until they all agreed. Then they returned to the King's presence and said: 'We have decided that the Prince of Baniyas should indemnify this man for the cattle that he has ruined.' The King ordered that the indemnity should be paid, but such was the pressure put on me and the courtesy shown me that in the end I accepted four hundred *dinar* from the Prince. Once the knights have given their judgment neither the King nor any other commander can alter or annul it, so great an influence do their knights have in their society. On this occasion the King swore to me that he had been made very happy the day before. When I asked him what had made him happy he said: 'They told me that you were a great knight, but I did not believe that you would be chivalrous.' 'Your Majesty,' I replied, 'I am a knight of my race and my people.' When a knight is tall and well-built they admire him all the more.

From *Arab Historians of the Crusades*, trans. from the Italian by E.J. Costello. ©1957 by Giullo Einaudi Editore S.P.A., Turin. This translation ©1969 by Routledge & Kegan Paul Ltd. The Regents of the University of California. Reprinted by permission of the publisher.

A very important Frankish knight was staying in the camp of King Fulk, the son of Fulk. He had come on a pilgrimage and was going home again. We got to know one another, and became firm friends. He called me 'brother' and an affectionate friendship grew up between us. When he was due to embark for the return journey he said to me: 'My brother, as I am about to return home, I should be happy if you would send your son with me,' (the boy, who was about fourteen years old, was beside me at the time), 'so that he could meet the noblemen of the realm and learn the arts of politics and chivalry. On his return home he would be a truly cultivated man.' A truly cultivated man would never be guilty of such a suggestion; my son might as well be taken prisoner as go off into the land of the Franks. I turned to my friend and said: 'I assure you that I could desire nothing better for my son, but unfortunately the boy's grandmother, my mother, is very attached to him, and she would not even let him come away with me without extracting a promise from me that I would bring him back to her.' 'Your mother is still alive?' 'Yes.' 'Then she must have her way.'

This is an example of Frankish barbarism, God damn them! When I was in Jerusalem I used to go to the Masjid al-Aqsa, beside which is a small oratory which the Franks have made into a church. Whenever I went into the Moseque, which was in the hands of Templars who were friends of mine, they would put the little oratory at my disposal, so that I could say my prayers there. One day I had gone in, said the *Allah akhbar* and risen to begin my prayers, when a Frank threw himself on me from behind, lifted me up and turned me so that I was facing east. 'That is the way to pray!' he said. Some Templars at once intervened, seized the man and took him out of my way while I resumed my prayer. But the moment they stopped watching him he seized me again and forced me to face east, repeating that this was the way to pray. Again the Templars intervened and took him away. They apologized to me and said: 'He is a foreigner who has just arrived today from his homeland in the north, and he has never seen anyone pray facing any other direction than east.' I have finished my prayers,' I said, and left stupefied by the fanatic who had been so perturbed and upset to see someone praying facing Mecca.

I paid a visit to the tomb of John the son of Zechariah—God's blessing on both of them—in the village of Sebastea in the province of Nablus. After saying my prayers, I came out into the square that was bounded on one side by the Holy Precinct. I found a half-closed gate opened it and entered a church. Inside were about ten old men, their bare heads as white as combed cotton. They were facing the east, and wore (embroidered?) on their breasts staves ending in crossbars turned up like the rear of a saddle. They took their oath on this sign, and gave hospitality to those who needed it. The sight of their piety touched my heart, but at the same time it displeased and saddened me, for I had never seen such zeal and devotion among the Muslims. For some time I brooded on this experience, until one day, as Mu'in ad-Din and I were passing the Peacock House, he said to me: 'I want to dismount here and visit the Old Men (the ascetics).' 'Certainly,' I replied, and we dismounted and went into a long building set at an angle to the road. For the moment I thought there was no one there. Then I saw about a hundred prayer-mats, and on each a sufi, his face expressing peaceful serenity, and his body humble devotion. This was a reassuring sight, and I gave thanks to Almighty God that there were among the Muslims men of even more zealous devotion than those Christian priests. Before I had never seen sufis in their monastery, and was ignorant of the way they lived.

76

The *Magna Carta*—1215 CE

Perhaps the most famous document in English history and the basis for England's constitution, the Great Charter *was actually a series of concessions forced out of King John by his rebellious nobles. Despite the fact that the freedoms it mentions were given to a very small percentage of the English people, the* Magna Carta *became the cornerstone of English liberty. What rights does the charter give to ordinary Englishman of the thirteenth century?*

John, by the grace of God, king of England, lord of Ireland, duke of Normandy and Aquitaine, and count of Anjou, to the archbishops, bishops, abbots, earls, barons, justiciars, foresters, sheriffs, stewards, servants, and to all his bailiffs and liege subjects, greeting. Know that, having regard to God and for the salvation of our souls, and those of all our ancestors and heirs, and unto the honor of God and the advancement of Holy Church, and for the reform of our realm . . .

I. In the first place we have granted to God, and by this our present charter confirmed for us and our heirs for ever that the English Church shall be free, and shall have her rights entire, and her liberties inviolate: and we will that it be thus observed . . .

II. If any of our earls or barons, or others holding of us in chief by military service shall have died, and at the time of his death his heir shall be full of age and owe relief he shall have his inheritance of payment of the ancient relief, namely the heir or heirs of an earl, £100 for a whole earl's barony: the heir or heirs of a baron, £100 for a whole barony; the heir or heirs of a knight, 100s. at most for a whole knight's fee: and whoever owes less let him give less, according to the ancient custom of fiefs.

From *Magna Carta*, ed. by W.S. McKechnie (Glasgow: Maclehose and Sons, 1914).

III. If, however, the heir of any one of the aforesaid has been under age and in wardship, let him have his inheritance without relief and without fine when he comes of age.

IV. The guardian of the land of an heir who is thus under age shall take from the land of the heir nothing but reasonable produce, reasonable customs, and reasonable services . . .

VII. A widow, after the death of her husband, shall forthwith and without difficulty have her marriage portion and inheritance; nor shall she give anything for her dower, or for her marriage portion, or, for the inheritance which her husband and she held on the day of the death of that husband; and she may remain in the house of her husband for forty days after his death, within which time her dower shall be assigned to her.

VIII. No widow shall be compelled to marry, so long as she prefers to live without a husband; provided always that she gives security not to marry without our consent, if she holds of us, or without the consent of the lord of whom she holds, if she holds of another.

IX. Neither we nor our bailiffs shall seize any land or rent for any debt, so long as the chattels of the debtor are sufficient to repay the debt . . .

XII. No scutage nor aid shall be imposed on our kingdom, unless by common counsel of our kingdom, except for ransoming our person, for making our eldest son a knight, and for once marrying our eldest daughter; and for these there shall not be levied more than a reasonable aid . . .

XIV. And for obtaining the common counsel of the kingdom anent the assessing of an aid (except in the three cases aforesaid) or of a scutage, we will cause to be summoned the archbishops, bishops, abbots, earls, and greater barons, severally by our letters; and we will moreover cause to be summoned generally, through our sheriffs and bailiffs, all others who hold of us in chief, for a fixed date, namely, after the expiry of at least forty days, and at a fixed place; and in all letters of such summons we will specify the reason of the summons. And when the summons has thus been made, the business shall proceed on the day appointed, according to the counsel of such as are present, although not all who were summoned have come . . .

XXVII. If any freeman shall die intestate, his chattels shall be distributed by the hands of his nearest kinsfolk and friends, under supervision of the Church, saving to everyone the debts which the deceased owed to him.

XXVIII. No constable or other bailiff of ours shall take corn or other provisions from anyone without immediately tendering money therefor, unless he can have postponement thereof by permission of the seller . . .

XXX. No sheriff or bailiff of ours, or other person, shall take the horses or carts of any freeman for transport duty, against the will of the said freeman . . .

XXXV. Let there be one measure of wine throughout our whole realm; and one measure of ale; and one measure of corn . . . and one width of cloth . . . of weights also let it be as of measures . . .

XXXVIII. No bailiff for the future shall, upon his own unsupported complaint, put anyone to his "law," without credible witnesses brought for his purpose.

XXXIX. No freeman shall be taken or imprisoned or disseised or exiled or in any way destroyed, nor will we go upon him nor send upon him, except by the lawful judgment of his peers or by the law of the land.

XL. To no one will we sell, to no one will we refuse or delay, right or justice . . .

LXI. . . . we give and grant . . . the underwritten security, namely, that the barons choose five-and-twenty barons of the kingdom, whomsoever they will, who shall be bound with all their might to observe and hold, and cause to be observed, the peace and liberties we have granted and confirmed to them by this our present charter, so that if we, or our justiciar, or our bailiffs, or any one of our officers, shall in anything be at fault toward any one, or shall have broken any one of the articles of the peace or of this security and the offense be notified to four barons of the aforesaid five-and-twenty, the said four barons shall repair to us . . . and . . . petition to have that transgression redressed without delay. And if we shall not have corrected the transgression . . . within forty days . . . those five-and-twenty barons shall, together with the community of the whole land, distrain and distress us in all possible ways, namely, by seizing our castles, lands, possessions, and in any other way they can, until redress has been obtained as they deem fit, saving harmless our own person, and the persons of our queen and children: and when redress has been obtained, they shall resume their old relations toward us. And let whoever in the country desires it swear to obey the orders of the said five-and-twenty barons for the execution of all the aforesaid matters, and along with them, to molest us to the utmost of his power: . . . All those, moreover, in the land who of themselves and of their own accord are unwilling to swear to the twenty-five to help them in constraining and molesting us, we shall by our command compel the same to swear to the effect aforesaid . . .

LXIII. . . . Given under our hand . . . on the fifteenth day of June, in the seventeenth year of our reign.

77

Address of Sultan Mehmed before the Battle of Constantinople—1453 CE

When Constantinople fell to the Seljuk Turks in 1453, the Byzantine Empire came to an end. What had been the center of Orthodox Christianity now came under the rule of the Islamic Ottoman Empire. Mehmed "The Conqueror" extended Ottoman territory to the banks of the Danube. What does Mehmed's speech to his troops tell us about what would happen to the inhabitants of Constantinople if his army were successful?

"My friends and my comrades in the present struggle! I have called you together here, not because I would accuse you of any laziness or carelessness in this business, nor try to make you more eager in the present struggle. For a long time past I have noted some of you showing such zeal and earnestness for the work that you would willingly undergo everything necessary rather than leave here without [conquering the city], and others of you not only zealous themselves but even inciting the rest of you with all their might to redouble their efforts.

So it is not for this that I have called you together, but simply in order to remind you, first of all, that whatever you have at present you have attained, not by sloth and carelessness, but by hard work and with great struggles and dangers together with us, and these things are yours as the rewards of your own valor and manliness rather than as gifts of fortune. And secondly, as to the rewards now put before you here, I wish to show you how many and how great they are and what great glory and honor accompany the winning. And I also wish that you may know well how to carry on the struggle for the very highest rewards.

First, then, there is great wealth of all sorts in this city [Constantinople], some in the royal palaces and some in the houses of the mighty, some in the homes of the common people and still other, finer and more abundant, laid up in the churches as votive offerings and treasures of all sorts, constructed of gold and silver and precious stones and costly pearls. Also there is countless wealth of magnificent furniture, without reckoning all the other articles and furnishings of the houses. Of all of these, you will be the masters!

From Kritovoulos, *History of Mehmed the Conqueror*, trans. by Charles T. Riggs (Princeton, NJ: Princeton University Press, 1954).

Then too, there are very many noble and distinguished men, some of whom will be your slaves, and the rest will be put up for sale; also very many and very beautiful women, young and good-looking, and virgins lovely for marriage, noble, and of noble families, and even till now unseen by masculine eyes, some of them, evidently intended for the weddings of great men. Of these, some will be your wives for you, while others will do for servants, and others you can sell. So you will gain in many ways, in enjoyment, and service, and wealth.

And you will have boys, too, very many and very beautiful and of noble families.

Further, you will enjoy the beauty of the churches and public buildings and splendid houses and gardens, and many such things, suited to look at and enjoy and take pleasure in and profit by. But I must waste time listing all these. A great and populous city, the capital of the ancient Romans, which has attained the very pinnacle of good fortune and luck and glory, being indeed the head of the whole inhabited globe—I give it now to you for spoil and plunder—unlimited wealth, men, women, children, all other adornments and arrangements. All these you will enjoy as if at a brilliant banquet, and will be happy with them yourselves and will leave very great wealth to your children.

And the greatest of all this, that you will capture a city whose renown has gone out to all parts of the world. It is evident that to whatever extent the leadership and glory of this city has spread, to a like extent the renown of your valor and bravery will spread for having captured by assault a city such as this. But think: what deed more brilliant, what greater enjoyment, or what inheritance of wealth better than that presented to you, along with honor and glory!

And, best of all, we shall demolish a city that has been hostile to us from the beginning and is constantly growing at our expense and in every way plotting against our rule. So for the future we shall be sure of guarding our present belongings and shall live in complete and assured peace, after getting rid of our neighboring enemies. We shall also open the way to further conquest. . . ."

. . .

CHAPTER 9

Science, Medicine and Technology— 500–1500 CE

D uring this period, the greatest scientists were found in the Muslim world. The study of science in the West lagged behind, except for the work of a few brilliant individuals such as Leonardo Da Vinci. Medicine made some strides, but also took some backward steps as physicians continued to use incantations and prayers rather than scientific knowledge to combat disease. In the first document, a Briton shows his admiration of the scholars he met in the Muslim world; in the last document, Leonardo brags about his ability to create weapons of war. The rest of the documents provide insight into the attitudes of doctors, philosophers, clergy, and ordinary citizens toward disease, especially the deadly Bubonic plague. How much did medicine seem to have advanced during the Middle Ages compared to the medicine practiced during the Classical Age?

78

The Impact of Muslim Science, From the Preface to *Natural Questions* by Adelard of Bath— ca. 1137 CE

Adelard was an English scholar who traveled to France and Salerno, Italy, which was the site of the first medical school in Europe, founded during the twelfth century. Through his travels, Adelard became an expert in the Arabic language as well as in Arabic science. He was the first to translate Euclid's Elements of Geometry *from Arabic sources into Latin. He also translated the astronomical tables of Al-Khwarezmi, a scholar in the House of Wisdom at Baghdad, who wrote a treatise on astronomy. Some consider Adelard to be the first English scientist and a pioneer in the scientific renaissance of the twelfth century. In the document that follows, Adelard discusses the information he gained from Arabic scholars in the form of a dialogue with his nephew. What seems to be the nephew's attitude toward Adelard's statements and his praise of Arabic knowledge?*

On my return the other day to England, in the reign of Henry [Henry I, r. 1100–35–, son of William,–it was he who had long maintained me abroad for the purpose of study-the renewal of intercourse with my friends gave me both pleasure and benefit.

After the first natural inquiries about my own health and that of my friends, my particular desire was to learn all I could about the manners and customs of my own country. Making this then the object of my inquiry, I learnt that its chief men were violent, its magistrates wine-lovers, its judges mercenary; that patrons were fickle, private men sycophants, those who made promises deceitful, friends full of jealousy, and almost all men self-seekers: this realised, the only resource, I said to myself, is to withdraw my thoughts from all misery.

Thereupon my friends said to me, "What do you think of doing, since you neither wish to adopt this moral depravity yourself, nor can you prevent it?" My reply was "to give myself up to oblivion, since oblivion is the only cure for evils that cannot be remedied; for he who gives heed to that which he hates in some sort endures that which he does not love." Thus we argued that matter together, and then as we still had time left for talking, a certain nephew of

From Adelard of Bath, *Dodi Ve-Nechdi*, ed. and trans. by H. Gollancz (London: Oxford University Press, 1920).

mine, who had come along with the others, rather adding to the tangle than unraveling it, urged me to publish something fresh in the way of Arabian learning. As the rest agreed with him, I took in hand the treatise which follows: of its profitableness to its readers I am assured, but am doubtful whether it will give them pleasure. The present generation has this ingrained weakness, that it thinks that nothing discovered by the moderns is worthy to be received -the result of this is that if I wanted to publish anything of my own invention I should attribute it to someone else, and say, "Someone else said this, not I." Therefore (that I may not wholly be robbed of a hearing) it was a certain great man that discovered all my ideas, not I. But of this enough.

Since I have yielded to the request of my friends so far as to write something, it remains for you to give your judgment as to its correctness. About this point I would that I felt less anxiety, for there is no essay in the liberal arts, no matter how well handled, to which you could not give a wider range. Grant me, therefore, your sympathy. I shall now proceed to give short answers to questions put by my nephew. Here begins Adelard's treatise to his Nephew.

★★★★

ADELARD: You will remember, Nephew, how seven years ago when you were almost a child in the learning of the French, and I sent you along with the rest of my hearers to study with a man of high reputation, it was agreed between us that I should devote myself to the best of my ability to the study of Arabic, while you on your part were to acquire the inconsistencies of French ideas.

NEPHEW: I remember, and all the more because, when departing, you bound me under a solemn promise to be a diligent student of philosophy.

The result was that I applied myself with great diligence to this study. Whether what I have said is correct, the present occasion will give you an opportunity of discovering; since when you have often set them forth, I, as hearer only, have marked the opinions of the Saracens, and many of them seem to me quite absurd; I shall, therefore, for a time cease to exercise this patience, and when you utter these views, shall attack them where it seems good to me to do so.

To me it seems that you go too far in your praise of the Arabs, and show prejudice in your disparagement of the learning of our philosophers. Our reward will be that you will have gained some fruit of your toil; if you give good answers, and I make a good showing as your opponent, you will see that my promise has been well kept.

ADELARD: You perhaps take a little more on you than you ought; but as this arrangement will be profitable not only to you but to many others, I will pardon your forwardness, making however this one stipulation, that when I adduce something unfamiliar, people are to think not that I am putting forward an idea of my own, but am giving the views of the Arabs. If anything I say displeases the less educated, I do not want them to be displeased with me also: I know too well what is the fate which attends upon the teachers of the truth with the common herd, and consequently shall plead the case of the Arabs, not my own.

NEPHEW: Let it be as you will, provided nothing causes you to hold your peace.

ADELARD: I think then that we should begin with lighter matters, and if here I fail to give you a reasonable account, you will know what to expect in more important subjects. Let us begin then at the bottom, and so proceed upwards. . . .

ADELARD: It is a little difficult for you and me to argue about animals. I, with reason for my guide, have learned one thing from my Arab teachers, you, something different; dazzled by the outward show of authority you wear a head-stall. For what else should we call authority but a head-stall? Just as brute animals are led by the head-stall where one pleases, without seeing why or where they are being led, and only follow the halter by which they are held, so many of you, bound and fettered as you are by a low credulity, are led into danger by the authority of writers. Hence, certain people arrogating to themselves the title of authorities have employed an unbounded licence in writing, and this to such an extent that they have not hesitated to insinuate into men of low intellect the false instead of the true. Why should you not fill sheets of paper, aye, fill them on both sides, when to-day you can get readers who require no proof of sound judgment from you, and are satisfied merely with the name of a time-worn title? They do not understand that reason has been given to individuals that, with it as chief judge, distinction may be drawn between the true and the false. Unless reason were appointed to be the chief judge, to no purpose would she have been given to us individually: it would have been enough for the writing of laws to have been entrusted to one, or at most to a few, and the rest would have been satisfied with their ordinances and authority. Further, the very people who are called authorities first gained the confidence of their inferiors only because they followed reason; and those who are ignorant of reason, or neglect it, justly desire to be called blind. However, I will not pursue this subject any further, though I regard authority as matter for contempt. This one thing, however, I will say. We must first search after reason, and when it has been found, and not until then, authority if added to it, may be received. Authority by itself can inspire no confidence in the philosopher, nor ought it to be used for such a purpose. Hence logicians have agreed in treating the argument from authority not as necessary, but probable only. if, therefore, you want to bear anything from me, you must both give and take reason. I am not the man whom the semblance of an object can possibly satisfy; and the fact is, that the mere word is a loose wanton abandoning herself now to this man, now to that.

★★★★

How the Globe Is Supported in the Middle of the Air

NEPHEW: . . . I will put the first question that comes into my head: How is it that this earth of ours which supports all weights (I am speaking not of simples, but of compounds), how is it that it remains in the same place, or by what is it supported? If all heavy bodies, such as stone, wood, etc., require support, and cannot through their weight be supported by the air, then much more does the earth, which is heavier than everything else put together, require to be supported, nor can it be held in position by so unstable a body as the air. Hence it is contrary to reason that it should maintain its position.

ADELARD: Certainly it is inexpedient that it should fall, and that we also shall not fall along with it. I will show that its remaining in its position is in accordance with reason. From the character of its primary qualities, we know that the earth has weight; that which has weight is more secure in the lowest position; and everything is naturally fond of that which preserves its life, and tends towards that for which it has a liking. It follows therefore that everything which is earthy tends towards the lowest possible position. But in the case of anything round, it is clear that the middle and the lowest are the same, and therefore all earthy things tend towards the middle position. Now the middle position is a simple and indivisible middle point, and it is therefore clear that all earthy things tend towards a local and simple point. But this local point is not several but one, and must necessarily be occupied by one thing, not by several; but to it, as has been said, all things tend: consequently each one thing presses on something else, since all and sundry are hastening to the same point. Now the point to which all weighty bodies are hastening is that to which they are falling, for the fall of weighty bodies is merely a hastening to a middle point. By the point to which they are falling I mean the fixed middle point. The place to which they are falling-the middle point -remains fixed; and therefore, while falling into a stable position, they yet remain fixed, unless some force be impressed on them as a result of which they are diverted from their natural course. The very opposite then is the case to what you thought; and you will now see clearly that it is what you thought to be a reason for falling which gives stability and coherence to heavy bodies. They are, therefore, in some way supported by the point to which they are hastening; and if it should move in any direction, all the things which are affected towards it would also of necessity move, though of course in that selfsame spot we have not the first but the second cause of stability: for, in accordance with the reason previously given, the first cause of this equilibrium is the property of the subject, the second the stability of the point which it makes for.

79

Ethical Conduct by Moses
Maimonides—ca. 1190 CE

Moses Maimonides (1135–1204 CE) was a Jewish Rabbi, philosopher, and physician during the Middle Ages. In the following excerpt, Maimonides draws from his knowledge in these three areas to discuss how the avoidance of sexual excess brings health and long life. What do you think was his main reason for writing this work?

Another great principle of hygiene, physicians say, is as follows: As long as a person takes active exercise, works hard, does not overeat and keeps his bowels open, he will be free from disease and will increase in vigor, even though the food he eats is coarse. . . .

Whosoever indulges in sexual dissipation becomes prematurely aged; his strength fails; his eyes become dim; a foul odor proceeds from his mouth and armpits; the hair of his head, eye-brows and eye-lashes drop out; the hair of his beard, armpits and legs grow abnormally; his teeth fall out; and besides these, he becomes subject to numerous other diseases. Medical authorities have stated that for each one who dies of other maladies, a thousand are the victims of sexual excess. A man should, therefore, be careful in this regard if he wishes to lead a happy life. He should only cohabit when he finds himself in good health and vigor, experiences involuntary erections which persist after he has diverted his mind to other things, is conscious of a heaviness from the loins downwards as if the spermatic cords were being drawn and his flesh is hot. Such a condition calls for cohabitation which then is conducive to health. One should not cohabit when sated with food, nor when one is hungry, but only after a meal has been digested. Before and after coition, attention should be paid to the excretory functions.

From Jacob Minkin, *The Teachings of Maimonides* (Northvale, NJ: Jason Aronson, 1987).

80

The Black Death, or the Plague, From *The Decameron* by Giovanni Boccacio— 14th century CE

Better known for the stories of The Decameron, *Giovanni Boccaccio (1313–1375 CE) here provides a detailed description of the effect of the plague, or Black Death, on Florence. It is not known whether he was living in Florence at the time of the plague, but his step-mother was one of its victims. According to Boccaccio, how did the people of Florence react to the plague?*

Let me say, then, that thirteen hundred and forty-eight years had already passed after the fruitful Incarnation of the Son of God when into the distinguished city of Florence, more noble than any other Italian city, there came a deadly pestilence. Either because of the influence of heavenly bodies or because of God's just wrath as punishment to mortals for our wicked deeds, the pestilence, originating some years earlier in the East, killed an infinite number of people as it spread relentlessly from one place to another until it had stretched its miserable length all over the West. And against this pestilence no human wisdom or foresight was of any avail; quantities of filth were removed from the city by officials charged with the task; the entry of any sick person into the city was prohibited; and many directives were issued concerning the maintenance of good health. Nor were the humble supplications rendered not once but many times by the pious to God, through public processions or by other means, in any way efficacious; for almost at the beginning of springtime of the year in question the plague began to show its sorrowful effects in an extraordinary manner. It did not assume the form it had in the East, where bleeding from the nose was a manifest sign of inevitable death, but rather it showed its first signs in men and women alike by means of swellings either in the groin or under the armpits, some of which grew to the size of an ordinary apple and others to the size of an egg (more or less), and the people called them *gavoccioli*. And from the two parts of the body already mentioned, in very little time, the said deadly *gavoccioli* began to spread indiscriminately over every part of the body; then, after this, the symptoms of the illness changed to black or livid spots appearing on the arms and thighs, and on every part of the body-sometimes there were large ones and other times a number of little ones scattered all around. And just as the *gavoccioli* were originally, and still are, a very definite indication of impending death, in like manner these spots came to mean the same thing for whoever contracted them. Neither a doctor's advice nor the strength of medicine could do anything to cure this illness; on the contrary, either the nature of the illness was such that they did not recognize its cause and, as a result, could not prescribe the proper remedy (in fact, the number of doctors, other than the well-trained, was increased by a large number of men and women who had never had any medical training); at any rate, few of the sick were ever cured, and almost all died after the third day of the appearance of the previously described symptoms (some sooner, others later), and most of them died without fever or any other side effects.

This pestilence was so powerful that it was transmitted to the healthy by contact with the sick, the way a fire close to dry or oily things will set them aflame. And the evil of the plague went even further: not only did talking to or being around the sick bring infection and a common death, but also touching the clothes of the sick or anything touched or used by them seemed to communicate this very disease to the person involved. What I am about to say is incredible to hear, and if I and others had not witnessed it with our own eyes, I should not dare believe it (let alone write about it), no matter how trustworthy a person I might have heard it from. Let me say, then, that the plague described here was of such virulence in spreading from one person to another that not only did it pass from one man to the next, but, what's more, it was often transmitted from the garments of a sick or dead man to animals that not only became contaminated by the disease but also died with a brief period of time. My own eyes, as I said earlier, were witness to such a thing one day when the rags of a poor man who died of this disease were thrown into the public street, two pigs came upon then, and, as they are wont to do, first with their snouts and then with their teeth they took the rags and shook them around; and within a short time, after a number of convulsions, both pigs fell dead upon the ill-fated rags, as if they had been poisoned. From these and many similar or worse occurrences there came about such fear that almost all of them took a very cruel attitude in the matter; that is, they completely avoided the sick and their possessions, and in so doing, each one believed that he was protecting his own good health.

There were some people who thought that living moderately and avoiding any excess might help a great deal in resisting this disease, and so they gathered in small groups and lived entirely apart from everyone else. They shut themselves up in those houses where there were no sick people and where one could live well by eating the most delicate of foods and drinking the finest of wines (doing so always in moderation) allowing no one to speak about or listen to anything said about the sick and the dead outside; these people lived, entertaining themselves with music and other pleasures that they could arrange. Others thought the opposite: they believed that drinking excessively, enjoying life, going about singing and celebrating, satisfying in every way the appetites as best one could, laughing, and making light of everything that happened was the best medicine for such a disease; so they practiced to the fullest what they believed by going from one tavern to another all day and night, drinking to excess; and they would often make merry in private homes, doing everything that pleased or amused them most. This they were able to do easily, for everyone felt he was doomed to die, and, as a result, abandoned his property, so that most of the houses had become common property, and any stranger who came upon them used them as if he were the rightful owner. In addition to this bestial behavior, they always managed to avoid the sick as best they could. And in this great affliction and misery of our city the revered authority of the laws, both divine and human, had fallen and almost completely disappeared, for, like other men, the ministers and executors of the laws were either dead or sick or so short of help that it was impossible for them to fulfill their duties; and as a result, everybody was free to do as he pleased.

Many others adopted a middle course between the two attitudes just described: neither did they restrict their food or drink so much as the first group nor did they fall into such dissoluteness and drunkenness as the second; rather, they satisfied their appetites to a moderate degree. They did not shut themselves up, but went around carrying in their hands flowers, or sweet-smelling herbs, or various kinds of spices; and they would often put these things their noses, believing that such smells were a wonderful means of purifying the brain, for all the air seemed infected with the stench of dead bodies, sickness, and medicines.

Others were of a crueler opinion (though it was, perhaps, a safer one): they maintained that there was no better medicine against the plague than to flee from it; convinced of this reasoning and caring only about themselves, men and women in great numbers abandoned their city, their houses, their farms, their relatives, and their possessions and sought other places, going at least as far away as the Florentine countryside—as if the wrath of God could not pursue them with this pestilence wherever they went but would only strike those it found within the walls of the city! Or perhaps they thought that Florence's last hour had come and that no one in the city would remain alive.

And not all those who adopted these diverse opinions died, nor did they all escape with their lives; on the contrary, many of those who thought this way were falling sick everywhere, and since they had given, when they were healthy, the bad example of avoiding the sick, they in turn were abandoned and left to languish away without care. The fact was that one citizen avoided another, that almost no one cared for his neighbor, and that relatives rarely or hardly ever visited each other—they stayed far apart. This disaster had struck such fear into the hearts of men and women that brother abandoned brother, uncle abandoned nephew, sister left brother, and very often wife abandoned husband, and—even worse, almost unbelievable—fathers and mothers neglected to tend and care for their children as if they were not their own.

Thus, for the countless multitude of men and women who fell sick, there remained no support except the charity of their friends (and these were few) or the greed of servants, who worked for inflated salaries without regard to the service they performed and who, in spite of this, were few and far between; and those few were men or women of little wit (most of them not trained for such service) who did little else but hand different things to the sick when requested to do so or watch over them while they died. . . . And so, many people died who, by chance, might have survived if they had been attended to. Between the lack of competent attendants, which the sick were unable to obtain, and the violence of the pestilence, there were so many, many people who died in the city both day and night that it was incredible just to hear this described, not to mention seeing it! Therefore, out of sheer necessity, there arose among those who remained alive customs which were contrary to the established practices of the time.

It was the custom, as it is again today, for the women, relatives, and neighbors to gather together in the house of a dead person and there to mourn with the women who had been dearest to him; on the other hand, in front of the deceased's home, his male relatives would gather together with his male neighbors and other citizens, and the clergy also came (many of them, or sometimes just a few) depending upon the social class of the dead man. Then upon the shoulders of his equals, he was carried to the church chosen by him before death with the funeral pomp of candles and chants. With the fury of the pestilence increasing, this custom, for the most part, died out and other practices took its place. And so, not only did people die without having a number of women around them, but there were many who passed away without even having a single witness present, and very few were granted the piteous laments and bitter tears of their relatives; on the contrary, most relatives were somewhere else, laughing, joking, and amusing themselves; even the women learned this practice too well, having put aside, for the most part, their womanly compassion for their own safety. Very few were the dead who bodies were accompanied to the church by more than ten or twelve of their neighbors, and these dead bodies were not even carried on the shoulders of honored and reputable citizens but rather by gravediggers from the lower classes that were called *becchini*. Working for pay, they would pickup the bier and hurry it off, not to the church the dead man had chosen before his death but, in most cases, to the church closest by, accompanied by four or six churchmen with just a few candles, and often none at all. With the help of these *becchini*, the churchmen would place the body as fast as they could in whatever unoccupied grave they could find, without going to the trouble of saying long or solemn burial services.

The plight of the lower class and, perhaps, a large part of the middle class, was even more pathetic: most of them stayed in their homes or neighborhoods either because of their poverty or their hopes for remaining safe, and every day they fell sick by the thousands; and not having servants or attendants of any kind, they almost always died. Many ended their lives in the public streets, during the day or at night, while many other who died in their homes were discovered dead by their neighbors only by the smell of their decomposing bodies. The city was full of corpses. The dead were usually given the same treatment by their neighbors, who were moved more by the fear that the decomposing corpses would contaminate them than by any charity they might have felt towards the deceased: either by themselves or with the assistance of porters (when they were available), they would drag the corpse out of the home and place it in front of the doorstep where, usually in the morning, quantities of dead bodies could be seen by any passerby; then, they were laid out on biers, or for lack of biers, on a plank. Nor did a bier carry only one corpse; sometimes it was used for two or three at a time. More than once, a single bier would serve for a wife and husband, two or three brothers, a father or son, or other relatives, all at the same time. And countless times it happened that two priests, each with a cross, would be on their way to bury someone, when porters carrying three or four biers would just follow along behind them; and where these priests thought they had just one dead man to bury, they had, in fact, six or eight and sometimes more. Moreover, the dead were honored with no tears or candles or funeral mourners but worse: things had reached such a point that the people who died were cared for as we care for goats today.

81

A Wholesome Medicine Against all Infirmities—ca. 14th–15th century

The unknown writer of the following document credits a Benedictine monk with the advice he records to prevent illness. Although his advice is mainly spiritual, what does it reveal about the medical treatment of the time?

The advice of the reverend father Dom Theophilus of Milan, of the order of St Benedict, against the plague; also a most wholesome medicine against all infirmities. Note it well.

Whenever anyone is struck down by the plague they should immediately provide themselves with a medicine like this. Let him first gather as much as he can of bitter loathing towards the sins committed by him, and the same quantity of true contrition of heart, and mix the two into an ointment with the

From Rosemary Horrox, *The Black Death* (Manchester: Manchester University Press, 1994), p. 149.

water of tears. Then let him make a vomit of frank and honest confession, by which he shall be purged of the pestilential poison of sin, and the boil of his vices shall be totally liquified and melt away. Then the spirit, formerly weighed down by the plague of sin, will be left all light and full of blessed joy. Afterwards let him take the most delightful and precious medicine: the body of our lord and saviour Jesus Christ. And finally let him have himself anointed on the seat of his bodily senses with holy oil. And in a little while he will pass from transient life to the incorruptible country of eternal life, safe from plague and all other infirmities.

Compared with this all other remedies of doctors are futile and profit little against the plague, which God keeps for the chastisement of sin and which is without remedy save through him and his power.

82

Leonardo Da Vinci in Search of a Job—1482 CE

Although Leonardo Da Vinci is best known for his paintings, including the Mona Lisa, he was also interested in science and technology. His notebooks, written backwards by the secretive Leonardo so that they had to be read in a mirror, contained many innovative ideas and designs, including those for weapons were quite modern. In this letter, Leonardo writes to Duke Ludovico of Milan detailing his many talents and skills in the hope that the Duke would hire him. He was successful, which is not surprising given the letter's contents. Which of Leonardo's claims do you think would have most intrigued the Duke? Why?

Having now sufficiently seen and considered the proofs of all those who count themselves masters and inventors of instruments of war, and finding that their invention and use of the said instruments does not differ in any respect from those in common practice, I am emboldened without prejudice to anyone else to put myself in communication with Your Excellency, in order to acquaint you with my secrets, thereafter offering myself at your

---

From Irma A. Richter, ed., *The Literary Works of Leonardo da Vinci* (Oxford: Oxford University Press, N.Y.—London, 1939).

pleasure effectually to demonstrate at any convenient time all those matters which are in part briefly recorded below.

1. I have plans for bridges, very light and strong and suitable for carrying very easily, with which to pursue and at times defeat the enemy; and others solid and indestructible by fire or assault, easy and convenient to carry away and place in position. And plans for burning and destroying those of the enemy.

2. When a place is besieged I know how to cut off water from the trenches, and how to construct an infinite number of bridges, mantlets, scaling ladders, and other instruments which have to do with the same enterprise.

3. Also if a place cannot be reduced by the method of bombardment, either through the height of its glacis or the strength of its position, I have plans for destroying every fortress or other stronghold unless it has been founded upon rock.

4. I have also plans for making cannon, very convenient and easy of transport, with which to hurl small stones in the manner almost of hail, causing great terror to the enemy from their smoke, and great loss and confusion.

5. Also I have ways of arriving at a certain fixed spot by caverns and secret winding passages, made without any noise, even though it may be necessary to pass underneath trenches or a river.

6. Also I can make armored cars, safe and unassailable, which will enter the serried ranks of the enemy with their artillery, and there is no company of men at arms so great that they will not break it. And behind these the infantry will be able to follow quite unharmed and without any opposition.

7. Also, if need shall arise, I can make cannon, mortars, and light ordnance, of very beautiful and useful shapes, quite different from those in common use.

8. Where it is not possible to employ cannon, I can supply catapults, mangonels, *trabocchi* [old war engines: trébuchets], and other engines of wonderful efficacy not in general use. In short, as the variety of circumstances shall necessitate, I can supply an infinite number of different engines of attack and defense.

9. And if it should happen that the engagement is at sea, I have plans for constructing many engines most suitable either for attack or defense, and ships which can resist the fire of all the heaviest cannon, and powder and smoke.

10. In time of peace I believe that I can give you as complete satisfaction as anyone else in architecture in the construction of buildings both public and private, and in conducting water from one place to another.

Also I can execute sculpture in marble, bronze, or clay, and also painting, in which my work will stand comparison with that of anyone else, whoever he may be.

Moreover, I would undertake the work of the bronze horse, which shall perpetuate with immortal glory and eternal honor the auspicious memory of the Prince your father and of the illustrious house of Sforza.

And if any of the aforesaid things should seem impossible or impracticable to anyone, I offer myself as ready to make trial of them in your park or in whatever place shall please Your Excellency to whom I commend myself with all possible humility.

CHAPTER 10

Daily Life in the Medieval World— 500–1500 CE

The daily life of peasants changed little during medieval times, despite the emergence of a small but growing class of merchants and clerks. This caused both the expansion of trade and the growth of educational and commercial opportunities for a lucky few. Contact with the more advanced cultures of the Middle East, which had long had universities, resulted in the establishment of the first Western universities.

Many societies began to look outside their borders for trading partners with which to exchange a variety products. At the same time, some established religious groups also sent missionaries abroad to spread the tenets of their beliefs. In some instances, missionaries traveled with trade missions to foreign peoples.

During the Middle Ages, travel to foreign lands was difficult but not impossible. The missionaries and traders who wrote accounts of their adventures showed both admiration and disdain for the customs of new lands they visited. Can you relate to the travelers' surprise or criticism of the foreign lands they visited?

Several documents deal with the way workers were treated during the Middle Ages. Do any of these documents show consideration for workers? Why or why not?

At the same time, the role of women began to decline both in the West and in the East. Increasingly, women were confined to the home and to traditional women's roles, with few opportunities for advancement in the world. Did women have more rights in the East or in the West? How can you explain their decline in status?

83

Chinese Impression of India— 7th century CE

Much of our knowledge of life in seventh century India comes from the writings of Chinese Buddhist monks who made many pilgrimages to Buddha's home during this period. The following document comes from the account of Hsuan Tsang (620-664 CE), a Chinese monk who traveled throughout India for 14 years beginning in 630 CE. What seems to have impressed Hsuan Tsang most about what he observed of Indian life?

TOWNS AND BUILDINGS

The towns and villages have inner gates; the walls are wide and high; the streets and lanes are tortuous, and the roads winding. The thoroughfares are dirty and the stalls arranged on both sides of the road with appropriate signs. Butchers, fishers, dancers, executioners, and scavengers, and so on, have their abodes without the city. In coming and going these persons are bound to keep on the left side of the road till they arrive at their homes. Their houses are surrounded by low walls, and form the suburbs. The earth being soft and muddy, the walls of the towns are mostly built of brick or tiles. The towers on the walls are constructed of wood or bamboo; the houses have balconies and belvederes, which are made of wood, with a coating of lime or mortar, and covered with tiles. The different buildings have the same form as those in China: rushes, or dry branches, or tiles, or boards are used for covering them. The walls are covered with lime and mud, mixed with cow's dung for purity. At different seasons they scatter flowers about. Such are some of their different customs.

The [monasteries] are constructed with extraordinary skill. A three-storied tower is erected at each of the four angles. The beams and the projecting heads are carved with great skill in different shapes. The doors, windows, and the low walls are painted profusely; the monks' cells are ornamental on the inside and plain on the outside. In the very middle of the building is the hall, high and wide. There are various storeyed chambers and turrets of different height and shape, without any fixed rule. The doors open towards the east; the royal throne also faces the east.

. . .

From Si-Yu-Ki, *Buddhist Records of the Western World*, trans. by Samuel Beal (London: Trubner & Co., 1874).

CLEANLINESS, ABLUTIONS, &C.

They are very particular in their personal cleanliness, and allow no remissness in this particular. All wash themselves before eating; they never use that which has been left over (*from a former meal*); they do not pass the dishes. Wooden and stone vessels, when used, must be destroyed; vessels of gold, silver, copper, or iron after each meal must be rubbed and polished. After eating they cleanse their teeth with a willow stick, and wash their hands and mouth.

Until these ablutions are finished they do not touch one another. Every time they perform the functions of nature they wash their bodies and use perfumes of sandalwood or turmeric.

When the king washes they strike the drums and sing hymns to the sound of musical instruments. Before offering their religious services and petitions, they wash and bathe themselves.

WRITING, LANGUAGE, BOOKS, THE VÊDAS, STUDY

The letters of their alphabet were arranged by Brahmâdêva, and their forms have been handed down from the first till now. They are forty-seven in number, and are combined so as to form words according to the object, and according to circumstances (*of time or place*): there are other forms (*inflexions*) used. This alphabet has spread in different directions and formed diverse branches, according to circumstances; therefore there have been slight modifications in the sounds of the words (*spoken language*); but in its great features there has been no change.

. . .

CASTES—MARRIAGE

With respect to the division of families, there are four classifications. The first is called the Brâhman . . . , men of pure conduct. They guard themselves in religion, live purely, and observe the most correct principles. The second is called Kshattriya . . . , the royal caste. For ages they have been the governing class: they apply themselves to virtue (*humanity*) and kindness. The third is called Vaiśyas . . . , the merchant class: they engage in commercial exchange, and they follow profit at home and abroad. The fourth is called Sûdra . . . , the agricultural class: they labour in ploughing and tillage. In these four classes purity or impurity of caste assigns to every one his place. When they marry they rise or fall in position according to their new relationship. They do not allow promiscuous marriages between relations. A woman once married can never take another husband. Besides these there are other classes of many kinds that intermarry according to their several callings. It would be difficult to speak of these in detail.

ROYAL FAMILY, TROOPS, WEAPONS

The succession of kings is confined to the Kshattriya caste, who by usurpation and bloodshed have from time to time raised themselves to power. Although a distinct caste, they are regarded as honourable (*or* lords).

The chief soldiers of the country are selected from the bravest of the people, and as the sons follow the profession of their fathers, they soon acquire a knowledge of the art of war. These dwell in garrison around the palace (*during peace*), but when on an expedition they march in front as an advanced guard. There are four divisions of the army, viz.—(1) the infantry, (2) the cavalry, (3) the chariots, (4) the elephants. The elephants are covered with strong armour, and their tusks are provided with sharp spurs. A leader in a car gives the command, whilst two attendants on the right and left drive his chariot, which is drawn by four horses abreast. The general of the soldiers remains in the chariot; he is surrounded by a file of guards, who keep close to his chariot wheels.

The cavalry spread themselves in front to resist an attack, and in case of defeat they carry orders hither and thither. The infantry by their quick movements contribute to the defence. These men are chosen for their courage and strength. They carry a long spear and a great shield; sometimes they hold a sword or sabre, and advance to the front with impetuosity. All their weapons of war are sharp and pointed. Some of them are these—spears, shields, bows, arrows, swords, sabres, battle-axes, lances, halberds, long javelins, and various kinds of slings. All these they have used for ages.

. . .

MEDICINES, FUNERAL CUSTOMS, &C.

When a person dies, those who attend the funeral raise lamentable cries and weep together. They rend their garments and loosen their hair; they strike their heads and beat their breasts. There are no regulations as to dress for mourning, nor any fixed time for observing it.

There are three methods of paying the last tribute to the dead: (1) by cremation—wood being made into a pyre, the body is burnt: (2) by water— the body is thrown into deep flowing water and abandoned: (3) by desertion— the body is cast into some forest-wild, to be devoured by beasts.

. . .

PLANTS AND TREES, AGRICULTURE, FOOD, DRINK, COOKERY

. . .

In cultivating the land, those whose duty it is sow and reap, plough and harrow (*weed*), and plant according to the season: and after their labour they rest awhile. Among the products of the ground, rice and corn are most plentiful. With respect to edible herbs and plants, we may name ginger and mustard, melons and pumpkins, . . . and others. Onions and garlic are little grown; and few persons eat them; if any one uses them for food, they are expelled beyond the walls of the town. The most usual food is milk, butter, cream, soft sugar, sugar-candy, the oil of the mustard-seed, and all sorts of cakes made of corn are used as food. Fish, mutton, gazelle, and deer they eat generally fresh, sometimes salted; they are forbidden to eat the flesh of the ox, the ass, the elephant, the horse, the pig, the dog, the fox, the wolf, the lion, the monkey, and all the hairy kind. Those who eat them are despised and scorned, and are universally reprobated; they live outside the walls, and are seldom seen among men.

With respect to the different kinds of wine and liquors, there are various sorts. The juice of the grape and sugarcane, these are used by the Kshattriyas as drink; the Vaiśyas use strong fermented drinks; the . . . Brâhmans drink a sort of syrup made from the grape or sugarcane, but not of the nature of fermented wine.

The mixed classes and base-born differ in no way (*as to food or drink*) from the rest, except in respect of the vessels they use, which are very different both as to value and material. There is no lack of suitable things for household use. Although they have saucepans and stewpans, yet they do not know the steamer used for cooking rice. They have many vessels made of dried clay; they seldom use red copper vessels: they eat from one vessel, mixing all sorts of condiments together, which they take up with their fingers. They have no spoons or cups, and in short no sort of chopstick. When sick, however, they use copper drinking cups.

Commercial Transactions.

Gold and silver, *tcou-shih* (native copper), white jade, fire pearls, are the natural products of the country; there are besides these abundance of rare gems and various kinds of precious stones of different names, which are collected from the islands of the sea. These they exchange for other goods; and in fact they always barter in their commercial transactions, for they have no gold or silver coins, pearl shells, or little pearls.

. . .

84

Account of the Rus by Ibn Fadlan—913 CE

Ibn Fadlan was a tenth century diplomat who was sent from Baghdad to a town on the Volga River in 913 CE. His first contact with the Swedish Vikings who had settled in what is now Russia caused some cross-cultural conflict. After the fall of the Roman Empire, a variety of cultures competed and traded throughout the continent of Europe and the Mediterranean Basin. Which customs of the Rus seemed to have most shocked Fadlan, and what does this tell us about his cultural values?

I saw the Rus when they arrived on their trading mission and anchored at the River Atul [Volga]. Never had I seen people of more perfect physique; they are tall as date-palms, and reddish in colour. They wear neither coat nor mantle, but each man carries a cape which covers one half of his body-leaving one hand free. Their swords are Frankish in pattern, broad, flat, and fluted. Each man has [tattooed upon him] trees, figures, and the like from the finger-nails to the neck. Each woman carries on her bosom a container made of iron, silver, copper, or gold—its size and substance depending on her man's wealth. Attached to the container is a ring carrying her knife which is also tied to her bosom. Round her neck she wears gold or silver rings; when a man amasses 10,000 *dirhems* he makes his wife one gold ring; when he has 20,000 he makes two; and so the woman gets a new ring for every 10,000 *dirhems* her husband acquires, and often a woman has many of these rings. Their finest ornaments are green beads made from clay. They will go to any length to get hold of these; for one *dirhem* they procure one such bead and they string these into necklaces for their women.

They are the filthiest of god's creatures. They do not wash after discharging their natural functions, neither do they wash their hands after meals. They are as stray donkeys. They arrive from their distant lands and lay their ships alongside the banks of the Atul, which is a great river, and there they build big wooden houses on its shores. Ten or twenty of them may live together in one house, and each of them has a couch of his own where he sits and diverts himself with the pretty slave-girls whom he has brought along to offer for sale. He will make love with one of them in the presence of his comrades, sometimes this develops into a communal orgy, and, if a customer should turn up to buy a girl, the Rus will not let her go till he has finished with her.

From Johanees Brondsted, *The Vikings*, trans. Kalle Skov, p. 264-266. Copyright © 1965.
Reprinted by permission of Penguin Group (USA), Inc.

Every day they wash their faces and heads, all using the same water which is as filthy as can be imagined. This is how it is done. Every morning a girl brings her master a large bowl of water in which he washes his face and hands and hair, combing it also over the bowl, then blows his nose and spits into the water. No dirt is left on him which doesn't go into the water. When he has finished the girl takes the same bowl to his neighbour—who repeats the performance—until the bowl has gone round to the entire household. All have blown their noses, spat, and washed their faces and hair in the water.

On anchoring their vessels, each man goes ashore carrying bread, meat, onions, milk, and *nabid* [beer?], and these he takes to a large wooden stake with a face like that of a human being, surrounded by smaller figures, and behind them tall poles in the ground. Each man prostrates himself before the large post and recites: 'O Lord, I have come from distant parts with so many girls, so many sable furs (and whatever other commodities he is carrying). I now bring you this offering.' He then presents his gift and continues 'Please send me a merchant who has many *dinars* and *dirhems*, and who will trade favourably with me without too much bartering.' Then he retires. If, after this, business does not pick up quickly and go well, he returns to the statue to present further gifts. If results continue slow, he then presents gifts to the minor figures and begs their intercession, saying, 'These are our Lord's wives, daughters, and sons.' Then he pleads before each figure in turn, begging them to intercede for him and humbling himself before them.

Often trade picks up, and he says 'My Lord has required my needs, and now it is my duty to repay him.' Whereupon he sacrifices goats or cattle, some of which he distributes as alms. The rest he lays before the statues, large and small, and the heads of the beasts he plants upon the poles. After dark, of course, the dogs come and devour the lot—and the successful trader says, 'My Lord is pleased with me, and has eaten my offerings.'

If one of the Rus falls sick they put him in a tent by himself and leave bread and water for him. They do not visit him, however, or speak to him, especially if he is a serf. Should he recover he rejoins the others; if he dies they burn him. If he happens to be a serf, however, they leave him for the dogs and vultures to devour. If they catch a robber they hang him in a tree until he is torn to shreds by wind and weather.

85

The Dialogue Between Master and Disciple: On Laborers— ca. 1000 CE

The anonymous author of the following dialogue provides considerable information about the lives of peasants and serfs in medieval Europe. Some of the workers discussed are serfs who have little choice in their occupation and are bound to obey the lord of their manor. Which of the workers interviewed seems to have the most freedom and the best working conditions?

Master: What do your companions know?

Disciple: They are plowmen, shepherds, oxherds, huntsmen, fishermen, falconers, merchants, cobblers, salt-makers, and bakers.

Master: What sayest thou plowman? How do you do your work?

Plowman: O my lord, I work very hard: I go out at dawn, driving the cattle to the field, and I yoke them to the plow. Nor is the weather so bad in winter that I dare to stay at home, for fear of my lord: but when the oxen are yoked, and the plowshare and coulter attached to the plow, I must plow one whole field a day, or more.

Master: Have you any assistant?

Plowman: I have a boy to drive the oxen with a goad, and he too is hoarse with cold and shouting.

Master: What more do you do in a day?

Plowman: Certainly I do more. I must fill the manger of the oxen with hay, and water them and carry out the dung.

Master: Indeed, that is a great labor.

Plowman: Even so, it is a great labor for I am not free.

Master: What have you to say shepherd? Have you heavy work too?

Shepherd: I have indeed. In the grey dawn I drive my sheep to the pasture and I stand watch over them, in heat and cold, with my dogs, lest the wolves devour them. And I bring them back to the fold and milk them twice a day. And I move their fold; and I make cheese and butter, and I am faithful to my lord.

Master: Oxherd, what work do you do?

From Thomas Wright, ed. *Anglo-Saxon and Old English Vocabularies* (London: Trubner, 1884), Vol. I, p. 88.

Oxherd: O my lord, I work hard. When the plowman unyokes the oxen I lead them to the pasture and I stand all night guarding them against thieves. Then in the morning I hand them over to the plowman well fed and watered.

Master: What is your craft?

Fisherman: I am a fisherman.

Master: What do you obtain from your work?

Fisherman: Food and clothing and money.

Master: How do you take the fish?

Fisherman: I get into a boat, and place my nets in the water, and I throw out my hook and lines, and whatever they take I keep.

Master: What if the fish should be unclean?

Fisherman: I throw out the unclean fish and use the clean as food.

Master: Where do you sell your fish?

Fisherman: In the town.

Master: Who buys them?

Fisherman: The citizens. I cannot catch as much as I can sell.

Master: What fish do you take?

Fisherman: Herring, salmon, porpoises, sturgeon, oysters, crabs, mussels, periwinkles, cockles, plaice, sole, lobsters, and the like.

Master: Do you wish to capture a whale?

Fisherman: No.

Master: Why?

Fisherman: Because it is a dangerous thing to capture a whale. It is safer for me to go to the river with my boat than to go with many ships hunting whales.

Master: Why so?

Fisherman: Because I prefer to take a fish that I can kill rather than one which with a single blow can sink or kill not only me but also my companions.

Master: Yet many people do capture whales and escape the danger, and they obtain a great price for what they do.

Fisherman: You speak the truth, but I do not dare because of my cowardice.

86

A Buddhist Commentary, "On the Salvation of Women"—ND

This brief excerpt from an Indian Buddhist commentary provides some insight into the status of women in that society. How does this view compare with that of Gratian in the Decretum?

A BUDDHIST'S COMMENTARY, "ON THE SALVATION OF WOMEN"

We must admit that there are great hindrances in the way of woman's attaining enlightenment . . . the reason is that her sin is grievous, and so she is not allowed to enter the lofty palace of the great Brahma, nor to look upon the clouds which hover over his ministers and people. She is always taken down to a lower seat than the soft-cushioned one of the divine, Indra, and she can never behold the flowers in his thirty-three-citied Heaven. . . .(6)

87

From *Precepts for a Social Life* by Yuan Ts'ai—1178 CE

Yüan Ts'ai, the author of this handbook for women, was a well-educated Chinese bureaucrat who eventually became a high-ranking government official during the Sung Dynasty. The excerpts that follow provide a guide for the role of women in Chinese society. It is difficult to know whether these conditions actually existed in twelfth century China. Yüan Ts'ai may have merely been setting up a model for women's roles and

From David John Lu, ed., *Japan: A Documentary History* (Armouk, New York: M.E. Sharpe, 1997), p. 131–132.

Omit – Source to come..

status during this period. According to this guide, what were the main functions of women in Sung China?

THE PROBLEMS OF WOMEN

WOMEN SHOULD NOT TAKE PART IN AFFAIRS OUTSIDE THE HOME

Women do not take part in extra-familial affairs. The reason is that worthy husbands and sons take care of everything for them, while unworthy ones can always find ways to hide their deeds from the women.

Many men today indulge in pleasure and gambling; some end up mortgaging their lands, and even go so far as to mortgage their houses without their wives' knowledge. Therefore, when husbands are bad, even if wives try to handle outside matters, it is of no use. Sons must have their mothers' signatures to mortgage their family properties, but there are sons who falsify papers and forge signatures, sometimes borrowing money at high interest from people who would not hesitate to bring their claim to court. Other sons sell illicit tea and salt to get money, which, if discovered by the authorities, results in fines. Mothers have no control in such matters. Therefore, when sons are bad, it is useless for mothers to try to handle matters relating to the outside world.

For women, these are grave misfortunes, but what can they do? If husbands and sons could only remember that their wives and mothers are helpless and suddenly repent, would that not be best?

WOMEN'S SYMPATHIES SHOULD BE INDULGED

Without going overboard, people should marry their daughters with dowries appropriate to their family's wealth. Rich families should not consider their daughters outsiders but should give them a share of the property. Sometimes people have incapable sons and so have to entrust their affairs to their daughters' families; even after their deaths, their burials and sacrifices are performed by their daughters. So how can people say that daughters are not as good as sons?

Generally speaking, a woman's heart is very sympathetic. If her parents' family is wealthy and her husband's family is poor, she wants to take her parents' wealth to help her husband's family prosper. If her husband's family is wealthy but her parents' family is poor, then she wants to take from her husband's family to enable her parents to prosper. Her parents and husband should be sympathetic toward her feelings and indulge some of her wishes. When her own sons and daughters are grown and married, if either her son's family or her daughter's family is wealthy while the other is poor, she wishes to take from the wealthy one to give to the poor one. Her sons and daughters should understand her feelings and be somewhat indulgent. But taking from the poor to make the rich richer is unacceptable, and no one should ever go along with it.

ORPHANED GIRLS SHOULD HAVE THEIR MARRIAGES ARRANGED EARLY

When a widow remarries she sometimes has an orphaned daughter not yet engaged. In such cases she should try to get a respectable relative to arrange a marriage for her daughter. She should also seek to have her daughter reared in the house of her future in-laws, with the marriage to take place after the girl has grown up. If the girl were to go along with the mother to her step-father's house, she would not be able to clear herself if she were subjected to any humiliations.

FOR WOMEN OLD AGE IS PARTICULARLY HARD TO BEAR

People say that, though there may be a hundred years allotted to a person's life, only a few reach seventy, for time quickly runs out. But for those destined to be poor, old age is hard to endure. For them, until about the age of fifty, the passage of twenty years seems like only ten; but after that age, ten years can feel as long as twenty. For women who live a long life, old age is especially hard to bear, because most women must rely on others for their existence. Before a woman's marriage, a good father is even more important than a good grandfather; a good brother is even more important than a good father; a good nephew is even more important than a good brother. After her marriage, a good husband is even more important than a good father-in-law; a good son is even more important than a good husband; and a good grandson is even more important than a good son. For this reason women often enjoy comfort in their youth but find their old age difficult to endure. It would be well for their relatives to keep this in mind.

IT IS DIFFICULT FOR WIDOWS TO ENTRUST THEIR FINANCIAL AFFAIRS TO OTHERS

Some wives with stupid husbands are able to manage the family's finances, calculating the outlays and receipts of money and grain, without being cheated by anyone. Of those with degenerate husbands, there are also some who are able to manage the finances with the help of their sons without ending in bankruptcy. Even among those whose husbands have died and whose sons are young, there are occasionally women able to raise and educate their sons, keep the affection of all their relatives, manage the family business, and even prosper. All of these are wise and worthy women. But the most remarkable are the women who manage a household after their husbands have died leaving them with young children. Such women could entrust their finances to their husbands' kinsmen or their own kinsmen, but not all relatives are honorable, and the honorable ones are not necessarily willing to look after other people's business.

When wives themselves can read and do arithmetic, and those they entrust with their affairs have some sense of fairness and duty with regard to food, clothing, and support, then things will usually work out all right. But in most of the rest of the cases, bankruptcy is what happens.

BEWARE OF FUTURE DIFFICULTIES IN TAKING IN FEMALE RELATIVES

You should take into your own house old aunts, sisters, or other female relatives whose children and grandchildren are unfilial and do not support them. However, take precautions. After a woman dies, her unfilial sons or grandsons might make outrageous accusations to the authorities, claiming that the woman died from hunger or cold or left valuables in trunks. When the authorities receive such complaints, they have to investigate and trouble is unavoidable. Thus, while the woman is alive, make it clear to the public and to the government that the woman is bringing nothing with her but herself. Generally, in performing charitable acts, it is best to make certain that they will entail no subsequent difficulties.

BEFORE BUYING A SERVANT GIRL OR CONCUBINE, MAKE SURE OF THE LEGALITY

When buying a female servant or concubine, inquire whether it is legal for her to be indentured or sold before closing the deal. If the girl is impoverished and has no one to rely on, then she should be brought before the authorities to give an account of her past. After guarantors have been secured and an investigation conducted, the transaction can be completed. But if she is not able to give an account of her past, then the agent who offered her for sale should be questioned. Temporarily she may be hired on a salaried basis. If she is ever recognized by her relatives, she should be returned to them.

HIRED WOMEN SHOULD BE SENT BACK WHEN THEIR PERIOD OF SERVICE IS OVER

If you hire a man's wife or daughter as a servant, you should return her to her husband or father on completion of her period of service. If she comes from another district, you should send her back to it after her term is over. These practices are the most humane and are widely carried out by the gentry in the Southeast. Yet there are people who do not return their hired women to their husbands but wed them to others instead; others do not return them to their parents but marry them off themselves. Such actions are the source of many lawsuits.

How can one not have sympathy for those separated from their relatives, removed from their hometowns, who stay in service for their entire lives with neither husbands nor sons? Even in death these women's spirits are left to wander all alone. How pitiful they are!

88

Marco Polo in China—ca. 1270 CE

Marco Polo, a merchant from Venice, traveled to China during the period of the Mongol conquest. The Mongols were disliked by the Chinese people and were often forced to use foreigners such as Polo to function as government officials. It is likely that Marco Polo did take a position in the Mongol government because he stayed in China for 20 years. The story of his travels was transcribed by a professional writer after Polo returned to Italy. If read carefully, this account provides a useful description of thirteenth century China. After reading Polo's account, do you think he was prone to exaggeration or does his account seem to "tell it like it was?"

Upon leaving Va-giu you pass, in the course of three days' journey, many towns, castle and villages, all of them well-inhabited and opulent. The people have an abundance of provisions. At the end of three days you reach the noble and magnificent city of Hangchow, a name that signifies. "The Celestial City." This name it merits from its preeminence, among all others in the world, in point of grandeur and beauty, as well as from its many charms, which might lead an inhabitant to imagine himself in paradise.

This city was frequently visited by Marco Polo, who carefully and diligently observed and inquired into every aspect of it, all of which he recorded in his notes, from which the following particulars are drawn. According to common estimate, this city is a hundred miles around. Its streets and canals are extensive, and there are squares or market places, which are frequented by a prodigious number of people and are exceedingly spacious. It is situated between a fresh, very clear lake and a river of great magnitude, the waters of which run via many canals, both large and small, through every quarter of the city, carrying all sewage into the lake and ultimately to the ocean. This furnishes communication by water, in addition to that by land, to all parts of the town, the canals being of sufficient width for boats and the streets for carriages.

It is commonly said that the number of bridges amounts to twelve thousand. Those which cross the principal canals and are connected with the main streets have arches so high and are built with so much skill that the masts of vessels can pass under them. At the same time, carts and horses can pass over them, so gradual is the upward slope of the arch. If they were not so numerous, there would be no way of crossing from one part to another.

Beyond the city, and enclosing it on that side, there is a moat about forty miles in length, very wide, and issuing from the river mentioned before. This

From Documents in World History, Vol. VI, ed. by Peter Stearns et al. (Glenview, Ill.: Longman, 2002).

was excavated by the ancient kings of the province so that when the river overflowed its banks, the floodwater might be drawn off into this channel. This also serves for defense. The earth dug from it was thrown to the inner side, and forms a mound around the place.

There are within the city ten principal squares or market places, besides innumerable shops along the streets. Each side of these squares is half a mile in length, and in front of them is the main street, forty paces in width and running in a straight line from one end of the city to the other. It is crossed by many low and convenient bridges. These market squares are four miles from each other. Parallel to the main street, but on the opposite side of the squares, runs a very large canal. On the nearer bank of this stand large stone warehouses provided for merchants who arrive from India and other parts with their goods and effects. They are thus situated conveniently close to the market squares. In each of these, three days in every week, from forty to fifty thousand persons come to the markets and supply them with every article that could be desired.

There is a great deal of game of all kinds, such as roebuck, stags, fallow deer, hares, and rabbits, together with partridges, pheasants, quail, hens, capon, and ducks and geese beyond number, for so easily are they bred on the lake that, for the value of a Venetian silver groat, you may purchase a pair of geese and two pair of ducks. There, too, are the houses where they slaughter cattle, such as oxen, calves, kids, and lambs, to furnish the tables of the rich and of leading citizens. . . .

At all seasons there is in the markets a great variety of herbs and fruits, especially pears of an extraordinary size, weighing ten pounds each, that are white inside and very fragrant. There are also peaches in season, both the yellow and white kinds, and of a delicious flavor. . . From the sea, fifteen miles distant, a vast quantity of fish is each day brought up the river to the city. There is also an abundance of fish in the lake, which gives employment at all times to a group of fisherman. . . .

Each of the ten market squares is surrounded with high dwelling houses, in the lower part of which are shops where every kind of manufacture is carried on and every article of trade is offered, including spices, drugs, trinkets, and pearls. In certain shops nothing is sold but the wine of the country, which they make continually and serve out fresh to their customers at a moderate price. Many streets connect with the market squares, and in some of them are many cold baths, attended by servants of both sexes. The men and women who frequent them have been accustomed from childhood to wash in cold water, which they consider highly conducive to health. At these baths, however, they have rooms provided with warm water for the use of strangers who cannot bear the shock of the cold. All are in the habit of washing themselves daily, and especially before their meals. . . .

On each side of the principal street mentioned earlier, which runs from one end of the city to the other, there are great houses and mansions with their gardens, and near these, the dwellings of the artisans who work in the shops of the various trades. At all hours you see such multitudes of people passing to and fro on their personal affairs that providing enough food for them might be thought impossible. But one notes that on every market day the squares are crowded with tradespeople and with articles brought by cart and boat—all of which they sell out. From the sale of a single article such as pepper, some notion may be formed of the vast quantity of meat, wine, groceries, and the like, required by the inhabitants of Hangchow. From an officer in the Great Khan's customs, Marco Polo learned that the amount of pepper bought daily was forty-three loads, each load being 243 pounds.

The inhabitants of the city are idolaters. They use paper money as currency. The men as well as the women are fair-skinned and handsome. Most of them always dress themselves in silk, as a result of the vast quantity of that material produced in Hangchow, exclusive of what the merchants import from other provinces.

Among the handicrafts in the city, twelve are considered superior to the rest as being more generally useful. For each of these there are a thousand workshops, and each shop employs ten, fifteen, or twenty workmen, and in a few instances as many as forty, under their respective masters. . . .

There are on the lake a great number of pleasure vessels or barges that can hold ten, fifteen, or twenty persons. They are from fifteen to twenty paces in length, broad-beamed, and not liable to rock. Men who want to enjoy this pastime in the company either of women friends or other men can hire one of these barges, which are always kept in excellent order, and have suitable seats and tables and every other furnishing needed for a party. The cabins have a flat roof or upper deck, where the boatmen stand; and by means of long poles, which they thrust to the bottom of the lake (which is not more than one or two fathoms in depth), shove the barges along. These cabins are painted inside with various colors and figures; all parts of the vessel are likewise adorned with painting. There are windows on either side, which may be opened to allow the company, as they sit at table, to look out in every direction and feast their eyes on the variety and beauty of the passing scene. The pleasure of this exceeds any that can be derived from amusements on land; for as the lake extends the whole length of the city, you have a distant view, as you stand in the boat, of all its grandeur and beauty, its palaces, temples, large convents, and gardens with great trees growing down to the water's edge, while at the same time you can enjoy the sight of other similar boats continually passing you, filled in like manner with parties in pursuit of amusement. . . .

It must be observed . . . that the streets of Hangchow are all paved with stone and brick, and so too are all the principal roads running from there through the province of Manzi [South China]. By means of these, travelers can go to every part without muddying their feet. But as his Majesty's couriers go on horseback in great haste and cannot ride on pavement, a strip of road is left unpaved for their benefit.

The main street of the city is paved with stone and brick to the width of ten paces on each side, the center strip being filled with gravel and having curved drains for carrying off rain water into nearby canals so that it remains always dry. On this gravel, carriages continually pass to-and-fro. . . .

In every street of this city there are stone buildings or towers. In case a fire breaks out in any quarter, which is by no means unusual since the houses are mostly made of wood, the inhabitants may move their possessions to the safety of these towers.

By a regulation of his Majesty, there is a guard of ten watchmen, stationed under cover on all the principal bridges, five on duty by day and five by night. Each of these guards is provided with a drumlike wooden instrument as well as one of metal, together with a water clock which tells the hours of the day and night. When the first hour of the night has passed, one of the watchmen strikes once on the wooden instrument, and also upon the gong. At the end of the second hour he strikes twice, and so on as the hours advance. The guard is not allowed to sleep and must be always on the alert. In the morning as soon as the sun rises, they strike a single stroke again, as in the evening before, and so on from hour to hour. . . .

In cases of rioting or insurrection among the citizens, this police guard is also utilized; but independently of them, his Majesty always keeps on hand a large body of troops, both infantry and cavalry, under the command of his ablest officers.

For the purposes of the nightly watch, towers of earth have been thrown up at a distance of more than a mile from each other. On top of these is a wooden drum, which, when struck with a mallet by the guard stationed there, can be heard at a great distance. If precautions of this nature were not taken there would be a danger that half the city would be consumed. The usefulness of these guards in case of a popular uprising is obvious. . . .

Every father, or head of a household, is required to list on the door of his house the names of each member of his family, as well as the number of his horses. When any person dies, or leaves the dwelling, the name is struck out; similarly, when anyone is born, the name is added to the list. Thus the authorities know at all times the exact number of inhabitants. The same practice is followed throughout the province of Cathay [North China] as well as Manzi. In like manner, all the keepers of inns and public hotels inscribe the names of those who stay with them, noting the day and the hour of their arrival and departure. A copy of this record is transmitted daily to the magistrates stationed in the market squares.

The *Decretum*: Not in God's Image by Gratian—1140 CE

Gratian, a jurist from Northern Italy, wrote the Decretum to codify canon law during the twelfth century CE. This brief excerpt shows that the status of women in the Catholic Church had changed by this time. As the Church became more established and powerful, the role of women declined both in religious life and within the family. Although the souls of women were equal to those of men, in all other areas their status was inferior. How is the subordinate position of women justified by Gratian? What might have been some of the consequences of these beliefs in later times?

Women should be subject to their men. The natural order for mankind is that women should serve men and children their parents, for it is just that the lesser serve the greater.

The image of God is in man and it is one. Women were drawn from man, who has God's jurisdiction as if he were God's vicar, because he has the image of the one God. Therefore woman is not made in God's image.

Woman's authority is nil; let her in all things be subject to the rule of man. . . . And neither can she teach, nor be a witness, nor give a guarantee, nor sit in judgment.

Adam was beguiled by Eve, not she by him. It is right that he whom woman led into wrongdoing should have her under his direction, so that he may not fail a second time through female levity. [*Corpus Iuris Canonici*]

From Julia O'Faolain and Julia Martines, eds., *Not in God's Image* (New York: Harper & Row, 1973), p. 130.

The Book of Nurture: A Guide for a Youth Serving a Nobleman—1260 CE

By the end of the Middle Ages, there was growing interest in proper dress and behavior for upper-class youth serving noblemen as pages and squires. The following document is ascribed to John Russell, the Marshall and Usher to Duke Henry of Gloucester, and provides rules for correct behavior in serving a lord as well as insight into the lives of the upper class. What seems to have been the main tasks of a page serving a lord at court?

Do not claw your head or your back as if you were after a flea, or stroke your hair as if you sought a louse.

Be not glum, nor twinkle with your eyes, nor be heavy of cheer; and keep your eyes free from winking and watering. [Difficult in days of poor chimneys or no chimneys at all.]

Do not pick your nose or let it drop clear pearls, or sniff, or blow it too loud, lest your lord hear.

Twist not your neck askew like a jackdaw; wring not your hands with picking or trifling or shrugging, as if ye would saw wood; nor puff up your chest, nor pick your ears, nor be slow of hearing.

Retch not, nor spit too far, nor laugh or speak too loud. Beware of making faces and scorning; and be no liar with your mouth. Nor yet lick your lips or drivel.

Do not have the habit of squirting or spouting with your mouth, or gape, or yawn, or pout. And do not lick a dish with your tongue to get out dust.

Be not rash or reckless—that is not worth a clout.

Do not sigh with your breast, or cough, or breathe hard in the presence of your sovereign, or hiccough, or belch, or groan never the more. Do not trample with your feet, or straddle your legs, or scratch your body—there is no sense in showing off. Good son, do not pick your teeth, or grind, or gnash them, or with puffing and blowing cast foul breath upon your lord. . . Other faults on this matter, I spare not to disapprove in my opinion, when a servant is waiting on his master at table. Every sober sovereign must despise all such things. . .

In the morning, against your lord shall rise, take care that his linen be clean, and warm it at a clear fire, not smoky, if the weather be cold or freezing.

From Edith Rickert, trans., *The Babees Book*, (London: Chatto and Windus, 1923).

When he rises make ready the foot-sheet, and forget not to place a chair or some other seat with a cushion on it before the fire, with another cushion for the feet. Over the cushion and chair spread this sheet so as to cover them; and see that you have a kerchief and a comb to comb your lord's head before he is fully dressed.

Then pray your lord in humble words to come to a good fire and array him thereby, and there to sit or stand pleasantly; and wait with due manners to assist him. First hold out to him his tunic, then his doublet while he puts in his arms, and have his stomacher well aired to keep off harm, as also his vamps and socks, and so shall he go warm all day.

Then draw on his socks and his hose by the fire, and lace or buckle his shoes, draw his hosen on well and truss them up to the height that suits him, lace his doublet in every hole, and put round his neck and on his shoulders a kerchief; and then gently comb his head with an ivory comb, and give him water wherewith to wash his hands and face.

Then kneel down on your knee and say thus: "Sir, what robe or gown doth it please you to wear today?" Then get him such as he asks for, and hold it out for him to put on, and do on his girdle, if he wear one, tight or loose, arrange his robe in the proper fashion, give him a hood or hat for his head, a cloak or house-cape, according as it be fair or foul, or all misty with rain; and so shall ye please him. Before he goes out, brush busily about him, and whether he wear satin, sendal, velvet, scarlet, or grain, see that all be clean and nice . . .

Then return in haste to your lord's chamber, strip the clothes off the bed and cast them aside, and beat the feather-bed, but not so as to waste any feathers, and see that the blankets and sheets be clean. When you have made the bed mannerly, cover it with a coverlet, spread out the bench-covers, and cushions, set up the head-sheet and pillow, and remove the basin. See that carpets be laid round the bed and dress the windows, and the cupboard with carpets and cushions. See there be a good fire conveyed into the chamber, with plenty of wood and fuel to make it up.

You must attend busily to your lord's wardrobe, to keep the clothes well, and to brush them cleanly. Use a soft brush, and remember that overmuch brushing easily wears out cloth.

Never let woolen clothes or furs go a seven-night without being brushed or shaken, for moths be always ready to alight in them and engender; so always keep an eye on drapery and skinnery.

If your lord take a long nap after his meal to digest his stomach, have ready kerchief and comb, pillow and headsheet; yet be not far from him—take heed what I say—for much sleep is not good in the middle of the day, and have ready water and towel so that he may wash after his sleep . . .

A BATH OR STEW SO-CALLED

If your lord wishes to bathe and wash his body clean, hang sheets round the roof, every one full of flowers and sweet green herbs, and have five or six sponges to sit or lean upon, and see that you have one big sponge to sit upon, and a sheet over so that he may bathe there for a while, and have a sponge also for under his feet, if there be any to spare, and always be careful that the door is shut. Have a basin full of hot fresh herbs and wash his body with a soft sponge, rinse him with fair warm rose-water, and throw it over him; then let him go to bed; but see that the bed be sweet and nice; and first put on his socks and slippers that he may go near the fire and stand on his foot-sheet, wipe him dry with a clean cloth, and take him bed to cure his troubles.

91

Sorbonne's Regulations for his College—13th century CE

The Sorbonne is the former name of the University of Paris, which was founded in 1257 CE by Robert de Sorbon (Sorbonne) as a college for theological studies. Sorbon was both chaplain and confessor to King Louis the IX of France; he was also a noted scholar. His college quickly gained such a good reputation that by the end of the thirteenth century CE, there were 20,000 foreign students attending the school, and Paris had become the seat of Western knowledge. Which of the following rules seem to be directed at controlling a large body of foreign students in Paris?

I wish that the custom which was instituted from the beginning in this house by the counsel of good men may be kept, and if anyone ever has transgressed it, that henceforth he shall not presume to do so.

No one therefore shall eat meat in the house on Advent, nor on Monday or Tuesday of Lent, nor from Ascension Day to Pentecost.

Also, I will that the community be not charged for meals taken in rooms. If there cannot be equality, it is better that the fellow eating in his room be charged than the entire community.

Also, no one shall eat in his room except for cause. If anyone has a guest, he shall eat in hall. If, moreover, it shall not seem expedient to the fellow to bring that guest to hall, let him eat in his room and he shall have the usual portion for himself, not for the guest. If, moreover, he wants more for himself or his guest, he should pay for it himself. . . .

Also, the fellows should be warned by the bearer of the roll that those eating in private rooms conduct themselves quietly and abstain from too much

From Lynn Thorndike, ed. and trans. *University Records and Life in the Middle Ages* (New York: Columbia University Press, 1944), p. 88–98.

noise, lest those passing through the court and street be scandalized and lest the fellows in rooms adjoining be hindered in their studies. . . .

Also, the rule does not apply to the sick. If anyone eats in a private room because of sickness, he may have a fellow with him, if he wishes, to entertain and wait on him, who also shall have his due portion. What shall be the portion of a fellow shall be left to the discretion of the dispenser. If a fellow shall come late to lunch, if he comes from classes or a sermon or business of the community, he shall have his full portion, but if from his own affairs, he shall have bread only. . . .

Also, all shall wear closed outer garments, nor shall they have trimmings of vair or grise[7] or of red or green silk on the outer garment or hood.

Also, no one shall have loud shoes or clothing by which scandal might be generated in any way.

Also, no one shall be received in the house unless he shall be willing to leave off such and to observe the aforesaid rules.

Also, no one shall be received in the house unless he pledges faith that, if he happens to receive books from the common store, he will treat them carefully as if his own and on no condition remove or lend them out of the house, and return them in good condition whenever required or whenever he leaves town.

Also, let every fellow have his own mark on his clothes and one only and different from the others. And let all the marks be written on a schedule and over each mark the name of whose it is. And let that schedule be given to the servant so that he may learn to recognize the mark of each one. And the servant shall not receive clothes from any fellow unless he sees the mark. And then the servant can return his clothes to each fellow. . . .

Also, for peace and utility we propound that no secular person living in town—scribe, corrector, or anyone else—unless for great cause eat, sleep in a room, or remain with the fellows when they eat, or have frequent conversation in the gardens or hall or other parts of the house, lest the secrets of the house and the remarks of the fellows be spread abroad.

Also, no outsider shall come to accountings or the special meetings of the fellows, and he whose guest he is shall see to this.

Also, no fellow shall bring in outsiders frequently to drink at commons, and if he does, he shall pay according to the estimate of the dispenser.

Also, no fellow shall have a key to the kitchen.

Also, no fellow shall presume to sleep outside the house in town, and if he did so for reason, he shall take pains to submit his excuse to the bearer of the roll. . . .

Also, no women of any sort shall eat in the private rooms. If anyone violates this rule, he shall pay the assessed penalty, namely, sixpence.[8] . . .

Also, no one shall form the habit of talking too loudly at table. Whoever after he has been warned about this by the prior shall have offended by speaking too loudly, provided this is established afterwards by testimony of several fellows to the prior, shall be held to the usual house penalty, namely two quarts of wine.

---

7 vair: squirrel fur. grise: any type of gray fur.

8 This was a substantial amount for most students to pay.

The penalty for transgression of statutes which do not fall under an oath is twopence, if the offenders are not reported by someone, or if they were, the penalty becomes sixpence in the case of fines. I understand "not reported" to mean that, if before the matter has come to the attention of the prior, the offender accuses himself to the prior or has told the clerk to write down twopence against him for such an offence, for it is not enough to say to the fellows, "I accuse myself."

92

The Goodman of Paris: Instructions on Being a Good Wife—late 14th century CE

There is relatively little information available regarding the history of women during the Middle Ages. However, the following excerpt—a letter purportedly written by a Parisian merchant to his wife—is actually a manual of wifely conduct. In it, the anonymous author provides some insight into the duties of a wealthy man's wife during the late Middle Ages. What kind of an education would have prepared a young woman to take on such duties?

THE FIRST SECTION

The first section of the three is necessary to gain the love of God and the salvation of your soul, and also to win the love of your husband and to give you in this world that peace which should be in marriage. And because these two things, namely the salvation of your soul and the comfort of your husband, be the two things most chiefly necessary, therefore are they here placed first. And this first section contains nine articles.

The first article speaketh of worshipping and thanking our Saviour and his Blessed Mother at your waking and your rising, and of apparelling yourself seemingly.

From Eileen Power, trans. *The Goodman of Paris* (London: Routledge & Kegan Paul, 1928), p. 43–46.

The second article is of fit companions, and of going to Church, and of choosing your place, of wise behaviour, of hearing mass and of making confession.

The third article is that you should love God and his Blessed Mother and serve them continually and set and keep yourself in their grace.

The fourth article is that you should dwell in continence and chastity, after the ensample of Susanna, of Lucrece, and others.

The fifth article is that you should love your husband (whether myself or another) after the ensample of Sarah, Rebecca and Rachel.

The sixth article is that you should be humble and obedient to him after the ensample of Griselda, of the woman who would not rescue her husband from drowning, and of the Mother of God who answered "fiat" etc., of Lucifer, of the *puys*, of the bailly of Tournay, of the monks and the husbands, of madame d'Andresel, of Chaumont and of the Roman woman.

The seventh that you be careful and heedful of his person.

The eighth that you be silent in hiding his secrets, after the ensample of Papirius, of the woman who laid eight eggs, of the Venetian woman, of the woman who returned from St James (of Compestollo), and of the advocate.

The ninth and last article showeth that if your husband try to act foolishly or so acteth, you must wisely and humbly withdraw him therefrom, like unto Melibeus and dame Jehanne la Quentine.

THE SECOND SECTION

The second section is necessary to increase the profit of the household, gain friends and save one's possessions; to succour and aid oneself against the ill fortunes of age to come, and it contains six [*sic*] articles.

The first article is that you have care of your household, with diligence and perseverence and regard for work; take pains to find pleasure therein and I will do likewise on my part, and so shall we reach the castle whereof it is spoken.

The second article is that at the least you take pleasure and have some little skill in the care and cultivation of a garden, grafting in due season and keeping roses in winter.

The third article is that you know how to choose varlets, doorkeepers, handymen or other strong folk to perform the heavy work that from hour to hour must be done, and likewise labourers etc. And also tailers, shoemakers, bakers, pastry-makers, etc. And in particular how to set the household varlets and chambermaids to work, to sift and winnow grain, clean dresses, air and dry, and how to order your folk to take thought for the sheep and horses and to keep and amend wines.

The fourth article is that you, as sovereign mistress of your house, know how to order dinners, suppers, dishes and courses, and be wise in that which concerns the butcher and the poulterer, and have knowledge of spices.

The fifth article is that you know how to order, ordain, devise and have made all manner of pottages, civeys, sauces and all other meats, and the same for sick folk.

THE THIRD SECTION

The third section tells of games and amusements that be pleasant enough to keep you in countenance and give you something to talk about in company, and contains three articles.

The first article is all concerned with amusing questions, which be shown forth and answered in strange fashion by the hazard of dice and by rooks and kings.

The second article is to know how to feed and fly the falcon.

The third article tells of certain other riddles concerning counting and numbering, which be subtle to find out and guess.

93

Travels in Africa
by Ibn Battuta—1304–1369 CE

The North African traveler Ibn Battuta traveled to Mali in sub-Saharan Africa in 1352. There, he encountered the kingdom of the fabulously weathly Mansa Musa, a convert to Islam. Battuta was the Arabic equivalent of Marco Polo, although he covered more territory. He was born in Morocco and returned there after his travels. Battuta's memoirs are preserved in a volume called the Ribla *("My Travels"). What seems to impress Battuta about the Malians? Of what does he disapprove?*

ANECDOTE CONCERNING THE MASSŪFA
WHO INHABIT IWĀLĀTAN

The condition of these people is strange and their manners outlandish. As for their men, there is no sexual jealousy in them. And none of them derives his genealogy from his father but, on the contrary, from his maternal uncle. A man does not pass on inheritance except to the sons of his sister to the exclusion of

From *Ibn Battuta in Black Africa*, ed. by Said Hamdum and Noel King (London: Rex Collings, 1975), 27–29, 36–39, 47–78. Reprinted by permission of Markus Weiner Publishers, Inc.

his own sons. Now that is a thing I never saw in any part of the world except in the country of the unbelievers of the land of Mulaībār [Malabar] among the Indians. As to the former [the Massūfa], they are Muslims keeping to the prayers, studying *fiqh* [Islamic jurisprudence], and learning the Qur'ān by heart. With regard to their women, they are not modest in the presence of men, they do not veil themselves in spite of their perseverance in the prayers. He who wishes to marry among them can marry, but the women do not travel with the husband, and if one of them wanted to do that, she would be prevented by her family. The women there have friends and companions amongst men outside the prohibited degrees of marriage [i.e., other than brothers, fathers, etc.]. Likewise for the men, there are companions from amongst women outside the prohibited degrees. One of them would enter his house to find his wife with her companion and would not disapprove of that conduct. . . .

The sultan [emperor of Mali] has a raised cupola which is entered from inside his house. He sits in it a great part of the time. It has on the audience side a chamber with three wooden arches, the woodwork is covered with sheets of beaten silver and beneath these, three more covered with beaten gold, or, rather, it is silver covered with gilt. The windows have woollen curtains which are raised on a day when the sultan will be in session in his cupola: thus it is known that he is holding a session. When he sits, a silken cord is put out from the grill of one of the arches with a scarf of Egyptian embroidery tied to it. When the people see the scarf, drums are beaten and bugles sounded. Then from the door of the palace come out about three hundred slaves. Some have bows in their hands and some small spears and shields. Some of the spearmen stand on the right and some on the left, the bowmen sit likewise. Then they bring two mares saddled and bridled, and with them two rams. They say that these are effective against the evil eye. When the sultan has sat down three of his slaves go out quickly to call his deputy, Qanjā Musā. The *farāriyya* [commanders] arrive, and they are the *amīrs* [officers], and among them are the preacher and the men of *fiqh*, who sit in front of the armed men on the right and left of the place of audience. The interpreter Dūghā stands at the door of the audience chamber wearing splendid robes of *zardkhuāna* [official] and others. On his head is a turban which has fringes, they have a superb way of tying a turban. He is girt with a sword whose sheath is of gold, on his feet are light boots and spurs. And nobody wears boots that day except he. In his hands there are two small spears, one of gold and one of silver with points of iron. The soldiers, the district governors, the pages and the Massūfa and others are seated outside the place of audience in a broad street which has trees in it. Each *farārī* [commander] has his followers before him with their spears, bows, drums and bugles made of elephant tusks. Their instruments of music are made of reeds and calabashes, and they beat them with sticks and produce a wonderful sound. Each *farārī* has a quiver which he places between his shoulders. He holds his bow in his hand and is mounted on a mare. Some of his men are on foot and some on mounts.

Inside the audience chamber under the arches a man is standing; he who wants to speak to the sultan speaks to Dūghā, Dūghā speaks to the man who is standing, and he speaks to the sultan.

AN ACCOUNT OF THE SESSIONS IN THE PLACE OF AUDIENCE

The sultan sits on certain days in the palace yard to give audience. There is a platform under a tree with three steps which they call *banbī*. It is covered with silk and has pillows placed on it. The *shatr* [umbrella] is raised, this is a shelter made of silk with a golden bird like a sparrowhawk above it. The sultan comes out from a gate in the corner of the palace, bow in hand, his quiver between his shoulders, and on his head a cap of gold tied with a golden band which has fringes like thin-bladed knives more than a span long. He often wears a robe which is soft and red, made from Roman cloth called *mutanfas*. The singers go out before him carrying gold and silver *qanābir* [guitars] and behind him come three hundred armed slaves. The sultan walks slowly and pauses often and sometimes he stops completely. When he comes to the *banbī* he stops and looks at the people. Then he mounts the steps with dignity in the manner of a preacher getting into the pulpit. When he sits down they beat the drums, blow the bugles and the horns, and three of the slaves go out in haste and call the deputy and the *farāriyya* [commanders]. They enter and sit down. The two mares are brought in with the two rams. Damughā stands at the door while the rest of the people are in the street under the tree. The blacks are the most humble of men before their king and the most extreme in their self-abasement before him. They swear by his name, saying 'Mansā Sulaimānkī' [the law of Mansā Sulaimānkī]. When he calls one of them while he is in session in his cupola which we described above, the man invited takes off his clothes and wears patched clothes, takes off his turban, puts on a dirty cap, and goes in raising his clothes and trousers up his legs half-way to his knees. He advances with humility looking like a beggar. He hits the ground with his elbows, he hits it hard. He stands bowed, like one in the *rukuʿ* position in prayer, listening to what the king says. When one of them speaks to the sultan and he gives him an answer, he removes his clothes from his back and throws dust on his head and back, as a person does when bathing with water. I used to wonder how they do not blind their eyes. When the sultan speaks in his council, at his word those present take their turbans off their heads and listen to the speech. . . .

Amongst their good qualities is the small amount of injustice amongst them, for of all people they are the furthest from it. Their sultan does not forgive anyone in any matter to do with justice. Among these qualities there is also the prevalence of peace in their country, the traveller is not afraid in it nor is he who lives there in fear of the thief or of the robber by violence. They do not interfere with the property of the white man who dies in their country even though it may consist of great wealth, but rather they entrust it to the hand of someone dependable among the white men until it is taken by the rightful claimant.

Another of the good habits amongst them is the way they meticulously observe the times of the prayers and attendance at them, so also it is with regard to their congregational services and their beating of their children to instill these things in them.

When it is Friday, if a man does not come early to the mosque he will not find a place to pray because of the numbers of the crowd. It is their custom for every man to send his boy with his prayer mat. He spreads it for him in a place commensurate with his position and keeps the place until he comes to the mosque. Their prayer-mats are made of the leaves of a tree like a date palm but it bears no fruit.

Among their good qualities is their putting on of good white clothes on Friday. If a man among them has nothing except a tattered shirt, he washes and cleans it and attends the Friday prayer in it. Another of their good qualities is their concern for learning the sublime Qur'ān by heart. They make fetters for their children when they appear on their part to be falling short in their learning of it by heart, and they are not taken off from them till they do learn by heart. I went in to visit the *qāī* on an 'Id day and his children were tied up. I said to him, 'Why do you not release them?' He said, 'I shall not do so until they learn the Qur'ān by heart.' One day I passed by a handsome youth from them dressed in fine clothes and on his feet was a heavy chain. I said to the man who was with me, 'What has this youth done—has he killed someone?' The youth heard my remark and laughed. It was told me, 'He has been chained so that he will learn the Qur'ān by heart.'

Among the bad things which they do—their serving women, slave women and little daughters appear before people naked, exposing their private parts. I used to see many of them in this state in Ramadān, for it was the custom of the *farāiyya* [commanders] to break the fast in the sultan's house. Everyone of them has his food carried in to him by twenty or more of his slave girls and they are naked, every one. Also among their bad customs is the way women will go into the presence of the sultan naked, without any covering; and the nakedness of the sultan's daughters—on the night of the twenty-seventh of Ramadān, I saw about a hundred slave girls coming out of his palace with food, with them were two of his daughters, they had full breasts and no clothes on. Another of their bad customs is their putting of dust and ashes on their heads as a sign of respect. And another is the laughing matter I mentioned of their poetic recitals. And another is that many of them eat animals not ritually slaughtered, and dogs and donkeys.

94

Tale of a Chinese
Weaver—1400 CE

*The weaving of silk and cotton fabrics was performed in peasant huts and merchant work-
shops during the Ming dynasty. Skilled weavers of brocade and other luxury cloth enjoyed
better working conditions than the average unskilled worker. Although this excerpt is actually a moral tale, the author, a Chinese scholar, provides us with considerable information
about a weaver's life in 1400 CE. What seems to be the moral of this story? What does
it tell you about the Confucian values that dominated Chinese society at this time?*

When I lived in Hsiang-an Ward in Ch'ien-t'ang, I had a wealthy
neighbor who employed live-in weavers. Late every evening one of
them would start to sing and the rest would join in. From the sound
of their voices, they seemed to be cheerful. "How happy they are!" I sighed.

One morning I walked over there and found it to be just a rickety old house.
There were four or five looms in a room, arranged in a row from the north to
south, and about ten workers, all of whom were laboring with both hands and
feet. They looked pale and spiritless. I called one worker over and said, "From
what I have seen, your work is very hard. Why are you still so happy?"

The worker replied, "Happiness is determined by the thoughts in a person's
mind. If he isn't greedy, he can be happy with very little. But those who are
greedy may earn a thousand strings of cash a day and still always feel unhappy.
Though my job is a humble one, I can earn two hundred strings of cash a day.
The master provides me with food and clothes, so I can use my wages to support
my parents, wife, and children. We are far from having delicious food, yet neither
are we suffering from hunger or cold. I consider my life a normal one; I am not
discontent, and the material I weave is very beautiful and highly valued by people. Thus, the master can easily sell the products and we are able to earn our
wages easily. Since this is all we really want, our inner contentment naturally
comes out in our voices as we sing together. We do not think of the hardship of
the work.

Not long ago, there was a weaver employed in another workshop. He
earned approximately the same amount of money as we do. Yet, after working
for a while, he started to complain: 'I am a more skillful weaver than anyone

From Patricia Ebrey, ed. Chinese Civilization and Society: A Sourcebook (New York: Free
Press, 1981). Reprinted by permission of Free Press, a division of Simon & Schuster Adult
Publishing.

else, but I still get the same wages. I am going to work for someone who will pay me twice as much. Later on, one workshop owner did offer him double. The master examined his work and noticed that it was indeed superior, and the other weavers, after seeing his skill, also respected him highly. The master was very happy, thinking, 'This one weaver's work is better than that of ten others put together. It is well worth doubling his pay.' After working for a while, the weaver again became dissatisfied. He thought, 'I am such a superior weaver that if I leave this occupation and engage in another, I will undoubtedly be superior in that one, too. If I take employment under a high official, by playing up to him and serving him wholeheartedly, I will be able to gain great wealth and glory for myself. Why should I work in a weaving factory forever?'

Eventually he did take a position serving a high official. He worked among the slaves taking care of carriages and horses, and for five years did not find anything he could consider an opportunity for wealth and glory. Then one day, after another five years had passed, he provoked the official, who became infuriated and dismissed him and refused to see him ever again. By that time, the weaver had already forgotten his former trade. Moreover, people were disgusted with his arrogance and inability to be content, and no one wanted to hire him to weave. In the end he died of hunger and cold.

I took this person as a warning. How could I fail to feel content and happy?"

This worker is indeed content and exemplifies what Lao Tzu meant when he said, "One who knows how to be satisfied will always be satisfied." This is why I recorded his story. At the time of our conversation, there were about ten workers present. The one who talked to me was named Yao.

CHAPTER 11

Arts and Culture— 500–1500 CE

The art of writing for nonreligious purposes first developed in the East. However, by the fourteenth century CE, Western writers had begun to produce tales in the vernacular that were written to amuse rather than edify the individual. This section contains documents primarily from the rich store of Eastern poems, fables, and novels that would later provide inspiration for Western writers. By this time, many Eastern societies held literate and elaborate courts that produced a large volume of literature. By contrast, Western rulers lived in a relatively simple style, and literacy was still somewhat limited. The Catholic Church was still influential, but Western writers had become increasingly critical of their civil society and religious institutions by the end of the Middle Ages. What do the poems and stories from China and Japan tell us about the values of their society? How does their literature compare with the examples from the West?

95

Stories from *The Panchatantra*—6th century CE

The Panchatantra are five volumes of stories dating from the golden age of India. Although their author is unknown, the tales were supposedly written by a teacher for the instruction of princes. These magical stories all contain a moral, yet they are so charming that many of them have found their way into Western literature and have certainly influenced medieval European writers. What can you learn from these tales about the values of India during the Gupta dynasty?

One Vishnusharman, shrewdly gleaning
All worldly wisdom's inner meaning,
In these five books the charm compresses
Of all such books the world possesses.
And this is how it happened.

In the southern country is a city called Maidens' Delight. There lived a king named Immortal-Power. He was familiar with the works treating of the wise conduct of life. His feet were made dazzling by the tangle of rays of light from jewels in the diadems of mighty kings who knelt before him. He had reached the far shore of all the arts that embellish life. This king had three sons. Their names were Rich-Power, Fierce-Power, Endless-Power, and they were supreme blockheads.

Now when the king perceived that they were hostile to education, he summoned his counselors and said: "Gentlemen, it is known to you that these sons of mine, being hostile to education, are lacking in discernment. So when I behold them, my kingdom brings me no happiness, though all external thorns are drawn. For there is wisdom in the proverb:

Of sons unborn, or dead, or fools,
    Unborn or dead will do;
They cause a little grief, no doubt;
    But fools, a long life through.

And again:

To what good purpose can a cow

From *The Panchatantra* trans. by Arthur W. Ryder (Chicago: University of Chicago Press, 1925).

That brings no calf nor milk, be bent?
Or why beget a son who proves
    A dunce and disobedient?

Some means must therefore be devised to awaken their intelligence."

And they, one after another, replied: "O King, first one learns grammar, in twelve years. If this subject has somehow been mastered, then one masters the books on religion and practical life. Then the intelligence awakens."

But one of their number, a counselor named Keen, said: "O King, the duration of life is limited, and the verbal sciences require much time for mastery. Therefore let some kind of epitome be devised to wake their intelligence. There is a proverb that says:

Since verbal science has no end,
Since life is short, and obstacles impend,
Let central facts be picked and firmly fixed,
As swans extract the milk with water mixed.

Now there is a Brahman here named Vishnusharman, with a reputation for competence in numerous sciences. Intrust the princes to him. He will certainly make them intelligent in a twinkling."

When the king had listened to this, he summoned Vishnusharman and said: "Holy sir, as a favor to me you must make these princes incomparable masters of the art of practical life. In return, I will bestow upon you a hundred land-grants."

And Vishnusharman made answer to the king: "O King, listen. Here is the plain truth. I am not the man to sell good learning for a hundred land-grants. But if I do not, in six months' time, make the boys acquainted with the art of intelligent living, I will give up my own name. Let us cut the matter short. Listen to my lion-roar. My boasting arises from no greed for cash. Besides, I have no use for money; I am eighty years old, and all the objects of sensual desire have lost their charm. But in order that your request may be granted, I will show a sporting spirit in reference to artistic matters. Make a note of the date. If I fail to render your sons, in six months' time, incomparable masters of the art of intelligent living, then His Majesty is at liberty to show me his Majestic bare bottom."

When the king, surrounded by his counselors, had listened to the Brahman's highly unconventional promise, he was penetrated with wonder, intrusted the princes to him, and experienced supreme content.

Meanwhile, Vishnusharman took the boys, went home and made them learn by heart five books which he composed and called: (I) "The Loss of Friends," (II) "The Winning of Friends," (III) "Crows and Owls," (IV) "Loss of Gains," (V) "Ill-Considered Action."

These the princes learned, and in six months' time they answered the prescription. Since that day this work on the art of intelligent living, called *Panchatantra*, or the "Five Books," has traveled the world, aiming at the awakening of intelligence in the young. To sum the matter up:

> Whoever learns the work by heart,
> Or through the story-teller's art
>   Becomes acquainted,
> His life by sad defeat—although
> The king of heaven be his foe—
>   Is never tainted.

When this had been done, the lion was brought to life, rose up, and killed all three. But the man of sense, after the lion had gone elsewhere, climbed down and went home.

And that is why I say:

> Scholarship is less than sense;
> Therefore seek intelligence:
> Senseless scholars in their pride
> Made a lion; then they died.

96

"Watching the Wheat Reapers" and Other Poems About Peasant Life From the Tang Dynasty—618–907 CE

The following poems were written by government officials during one of China's golden ages of artistic development. Po Chu-yi (772-846 CE) was the first great popular poet in China. His verses were often inscribed on the walls of inns and monasteries. Though educated men, government officials such as Po Chu-yi were able to describe the daily lives of simple peasant farmers in sympathetic yet elegant verse. Evading military service is a popular theme in the poetry of the Tang dynasty; what does this tell you about the regard the Chinese had for military service? How do you think the authors felt about the

Poems by PO CHÜ-YI (772–846) and FROM P ʻI JIH-HSIU (ca. 833–883).

people they wrote about? How do these poems compare with the literary works of other societies during the Middle Ages?

FROM PO CHÜ-YI (772–846)

Watching the Wheat-reapers

Farm families have few leisure months,
In the fifth month chores double up.
When south wind rises at night,
Fields and dikes are covered with golden wheat.

Women old and young carry baskets of food,
Children and toddlers bring out porridge in pots,
Following each other with food for the farmhands,
Those stout fellows on the southern knoll.

Their feet steamed by the sultry vapor from the soil,
Their backs scorched by the sun's burning light;
Drained of all strength to feel any heat,
Their only regret, summer days are too short.

Then there are those poor womenfolk,
Their children clinging to their side.
With their right hand they pick up leftover grains;
On their left arm dangles a broken basket.

To hear their words of complaint—
All who listen will grieve for them:
Their family land stripped clean to pay tax,
They now glean the field to fill their stomach.

What deeds of merit have I done?
I've neither farmed nor raised silkworms;
My official's salary, three hundred piculs of rice,
And at year's end there is surplus grain to eat.

Thinking of this, I feel guilty and ashamed;
All day long I cannot keep it out of my mind.

The Old Man of Hsin-feng with the Broken Arm

An old man from Hsin-feng, eighty-eight years old,
Hair on his temples and his eyebrows white as snow.
Leaning on his great-great-grandson, he walks to the front of the inn,

His left arm on the boy's shoulder, his right arm broken.
I ask the old man how long has his arm been broken,
And how it came about, how it happened.
The old man said he grew up in the Hsin-feng district.
He was born during blessed times, without war or strife,
And he used to listen to the singing and dancing in the Pear Garden,
Knew nothing of banner and spear, or bow and arrow.
Then, during the T'ien-pao period, a big army was recruited:
From each family, one was taken out of every three,
And of those chosen, where were they sent?
Five months, ten thousand miles away, to Yunnan,
Where, it is said, the Lu River runs,
Where, when flowers fall from pepper trees, noxious fumes rise;
Where, when a great army fords the river, with its seething eddies,
Two or three out of ten never reach the other side.

The village, north and south, was full of the sound of wailing,
Sons leaving father and mother, husbands leaving wives.
They all said, of those who went out to fight the barbarians,
Not one out of a thousand lived to come back.
At the time, this old man was twenty-four,
And the army had his name on their roster.

"Then, late one night, not daring to let anyone know,
By stealth, I broke my arm, smashed it with a big stone.
Now I was unfit to draw the bow or carry the flag,
And I would be spared the fighting in Yunnan.
Bone shattered, muscles ached, it wasn't unpainful,
But I could count on being rejected and sent home.

"This arm has been broken now for over sixty years:
I've lost one limb, but the body's intact.
Even now, in cold nights, when the wind and rain blow,
Right up to daybreak, I hurt so much I cannot sleep,
But I have never had any regrets.
At least, now I alone have survived.
Or else, years ago at the River Lu,
I would have died, my spirit fled, and my bones left to rot:
I would have wandered, a ghost in Yunnan looking for home,
Mourning over the graves of ten thousands."
So the old man spoke: I ask you to listen.
Have you not heard the Prime Minister of the K'ai-yüan period, Sung
    K'ai-fu?
How he wouldn't reward frontier campaigns, not wanting to glorify war?
And, have you not heard of Yang Kuo-chung, the Prime Minister of the
    T'ien-pao period,
Wishing to seek favor, achieved military deeds at the frontier,

But, before he could pacify the frontier, the people became disgruntled:
Ask the old man of Hsin-feng with the broken arm!

An Old Charcoal Seller

An old charcoal seller
Cuts firewood, burns coal by the southern mountain.
His face, all covered with dust and ash, the color of smoke,
The hair at his temples is gray, his ten fingers black.
The money he makes selling coal, what is it for?
To put clothes on his back and food in his mouth.
The rags on his poor body are thin and threadbare;
Distressed at the low price of coal, he hopes for colder weather.
Night comes, an inch of snow has fallen on the city,
In the morning, he rides his cart along the icy ruts,
His ox weary, he hungry, and the sun already high.
In the mud by the south gate, outside the market, he stops to rest.
All of a sudden, two dashing riders appear;
An imperial envoy, garbed in yellow (his attendant in white),
Holding an official dispatch, he reads a proclamation.
Then turns the cart around, curses the ox, and leads it north.
One cartload of coal—a thousand or more catties!
No use appealing to the official spiriting the cart away:
Half a length of red lace, a slip of damask
Dropped on the ox—is payment in full!

FROM P'I JIH-HSIU (ca. 833–883)

Lament of a Woman Acorn-gatherer

Deep into autumn the acorns ripen,
Scattering as they fall into the scrub on the hill.
Hunched over, a hoary-haired crone
Gathers them, treading the morning frost.
After a long time she's got only a handful,
An entire day just fills her basket.
First she suns them, then steams them,
To use in making late winter provisions.

At the foot of the mountain she has ripening rice,
From its purple spikes a fragrance pervades.
Carefully she reaps, then hulls the grain,
Kernel after kernel like a jade earring.
She takes the grain to offer as government tax,
In her own home there are no granary bins.
How could she know that well over a picul of rice
Is only five pecks in official measurement?

Those crafty clerks don't fear the law,
Their greedy masters won't shun a bribe.
In the growing season she goes into debt.
In the off season sends grain to government bin.
From winter even into spring,
With acorns she tricks her hungry innards.

. . .

Aah, meeting this old woman acorn-gatherer,
Tears come uncalled to moisten my robe.

97

From *The Pillow Book* by Sei Shonagon—10th century CE

The Pillow Book *is both diary and memoir and tells us much about the Japanese lady-in-waiting who wrote it. Sei Shonagon entered the service of the Japanese Empress Sadako when she was 24; little is known of her life after she left the Empress' service. Shonagon means "minor counselor" and does not refer to her surname but rather to her position at court. Shonagon's writing stands out because of its free expression of her opinions about life and society. What picture of Japanese life at court do you gain from this brief excerpt? How does it differ from that of Lady Sarashina's account?*

A LOVER'S COURTESY-NOTES

I like to think of a bachelor—an adventurous disposition has left him single—returning at dawn from some amorous excursion. He looks a trifle sleepy; but, as soon as he is home, draws his writing-case towards him, carefully grinds himself some ink and begins his next-morning letter—not simply dashing off whatever comes into his head, but spreading himself to the task and taking trouble to write the characters beautifully. He should be clad in an azalea-yellow or vermilion cloak worn over a white robe. Glancing from time to time at the dewdrops that

From *The Pillow Book of Sei Shonagon*, trans. by Arthur Waley (London: George Allen and Unwin Ltd., 1929).

still cling to the thin white fabric of his dress, he finishes his letter, . . . he gets up and, choosing from among his page-boys one who seems to him exactly appropriate to such a mission, calls the lad to him, and whispering something in his ear puts the letter in his hand; then sits gazing after him as he disappears into the distance. While waiting for the answer he will perhaps quietly murmur to himself this or that passage from the *Sūtras*. Presently he is told that his washing-water and porridge are ready, and goes into the back room, where, seated at the reading-table, he glances at some Chinese poems, now and then reciting out loud some passage that strikes his fancy. When he has washed and got into his Court cloak, which he wears as a dressing-gown (without trousers), he takes the 6th chapter of the Lotus Scripture and reads it silently. Precisely at the most solemn moment of his reading—the place being not far away—the messenger returns, and by his posture it is evident that he expects an instant reply. With an amusing if blasphemous rapidity the lover transfers his attention from the book he is reading to the business of framing his answer. . . .

THINGS THAT MAKE ONE HAPPY

Getting hold of a lot of stories none of which one has read before.

Or finding Volume Two of a story one is in a great state of excitement about, but was previously only able to secure the first volume. However, one is often disappointed.

To pick up a letter that someone has torn up and thrown away, and find that one can fit the pieces together well enough to make sense.

When one has had a very upsetting dream and is sure it means that something disagreeable is going to happen, it is delightful to be told by the interpreter that it does not signify anything in particular.

98

The Rubáiyát by Omar Khayyam—11th century CE

Best known in our time for his poetry, Omar Khayyám (ca. 1048-1131 CE) was also a mathematician, astronomer, and philosopher. Born in the great city of Nishapour, Iran, in the golden days before its destruction during the thirteenth century CE, Khayyám studied both philosophy and mathematics. He eventually headed a commission charged with reforming the Eastern calendar, called the Jalali calendar, which is considered by some to be more accurate than the Western calendar. Writing over many years, Khayyám revealed his thoughts and inner self through the 1,200 individual quatrains of The Rubáiyát. *A quatrain is four-line set of verse in which the first, second, and fourth lines rhyme. What does Khayyám tell us in these verses about the meaning of life?*

Come, fill the Cup, and in the fire of Spring
Your Winter-garment of Repentance fling:
    The Bird of Time has but a little way
To flutter—and the Bird is on the Wing.

Whether at Naishápúr or Babylon,
Whether the Cup with sweet or bitter run,
    The Wine of Life keeps oozing drop by drop,
The Leaves of Life keep falling one by one. . . .

A Book of Verses underneath the Bough,
A Jug of Wine, a Loaf of Bread—and Thou
    Beside me singing in the Wilderness—
Oh, Wilderness were Paradise enow!

Some for the Glories of This World; and some
Sigh for the Prophet's Paradise to come;
Ah, take the Cash, and let the Credit go,
Nor heed the rumble of a distant Drum!. . .

And those who husbanded the Golden grain,
And those who flung it to the winds like Rain,
    Alike to no such aureate Earth are turn'd
As, buried once, Men want dug up again.

From *The Rubaiyat of Omar Khayyam*, trans. by Edward Fitzgerald, originally published 1859.

The Worldly Hope men set their Hearts upon
Turns Ashes—or it prospers; and anon,
    Like Snow upon the Desert's dusty Face,
Lighting a little hour or two—is gone. . . .

Why, all the Saints and Sages who discuss'd
Of the Two Worlds so wisely—they are thrust
    Like foolish Prophets forth; their Words to Scorn
Are scatter'd, and their Mouths are stopt with Dust.

Myself when young did eagerly frequent
Doctor and Saint, and heard great argument
    About it and about: but evermore
Came out by the same door where in I went.

With them the seed of Wisdom did I sow,
And with mine own hand wrought to make it grow;
    And this was all the Harvest that I reap'd—
"I came like Water, and like Wind I go."

Into this Universe, and *Why* not knowing
Nor *Whence*, like Water willy-nilly flowing;
    And out of it, as Wind along the Waste,
I know not *Whither*, willy-nilly blowing.

What, without asking, hither hurried *Whence?*
And, without asking, *Whither* hurried hence!
    Oh, many a Cup of this forbidden Wine
Must drown the memory of that insolence!

Up from Earth's Centre through the Seventh Gate
I rose, and on the Throne of Saturn sate;
    And many a Knot unravel'd by the Road;
But not the Master-knot of Human Fate.

There was the Door to which I found no Key;
There was the Veil through which I might not see:
    Some little talk awhile of ME and THEE
There was—and then no more of THEE and ME.

Earth could not answer; nor the Seas that mourn
In flowing Purple, of their Lord forlorn;
    Nor rolling Heaven, with all his Signs reveal'd
And hidden by the sleeve of Night and Morn. . . .

Then to the lip of this poor earthen Urn
I lean'd, the Secret of my Life to learn:
    And Lip to Lip it murmur'd—"While you live,
Drink!—for, once dead, you never shall return.". . .

Waste not your Hour, nor in the vain pursuit
Of This and That endeavor and dispute;
   Better be jocund with the fruitful Grape
Than sadden after none, or bitter, Fruit. . . .

99

"As I Crossed a Bridge of Dreams"—11th century CE

*A lady-in-waiting at the court of Heian Japan, Sarashina enjoyed books more than peo-
ple, perhaps because she and the other ladies of the court had little privacy. Unlike her
near contemporary Sei Shonagon, who seems to have been more outgoing and optimistic,
Sarashina shows both sensitivity and sadness in her writing, which reflects the many
losses she experienced in her life. What are the main themes of Sarashina's prose, and
what does her work tell you about the life of a lady at Japanese court?*

Late one Spring night, while immersed in a Tale, I heard a prolonged miaow.
I looked up with a start and saw an extremely pretty cat. Where on earth
was it from, I wondered. Just then my sister came behind the curtain.
"Hush!" she said. "Not a word to anyone! It's a darling cat. Let's keep it!"

The cat was very friendly and lay down beside us. Since we were afraid that
people might come looking for her, we kept her hidden in our part of the house.
There she stayed faithfully, cuddled up between us; she never went near the servants' quarters and would eat only the daintiest food. We looked after her with
great care until one day my sister fell ill and in the confusion I decided to keep
our cat in the northern wing of the house. She miaowed loudly at not being
allowed into our rooms, but I had expected this and, pitiful though her cries
were, I thought it better to keep her away during my sister's illness.

One day my sister suddenly said, "What's happened? Where's our cat?
Bring her here!"

"Why?" I asked.

"I've had a dream," she explained. "Our cat came to me and said, 'I am the
daughter of the Chamberlain Major Counsellor, and it is in this form that I have

From "*Diary of Lady Sarashina*" trans. by Annie Shipley Omori and Lochi Doi, in Diaries of
Court Ladies of Old Japan (Boston: Houghton Mifflin, 1920).

been reborn. Because of some karma between us, your sister grew very fond of me and so I have stayed in this house for a time. But recently she has put me in the servants' quarters, which I find terrible.' She cried and cried, and I thought she looked like a very beautiful and elegant woman. When I awoke, I realized that the words in my dream were the miaowing of our cat. This dream has moved me deeply." I too was moved by my sister's story and thereafter never sent the cat to the northern wing, but looked after her carefully in my own room.

Once when I was alone she came and sat beside me. I stroked her for a long time. "So you are the Major Counsellor's daughter!" I said. "If only I could let His Excellency know that you are here!" Hearing this, she gazed at me intently and gave a long miaow. It may have been my imagination but that moment her eyes were not those of an ordinary cat; they seemed to understand exactly what I was saying.

I heard of a family that owned a copy of *The Song of Everlasting Regret* rewritten as a Tale. I longed to see it, but could not bring myself to ask them. On the seventh day of the Seventh Month I found a suitable opportunity and sent them the poem,

> Long ago the Herdsman and the Weaver
>   made their vow.
> Today my fond thoughts go to them, and
>   yearning waves of Heaven's River surge
>   within my heart.

This was their reply:

> Fondly indeed one views the river where
>   those lovers meet,
> And forgets the sadness of their ill-starred love.

On the thirteenth night of that month the moon shone brightly, lighting every corner of the earth. At about midnight, when the rest of our household was asleep, my sister and I sat on the veranda. "If I flew away now all of a sudden and disappeared without a trace," she said, gazing at the sky, "what would you think?" Then, seeing the anxious look on my face, she changed the subject and soon she was laughing and chatting merrily. Presently a carriage approached with a forerunner and stopped by our house. The passenger ordered his attendant to call for someone, "Oginoha, Oginoha!" cried the man, but there was no reply from inside the house and presently he gave up. The gentleman played his flute for a while in a beautiful, clear tone; then the carriage moved away. After it had left I said,

> That flute was like the Autumn wind.
> Why did the Reed Leaf make no gentle
>   answering sound?

My sister nodded and replied,

> It was the flute's fault, for it passed too soon
> And did not wait for Reed Leaf to reply.

We sat there all night, looking at the sky; at dawn we went to bed.

In the Fourth Month of the following year there was a fire in our house and the cat whom we had tended so carefully as the daughter of His Excellency the Major Counsellor was burnt to death. Whenever I used to call out "Counsellor's daughter!" this cat had miaowed and come to me with a look of understanding on her face. "It really is extraordinary," Father used to say. "I must tell His Excellency about it." How pathetic that she should have died like this!

100

From *De Arte Honeste Amandi,* by Andreas Capellanus— ca. 1174–1186 CE

At the court of Champagne, the idea of a nonsexual, spiritual relationship between noblemen and noblewomen was promoted by Marie, the Countess of Champagne and daughter of Eleanor of Acquitaine. In the following document, Andreas Capellanus, the Countess' chaplain, set out the rules and code of etiquette to be followed at her court. This idealistic document seems to raise the status of women by showing some consideration for their emotions. Would the Catholic Church have approved of the concepts detailed in this document? Why or why not?

Love is a certain inborn suffering derived from the sight of and excessive meditation upon the beauty of the opposite sex, which causes each one to wish above all things the embraces of the other and by common desire to carry out all of love's precepts in the other's embrace.

That love is suffering is easy to see, for before the love becomes equally balanced on both sides there is no torment greater, since the lover is always in fear that his love may not gain its desire and that he is wasting his efforts. He fears, too, that rumors of it may get abroad, and he fears everything that might harm it in any way, for before things are perfected a slight disturbance often spoils them. If he is a poor man, he also fears that the woman may scorn his poverty; if he is ugly, he fears that she may despise his lack of beauty or may give her love to a more handsome man; if he is rich, he fears that his parsimony in the past may stand in his way. To tell the truth, no one can number the fears of one single lover. This kind of love, then, is a suffering which is felt by only one of the persons and may be called "single love." But even after both are in love the fears that arise are just as great, for each of the lovers fears that what he has acquired with so much effort may be lost through the effort of someone else, which is certainly much worse for a man than if, having no hope, he sees that his efforts are accomplishing nothing, for it is worse to lose the things you are seeking than to be deprived of a gain you merely hope for. The lover fears, too, that he may offend his loved one in some way; indeed he fears so many things that it would be difficult to tell them.

. . .

Now, in love you should note first of all that love cannot exist except between persons of opposite sexes. Between two men or two women love can find no place, for we see that two persons of the same sex are not at all fitted for giving each other the exchanges of love or for practicing the acts natural to it. Whatever nature forbids, love is ashamed to accept.

. . .

An excess of passion is a bar to love, because there are men who are slaves to such passionate desire that they cannot be held in the bonds of love—men who, after they have thought long about some woman or even enjoyed her, when they see another woman straightway desire her embraces, and they forget about the services they have received from their first love and they feel no gratitude for them. Men of this kind lust after every woman they see; their love is like that of a shameless dog. They should rather, I believe, be compared to asses, for they are moved only by that low nature which shows that men are on the level of the other animals rather than by that true nature which sets us apart from all the other animals by the difference of reason.

. . .

The readiness to grant requests is, we say, the same thing in women as over-voluptuousness in men—a thing which all agree should be a total stranger in the court of Love. For he who is so tormented by carnal passion that he cannot embrace anyone in heartfelt love, but basely lusts after every woman he sees, is not called a lover but a counterfeiter of love and a pretender, and he is lower than a shameless dog. Indeed the man who is so wanton that he cannot confine himself to the love of one woman deserves to be considered an impetuous ass. It will therefore be clear to you that you are bound to avoid an overabundance of passion and that you ought not to seek the love of a woman who you know will grant easily what you seek.

. . .

Furthermore a lover ought to appear to his beloved wise in every respect and restrained in his conduct, and he should do nothing disagreeable that might annoy her. And if inadvertently he should do something improper that offends her, let him straightway confess with downcast face that he has done wrong, and let him give the excuse that he lost his temper or make some other suitable explanation that will fit the case. And every man ought to be sparing of praise of his beloved when he is among other men; he should not spend a great deal of time in places where she is. When he is with other men, if he meets her in a group of women, he should not try to communicate with her by signs, but should treat her almost like a stranger lest some person spying on their love might have opportunity to spread malicious gossip. Lovers should not even nod to each other unless they are sure that nobody is watching them. Every man should also wear things that his beloved likes and pay a reasonable amount of attention to his appearance—not too much because excessive care for one's looks is distasteful to everybody and leads people to despise the good looks that one has. If the lover is lavish in giving, that helps him retain a love he has acquired, for all lovers ought to despise all worldly riches and should give alms to those who have need of them. Also, if the lover is one who is fitted to be a warrior, he should see to it that his courage is apparent to everybody, for it detracts very much from the good character of a man if he is timid in a fight. A lover should always offer his services and obedience freely to every lady, and he ought to root out all his pride and be very humble. Then, too, he must keep in mind the general rule that lovers must not neglect anything that good manners demand or good breeding suggests, but they should be very careful to do everything of this sort. Love may also be retained by indulging in the sweet and delightful solaces of the flesh, but only in such manner and in such number that they may never seem wearisome to be the loved one. Let the lover strive to practice gracefully and manfully any act or mannerism which he has noticed is pleasing to his beloved. A clerk should not, of course, affect the manners or the dress of the laity, for no one is likely to please his beloved, if she is a wise woman, by wearing strange clothing or by practicing manners that do not suit his status. Furthermore a lover should make every attempt to be constantly in the company of good men and to avoid completely the society of the wicked. For association with the vulgar makes a lover who joins them a thing of contempt to his beloved.

. . .

Too many opportunities for exchanging solaces, too many opportunities of seeing the loved one, too much chance to talk to each other all decrease love, and so does an uncultured appearance or manner of walking on the part of the lover or the sudden loss of his property. Love decreases, too, if the woman finds that her lover is foolish and indiscreet, or if he seems to go beyond reasonable bounds in his demands for love, or if she sees that he has no regard for her modesty and will not forgive her bashfulness. Love decreases, too, if the woman considers that her lover is cowardly in battle, or sees that he is unrestrained in his speech or spoiled by the vice of arrogance.

Other things which weaken love are blasphemy against God or His saints, mockery of the ceremonies of the Church, and a deliberate withholding of charity from the poor. We find that love decreases very sharply if one is unfaithful to his friend, or if he brazenly says one thing while he deceitfully conceals a different idea in his heart. Love decreases, too, if the lover piles up more wealth than is proper, or if he is too ready to go to law over trifles.

. . .

. . . [L]ove comes to an end if one of the lovers breaks faith or tries to break faith with the other, or if he is found to go astray from the Catholic religion. It comes to an end also after it has been openly revealed and made known to men. So, too, if one of the lovers has plenty of money and does not come to the aid of the other who is in great need and lacks a great many things, then love usually becomes very cheap and comes to an ignominious end. An old love also ends when a new one begins, because no one can love two people at the same time. Furthermore, inequality of love and a fraudulent and deceitful duplicity of heart always drive out love, for a deceitful lover, no matter how worthy he is otherwise, ought to be rejected by any woman. Again, if by some chance one of the lovers becomes incapable of carrying out love's duties, love can no longer last between them and deserts them and deserts them completely. Likewise if one of the lovers becomes insane or develops a sudden timidity, love flees and becomes hateful.

These are the rules.

I. Marriage is no real excuse for not loving.

II. He who is not jealous cannot love.

III. No one can be bound by a double love.

IV. It is well known that love is always increasing or decreasing.

V. That which a lover takes against his will of his beloved has no relish.

VI. Boys do not love until they arrive at the age of maturity.

VII. When one lover dies, a widowhood of two years is required of the survivor.

VIII. No one should be deprived of love without the very best of reasons.

IX. No one can love unless he is impelled by the persuasion of love.

X. Love is always a stranger in the home of avarice.

XI. It is not proper to love any woman whom one should be ashamed to seek to marry.

XII. A true lover does not desire to embrace in love anyone except his beloved.

XIII. When made public love rarely endures.

XIV. The easy attainment of love makes it of little value; difficulty of attainment makes it prized.

XV. Every lover regularly turns pale in the presence of his beloved.

XVI. When a lover suddenly catches sight of his beloved his heart palpitates.

XVII. A new love puts to flight an old one.

XVIII. Good character alone makes any man worthy of love.

XIX. If love diminishes, it quickly fails and rarely revives.

XX. A man in love is always apprehensive.

XXI. Real jealousy always increases the feeling of love.

XXII. Jealousy, and therefore love, are increased when one suspects his beloved.

XXIII. He whom the thought of love vexes, eats and sleeps very little.

XXIV. Every act of a lover ends in the thought of his beloved.

XXV. A true lover considers nothing good except what he thinks will please his beloved.

XXVI. Love can deny nothing to love.

XXVII. A lover can never have enough of the solaces of his beloved.

XXVIII. A slight presumption causes a lover to suspect his beloved.

XXIX. A man who is vexed by too much passion usually does not love.

XXX. A true lover is constantly and without intermission possessed by the thought of his beloved.

XXXI. Nothing forbids one woman being loved by two men or one man by two women.

101

Piers the Ploughman by William Langland—1370 CE

The excerpt below comes from an allegorical discussion about the search for truth and moral purity that preoccupied many people during the Middle Ages; it was written by an obscure English priest, William Langland. A plowman of low class, Piers convinces a group of nobles to plow his field in exchange for guidance on the path to righteousness. What is the main message of this excerpt? What insights does it provide about middle-class society during this period?

THE PILGRIMAGE

Announce the Pilgrimage to the people. They will come to you on foot and riding along distant roads on lean and slender beasts . . . let them then attend to their persons and complete the rites of pilgrimage, fulfil their vows and circuit round the ancient House.

"Do you know anything about a saint called Truth?" they said. "Can you tell us where to find him?"

"Good Heavens, no!" said the man. . . .

"By Saint Peter!" said a plowman, pushing his way through the crowd, "I know Him, as well as a scholar knows his books. Conscience and Common Sense showed me the way to His place, and they made me swear to serve Him forever, and do His sowing and planting for as long as I can work. I've been his man for the last fifty years; I've sown His seed and herded His beasts, and looked after all His affairs, indoors and out. I ditch and dig, sow and thresh, and do whatever Truth tells me—tailoring and tinkering, spinning and weaving—I put my hand to anything He bids me. And Truth is pleased with my work, though I say it myself. He pays me well, and sometimes gives me extra; for He's as ready with His wages as any poor man could wish, and never fails to pay His men each night. Besides, He's as mild as a lamb, and always speaks to you kindly. So if you would like to know where He lives, I'll put you on the track in no time."

"Thank you, Piers old fellow," the pilgrims said; and they offered him money to guide them to Truth's castle.

"No, by my soul!" swore Piers, "I wouldn't take a farthing [money] not for all the riches in St. Thomas' shrine! Truth would find it hard to forgive me for

From *Piers the Ploughman* by William Langland, trans. by J.F. Goodridge (London: Penguin Books, 1966), p. 77–82, 84. Reprinted by permission of Penguin Books UK.

that! But if you want to go the right way, listen now, while I set you on Truth's path.

You must all set out through *Meekness*, men and women alike, and continue until you come to *Conscience*; for Christ may know by this that you love God above all things, and your neighbor next, and treat others as you would like them to treat you. Then turn down by the stream *Be-gentle-in-speech*, till you come to a ford [shallow crossing], *Honor-thy-father-and-mother*. There you must wade into the water and wash yourselves thoroughly, then you'll step more lightly for the rest of your life. Next, you will see a place called *Swear-not-with-out-necessity-and-above-all-take-not-the-name-of-the-Lord-thy-God-in-vain*. After that, you will pass by a farm where you must not trespass on any account, for its name is *Thou-shalt-not-covet-thy-neighbor's-cattle-nor-his-wives-nor-any-of-his-servants-lest-you-do-him-an-injury*. So take care not to break any branches there, unless they are on your property.

You will also see two pairs of stocks;[†] but do not stop, for they are *Steal-not*-and *Kill-not*. Go round and leave them on your left, and don't look back at them. And remember to observe Holy Days, and keep them holy from morning till night-fall. Then you will come to a hill, *Bear-no-false-witness*. Turn right away from it, for it is thickly wooded with bribes, and bristling with florins [money]. At all costs gather no blossoms there, or you will lose your soul. And so you will arrive at a place called *Speak-the-truth-and-mean-it-and-never-swerve-from-the-truth-for-any-man*. From there you will see a mansion as bright as the sun, surrounded by a moat of *Mercy*, with walls of *Wisdom*, to keep out passion. It has battlements of *Christendom* to save mankind, and is buttressed with *Believe-or-you-cannot-be-saved*.

And all the buildings, halls, and chambers are roofed, not with lead, but with Love, and are covered with the *Lowly-speech-of-brothers*. The drawbridge is of *Ask-and-you-shall-receive*, and each pillar is built of penance and prayers to the saints, and all the gates are hung on hinges of almsdeeds. The doorkeeper's name is Grace, a good man, who has a servant, Amendment, well known among men. And this is the password you must give him so that Truth may know you are honest: 'I have done penance which the priest gave me; I am very sorry for my sins, I always shall be whenever I think of them, and still should be even if I were Pope!'

Then you must ask Amendment to beg his Master to open the wicket-gate that Eve shut in the beginning, when she and Adam ate the sour apples. For 'Through Eve the door was closed to all men, and through the Virgin Mary it was opened again.' So Mary always has the key, even when the King is sleeping. And if Grace gives you leave to enter by this gate, you will find Truth dwelling in your heart, hung on a chain of charity. And you will submit to Him as a child to its father, never opposing His will.

But then beware of the villain Wrath, who envies Him who dwells in your heart. For he will push Pride in your way and make you feel so pleased with

---

† A "stock" was a device for the public punishment of criminals. It consisted of a wooden frame that held both head and hands in place.

yourself that you are blinded by the glory of your own good deeds. So you will be driven out 'as the early dew,' the door will be locked and bolted against you, and it may be a hundred years before you enter again. Thus by thinking too much of yourself, you may lose God's love, and enter His courts no more, unless His grace intervenes.

But there are also seven sisters, the eternal servants of Truth, who keep the postern-gates of the castle. These are Abstinence and Humility, Chastity and Charity. His chief maidens, Patience and Peace, who help many people, and the Lady Bountiful, who opens the gates to still more, and has helped thousands out of the Devil's pound. Anyone related to these seven is wonderfully welcome there, and received with honor. But if you are kin to none of them, it is very hard for you to get in at all, except by the special mercy of God."

. . .

Then the people complained to Piers and said, "This is a grim way you've described to us. We should need a guide for every step of the road." "Now look," said Piers the Plowman, "I have half an acre of land here by the highway. Once I can get it plowed and sown, I will go with you and show you the way myself." "We should have a long time to wait," said a veiled lady. "What work could we women be doing to pass the time?"

"Why, some of you can sew up the sacks," said Piers, "to keep the seed from spilling. And you fair ladies with slender fingers—you have plenty of silks and fine stuffs to sew. Make some vestments for priests, while you've got the time, and lend a hand in beautifying the churches. And those of you who are married or widows can spin flax and make some cloth, and teach your daughters to do it too. For Truth commands us to take care of the needy and clothe the naked. I'll give them food myself, so long as the harvest doesn't fail. For if I don't mind working all my life for the love of God, to provide meat and bread for the rich and poor. So come along now, all you men who live by food and drink—lend a hand to the man who provides you with it, and we will finish the job quickly."

"By Heavens!" said a knight, "this fellow knows what's good for us! But to tell the truth, I've never handled a team of oxen. Give me a lesson, Piers, and I'll do my best by God!" "That's a fair offer," said Piers. "And for my part, I'll sweat and toil for both of us as long as I live, and gladly do any job you want. But you must promise in return to guard over [the] Holy Church, and protect me from the thieves and wasters who ruin the world. And you'll have to hunt down all the hares and foxes and boars and badgers that break down my hedges, and tame falcons to kill the wild birds that crop my wheat."

Then the knight answered courteously and said, "I give you my word, Piers, as I am a true knight; and I'll keep this promise through thick and thin and protect you to the end of my days."

"Ah, but there's one thing more I must ask you," said Piers. "Never ill-treat your tenants, and see that you punish them only when Truth compels you to—even then, let Mercy assess the fine, and be ruled by Meekness. . . . And take care also that you never ill-use your serfs. It will be better for you in the long run, for though they are your underlings here on earth, they may be above you in Heaven, in greater happiness, unless you lead a better life than they do."

. . .

And now Piers and his pilgrims have gone to the plough, and many folk are helping him to till his half acre. Ditchers and diggers are turning up the headlands, and others, to please Piers, are hoeing up the weeds, while he is delighted with their labors and quick to praise them. They are all eager to work, and every man finds something useful to do. Then at nine o'clock in the morning Piers left his plough in order to see how things were going, and pick out the best workers to hire again at harvest-time. At this, some of them sat down to drink their ale and sing songs. . . .

"By the Lord!" said Piers, bursting with rage, "Get up and go back to work at once—or you'll get no bread to sing about when famine comes. You can starve to death, and to hell with the lot of you!"

102

Excerpt From *The Canterbury Tales* by Geoffrey Chaucer—14th century CE

Geoffrey Chaucer was a politician and soldier as well as a writer familiar with the manners and customs of his society. In The Canterbury Tales, Chaucer relates stories told by an imaginary group of pilgrims on their way to the shrine of Thomas Becket at Canterbury. In this short excerpt, he provides a brief description of the pilgrims. Based on what you have learned about this era, do you think this an eyewitness account or a somewhat satirical view of late medieval society? Why?

From Geoffrey Chaucer, *The Canterbury Tales*, trans. David Wright (New York: Random House, 1965), p. 3–8, 11–12. Copyright © 1964 by David Wright. Reprinted by permission of Sterling Lord Literistic Inc.

The KNIGHT was a very distinguished man. From the beginning of his career he had loved chivalry, loyalty, honourable dealing, generosity, and good breeding. He had fought bravely in the king's service, beside which he had travelled further than most men in heathen as well as in Christian lands. Wherever he went he was honoured for his valour. . . .

He was always outstandingly successful; yet though distinguished he was prudent, and his bearing as modest as a maid's. In his whole life he never spoke discourteously to any kind of man. He was a true and perfect noble knight. But, speaking of his equipment, his horses were good, yet he was not gaily dressed. He wore a tunic of thick cotton cloth, rust-marked from his coat of mail; for he had just come back from his travels and was making his pilgrimage to render thanks.

With him came his son, a young SQUIRE; a spirited apprentice-knight, a lover with hair as curly as if it had just been pressed in the tongs—I suppose his age was about twenty. He was of average height, wonderfully active and strong. In Flanders, Artois, and Picardy he had taken part in cavalry forays and in that short space of time had borne himself well, for he hoped to win favour in his lady's eyes. He was decked out like a meadow full of fresh flowers, white and red; he whistled or sang the whole day long, as lively as the month of May. His gown was short, with long wide sleeves. He was a good rider and sat his horse well; he was able to compose songs and set them to music, joust and also dance; and he could draw and write. Being passionately in love, at night he slept no more than a nightingale. Courteous, modest, and willing to serve, he carved for his father at table. . . .

There was also a NUN, a Prioress, who smiled in an unaffected and quiet way; her greatest oath was only, 'By St Loy!' Her name was Madame Eglantine. She sang the divine service prettily, becomingly intoned through the nose. She spoke French elegantly and well but with a Stratford-at-Bow accent, for she did not know the French of Paris. At table she showed her good breeding at every point: she never let a crumb fall from her mouth or wetted her fingers by dipping them too deeply into the sauce; and when she lifted the food to her lips she took care not to spill a single drop upon her breast. Etiquette was her passion. So scrupulously did she wipe her upper lip that no spot of grease was to be seen in her cup after she had drunk from it; and when she ate she reached daintily for her food. Indeed she was most gay, pleasant and friendly. She took pains to imitate courtly behaviour and cultivate a dignified bearing so as to be thought a person deserving of respect. Speaking of her sensibility, she was so tender-hearted and compassionate that she would weep whenever she saw a mouse caught in a trap, especially if it were bleeding or dead. She kept a number of little dogs whom she fed on roast meat, milk, and the best bread. But if one of them died or someone took a stick to it she would cry bitterly, for with her all was sensitivity and tender-heartedness. . . .

With her she had another NUN, her chaplain and three PRIESTS.

There was a remarkable fine-looking MONK, who acted as estate-steward to his monastery and loved hunting: a manly man, well fitted to be an abbot. He kept plenty of fine horses in his stable, and when he went out riding people could hear the bells on his bridle jingling in the whistling wind as clear and loud as the chapel bell of the small convent of which he was the head. Because the Rule of St Maur or of St Benedict was old-fashioned and somewhat strict, this Monk neglected the old precepts and followed the modern custom. He did not give two pins for the text which says hunters cannot be holy men, or that a monk who is heedless of his Rule—that is to say a monk out of his cloister—is like a fish out of water. In his view this saying was not worth a bean; and I told him his opinion was sound. Why should he study and addle his wits with everlasting poring over a book in cloisters, or work with his hands, or toil as St Augustine commanded? How is the world to be served? Let St Augustine keep his hard labour for himself! Therefore the Monk, whose whole pleasure lay in riding and the hunting of the hare (over which he spared no expense) remained a hard rider and kept greyhounds swift as birds. . . .

Next there was a MERCHANT with a forked beard who rode seated on a high saddle, wearing a many-coloured dress, boots fastened with neat handsome clasps, and upon his head a Flanders beaver hat. He gave out his opinions with great pomposity and never stopped talking about the increase of his profits. In his view the high seas between Harwich and Holland should be cleared of pirates at all costs. He was an expert at the exchange of currency. This worthy citizen used his head to the best advantage, conducting his money-lending and other financial transactions in a dignified manner; none guessed he was in debt. He was really a most estimable man; but to tell the truth his name escapes me. . . .

With us there was a good religious man, a poor PARSON, but rich in holy thoughts and acts. He was also a learned man, a scholar, who truly preached Christ's Gospel and taught his parishioners devoutly. Benign, hardworking, and patient in adversity—as had often been put to the test—he was loath to excommunicate those who failed to pay their tithes. To tell the truth he would rather give to the poor of his parish what had been offered him by the rich, or from his own pocket; for he managed to live on very little. Wide as was his parish, with houses few and far between, neither rain nor thunder nor sickness nor misfortune stopped him from going on foot, staff in hand, to visit his most distant parishioners, high or low. To his flock he set this noble example: first he practised, then he preached. This was a precept he had taken from the Gospel; and to it he added this proverb: 'If gold can rust, what will iron do?' For if the priest in whom we trust be rotten, no wonder an ordinary man corrupts. Let priests take note: shame it is to see the shepherd covered in dung while his sheep are clean! It's for the priest to set his flock the example of a spotless life! He did not farm his benefice and leave his sheep to flounder in the mud while he ran off to St Paul's in London to seek some easy living such as a chantry where he would be paid to sing masses for the souls of the dead, or a chaplaincy in one of the guilds; but dwelt at home and kept watch over his flock so that it was not harmed by the wolf. He was a shepherd, not a priest for hire.

And although he was saintly and virtuous he did not despise sinners. His manner of speaking was neither distant nor severe; on the contrary he was considerate and benign in his guidance. His endeavour was to lead folk to heaven by the example of a good life. Yet if anyone—whatever his rank—proved obstinate, he never hesitated to deliver a stinging rebuke. I'd say that there was nowhere a better priest. He never looked for ceremony and deference, nor was his conscience of the over-scrupulous and specious sort. He taught the Gospel of Christ and His twelve apostles: but first he followed it himself.